ALBERT CAMUS

Speaking Out

Albert Camus was born in Algeria in 1913. He spent the early years of his life in North Africa, where he became a journalist. During World War II, he was one of the leading writers of the French Resistance and editor of *Combat*, an underground newspaper he helped found. His fiction, including *The Stranger*, *The Plague*, *The Fall*, and *Exile and the Kingdom*; his philosophical essays, *The Myth of Sisyphus* and *The Rebel*; and his plays have assured his preeminent position in modern letters. In 1957, Camus was awarded the Nobel Prize in Literature. On January 4, 1960, he was killed in a car accident.

INTERNATIONAL

Also by Albert Camus

ALBERT CAMUS

Speaking Out

Lectures and Speeches, 1937–1958

*Translated from the French
and with a foreword by Quintin Hoare*

Vintage International
VINTAGE BOOKS
A DIVISION OF PENGUIN RANDOM HOUSE LLC
NEW YORK

A VINTAGE INTERNATIONAL ORIGINAL, FEBRUARY 2022

*English-language translation and additional
  notes copyright © 2021 by Quintin Hoare*
Foreword copyright © 2017 by Éditions Gallimard

The Cataloging-in-Publication Data is on file at the Library of Congress.

Vintage International Trade Paperback ISBN: 978-0-525-56723-3
eBook ISBN: 978-0-525-56724-0

Book design by Nicholas Alguire

www.vintagebooks.com

Printed in the United States of America
10   9   8   7   6   5   4   3   2   1

Contents

Contents

Foreword

This volume brings together the thirty-four known texts of public statements by Albert Camus, concluding with the unpublished transcript of his speech at the November 13, 1958, Algerian Club dinner in Paris. Apart from his 1937 talk "The New Mediterranean Culture," these speeches and lectures were delivered after the Second World War. By then, the fame of the novelist, essayist, playwright and editorialist meant that his viewpoint on the state of the world and the public mood was regularly sought and awaited, both in France and abroad.

However, Camus was not at heart a lecturer, a role that exposed him to the risk of having to pronounce on subjects about which he felt he had neither the competence nor the legitimacy to speak. "I'm not old enough for lectures," he warned in 1946. Despite his misgivings, public statements were to be one of the chosen forms of his political commitment, involving both testimony and polemic.

In none of the texts in the current volume does the writer evoke or quote any of his works or his fictional characters, as if the experience of the creator had little in common with that of the occasional orator. Yet the question of the artist's commitment remains at the heart of these platform pronouncements, from "The Crisis of Man" (delivered in New York, 1946) to the famous speeches in Sweden (Stockholm and Uppsala, 1957). There is no rupture, he seems to tell us, between the commitment of the citizen and that of the writer, inasmuch as the latter, through his work, seeks to keep as close as possible to a human truth more than ever exposed to terror, to lies, to bureaucratic and ideological abstraction, to injustice. "The artist distinguishes where the conqueror evens out. The artist who lives and creates at the level of the flesh and passion knows that nothing is simple and the other exists" (see p. 80). And he knows the flesh may be happy or unhappy.

The Camusian revolt is situated at the heart of the absurd, in the simultaneous recognition of common destiny and individual freedom. That is what underpins these public pronouncements. From one lecture to the next, Camus makes explicit and manifest his commitment as a man who aims to restore voice, face and dignity to those who have been stripped of them by half a century of sound and fury, in which the misuse of words and the excess of ideas have made man a wolf to himself.[1] It is necessary to break that hellish post-war movement, to "transform our appetite for hatred into desire for justice" (see p. 12) and suppress the poison of death within ourselves. Such is the generational experience to which the writer here bears witness.

There is a "Crisis of Man" which needs to be registered and explained. And the speaker sets about this here, repeatedly formulating and reformulating its causes and symptoms. But most important is to find a remedy for it, with the hope that humankind can recover, of his own accord, "that taste for man without which the world will never be anything but a vast solitude" (see p. 14). Artists and writers have their role to play, modest but necessary.

For Camus, man has a vocation that consists in opposing the world's unhappiness in order to diminish its intensity, within each individual's particular limits. Camus's authority as an intellectual and his specific journey give his words a special audience, in a world that has already become globalized—particularly under totalitarian and imperialist pressures. He does not limit his commitments to national frontiers: Europe is at the heart of his concerns, indeed his indignation, when it is the Europe of Franco and meets with no condemnation. He also takes to the rostrum when his brethren in Eastern Europe are subjected to an insane totalitarianism, crushing all liberties with the utmost contempt for human individuality and justice.

What is at stake is not just culture but civilization, and the fraternal sentiment that unites individuals in the struggle against their destiny. Thereby is traced an ethics for himself: this vocation of man is an apprenticeship, a discipline, played out daily and throughout life: "I prefer committed men to committed literature," he wrote in his *Notebooks*. "Courage in one's life and talent in one's work, that's not too bad."[2]

—Quintin Hoare

Speaking Out

Lectures and Speeches, 1937–1958

Indigenous Culture: The New Mediterranean Culture

1937

A member of the Parti Communiste Algérien (PCA) since late summer 1935, Albert Camus involved himself in cultural action by founding the Théâtre du Travail, a company that he managed at the same time as being a scriptwriter, director and actor. Meanwhile, he became general secretary of the Algiers Cultural Center, which organized cinema shows, concerts and lectures. It was at the inauguration of this body on February 8, 1937, that Camus, then twenty-two years old, delivered the following lecture. The text was published in the first issue of the Cultural Center's bulletin, Jeune Méditerranée, *in April 1937. In the autumn of that year Albert Camus left the PCA.*

I

The Cultural Center being introduced to you today claims to serve Mediterranean culture. Faithful to the general prescriptions governing centers of this type, it aims in the regional context to help promote a culture whose existence and greatness no longer need to be proved. In that respect, there is perhaps something surprising in the fact that left-wing intellectuals can place themselves at the service of a culture which seems in no way to concern their own cause, and which has even in some cases been taken over (as with Maurras[1]) by right-wing ideologues.

Serving the cause of a Mediterranean regionalism may indeed restore a useless and doomed traditionalism, or even exalt the superiority of one culture over another: for instance, in a reprise of fascism in reverse, by pitting the Latin against the Nordic peoples. Therein lies a perpetual misunderstanding. The purpose of this lecture is an attempt to resolve this. The fundamental error consists in confusing the Mediterranean with Latinity, and placing in Rome what began in Athens. For us the matter is clear: what is involved cannot be some kind of sunshine nationalism. We could never subject ourselves to traditions, or bind our living future to feats already defunct. A tradition is a past that counterfeits the present. The Mediterranean that surrounds us is by contrast a living land, filled with play and smiles. Meanwhile, nationalism has condemned itself by its actions. Nationalism always appears in history as a sign of decadence. When the vast edifice of the Roman Empire crumbled, when its spiritual unity, from which so many different regions drew their reason for living, broke apart, only then at the hour of decadence did nationalities appear. Since then, the West has never recovered its unity. At the present time, internationalism seeks to reinvest it with its true meaning and its vocation. But the principle is no longer Christian, no longer the papal Rome of the Holy Empire. The principle is man. Unity is no longer in belief but in hope. A civilization can last only insofar as, all nations suppressed, it derives its unity and its greatness from a spiritual principle. India, almost as large as Europe, without nations or a sovereign, has kept its own physiognomy even after two centuries of English domination.

This is why we shall reject out of hand the principle of a Mediterranean nationalism. Besides, any superiority of Mediterranean culture is out of the question. Man expresses himself in harmony with his land. And in the domain of culture, superiority resides only in that harmony. There is no culture which is greater or less great. There are cultures which are truer or less true. We wish only to help a land express itself. Locally. Nothing more. The real question: is a new Mediterranean culture achievable?

II. Proofs

1. There is a Mediterranean sea, a basin linking a dozen countries. The men wailing in the *cafés cantantes* of Spain, those roaming the port of Genoa or the quays of Marseilles, the strange, strong race inhabiting our shores—all spring from the same family. When traveling through Europe, as you come back down toward Italy or Provence, it is with a sigh of relief that you once more encounter disheveled men and that heady, colorful life we all know. I spent two months in Western Europe, between Austria and Germany, wondering about the source of that strange unease weighing upon my shoulders, that dull anxiety pervading me. Lately I have understood. Those people were always buttoned up to the neck. They did not know how to relax. They knew nothing about what joy is, so different from laughter. Yet it is with details like this that the word Fatherland can be imbued with a valid meaning. The Fatherland is not the abstraction driving men to massacre; it is a certain taste for life that is common to certain individuals, through which you can feel closer to a Genoese or a Mallorcan than to a Norman or an Alsatian. This is what the Mediterranean is: this smell or scent which it is pointless to express—we all feel it with our skin.

2. There are other proofs, historical ones. Whenever a doctrine has encountered the Mediterranean basin, in the resulting clash of ideas it is always the Mediterranean that has remained intact, the land that has conquered the doctrine. Christianity was originally a moving but closed doctrine, primarily Judaic, eschewing concessions, harsh, exclusive and admirable. From its encounter with the Mediterranean a new doctrine emerged: Catholicism. The initial complex of emotional aspirations was supplemented by a philosophical doctrine. The monument was completed, embellished—adapted to man. Thanks to the Mediterranean, Christianity was able to enter the world and begin there the miraculous career known to all.

It was another man of the Mediterranean, Francis of Assisi, who made from Christianity, all inward and tormented, a hymn to nature and naive joy. And the sole attempt made to separate Christianity from the world we owe to a man of the North, to Luther. Protestantism, properly speaking, is Catholicism torn away from the Mediterranean and its fatal, thrilling influence.

Let us look more closely. For those who have lived in both Germany and Italy, it is an obvious fact that fascism does not wear the same countenance in both countries. You feel it everywhere in Germany, on faces and in the city streets. Dresden, a military city, suffocates beneath an invisible enemy. What you feel first in Italy is the land. What you see at first sight in a German is the Nazi, greeting you with the words: "Heil Hitler!" With an Italian, it is the friendly, cheerful man. Here again, the doctrine seems to have retreated before the land; and it is a miracle of the Mediterranean to allow men who think humanely to live without oppression in a country with inhuman laws.

III

Yet this living reality which is the Mediterranean is nothing new for us. And it seems that this culture is the image of that Latin antiquity which the Renaissance sought to rediscover from across the Middle Ages. It is that Latinity which Maurras and his people are seeking to annex. It is in the name of that Latin order that, in the Ethiopian affair, twenty-four Western intellectuals signed a shameful manifesto exalting Italy's civilizing work in barbaric Ethiopia.

But no. That is not the Mediterranean to which our Cultural Center lays claim. Because it is not the true one. It is the abstract, conventional Mediterranean symbolized by Rome and the Romans. Yet that people of imitators without imagination did imagine replacing the artistic genius and feeling for life that they lacked by martial genius. And that order so warmly extolled to us was the one imposed by force, not the one which draws breath in intelligence. Even when they copied something, they made it dull. And it is not even the essential genius of Greece that they imitated, but the fruits of its decadence and its mistakes. Not the strong, harsh Greece of the great tragic or comic writers, but the charm and affectation of the final centuries. It is not life that Rome took from Greece, but childish, quibbling abstraction. The Mediterranean is elsewhere. It is the very negation of Rome and the Latin genius. Alive, it could not care less about abstraction. And we may readily concede to Monsieur Mussolini that he is the worthy continuator of the ancient Caesar and Augustus, if we mean by this that, like them, he sacrifices truth and greatness to soulless violence.

It is not the taste for argument and abstraction to which we lay claim in the Mediterranean, but its life—the courtyards, the cypresses, the strings of peppers; Aeschylus and not Euripides—the Doric Apollos, not the Vatican copies. It is Spain, its strength and its pessimism, not the swagger of Rome; the landscapes crushed by sunlight, not the stage sets where a dictator gets drunk on his own voice and subdues crowds. What we want is not the lie that triumphed in Ethiopia, but the truth being murdered in Spain.[2]

IV

An international basin criss-crossed by every current, the Mediterranean is of all lands perhaps the only one to converge with the great Oriental ways of thinking. For it is not classical and ordered, but diffuse and turbulent, like those Arab neighborhoods or those ports of Genoa and Tunisia. That triumphant taste for life, that sense of crushing boredom, the deserted squares at noon in Spain, the siesta: those are the true Mediterranean—and what it resembles is the Orient. Not the Latin West. North Africa is one of the rare lands where East and West cohabit. And at this confluence there is no difference between the way a Spaniard or Italian on the quays of Algiers lives and the Arabs who live all around them. What is most essential in the Mediterranean genius springs perhaps from that historically and geographically unique encounter born between East and West. (In this regard, reference to Audisio[3] is obligatory.)

That Mediterranean culture and truth exists and is displayed in every aspect: (1) linguistic unity—ease of learning one Latin language once you know another; (2) unity of origin—prodigious collectivism of the Middle Ages—order of knights, order of monks, feudal powers, etc. The Mediterranean, in all these aspects, gives us here the image of a living, colorful, concrete civilization transforming doctrines into its image—and absorbing ideas without changing its own nature.

But then, you will say, why go further?

V

Because the very land that transformed so many doctrines must transform the doctrines of today. A Mediterranean collectivism will be different from a Russian collectivism, strictly speaking. The game of collectivism is not being played out in Russia; it is being played out in the Mediterranean basin and in Spain at the present moment. To be sure, the game of man has been played out for a long while, but it is perhaps here that it has reached the peak of tragedy and that so many trump cards are concentrated in our hands. Before our eyes, there are realities that are stronger than us. Our ideas will bend before them and adapt. That is why our adversaries are mistaken in all their objections. No one has the right to prejudge the fate of a doctrine and judge our future in the name of the past, even if it is that of Russia.

Our task precisely here is to rehabilitate the Mediterranean, take it back from those who unjustly lay claim to it and make it ready to receive the economic forms that await it. It is to discover what is concrete and alive in it, and promote at every opportunity the diverse aspects of that culture. We are all the more prepared for this task in that we are in direct contact with the Orient, which can teach us so much in that respect. We are here with the Mediterranean against Rome. And the essential role that cities like Algiers and Barcelona can play in their own poor way is to serve that aspect of Mediterranean culture which promotes man rather than crushing him.

VI

The role of the intellectual is hard in our epoch. It is not up to him to modify history. Whatever people say, revolutions are made first and the ideas come later. So great courage is needed today to declare oneself faithful to things of the mind. But at least that courage is not useless. If so much scorn and so much disapproval is attached to the label intellectual, that is insofar as it implies the notion of the argumentative, abstract gentleman, incapable of devoting himself to life and preferring his own personality to the rest of the world. But for those who do not wish to avoid their responsibilities, the essential task is to rehabilitate intelligence by regenerating the matter upon which it works, and to give the mind back all its true meaning by restoring to culture its true face of health and sunlight. And, as I was saying, that courage is not useless. For if it is not in fact up to intelligence to modify history, then its proper task will be to act upon man who himself makes history. We have a contribution to make to that task. We want to reconnect culture with life. The Mediterranean, which surrounds us with smiles, sunlight and sea, provides us with the lesson for this. Xenophon, in his *Retreat of the Ten Thousand*, recounts how the Greek soldiers who had ventured into Asia, returning to their own land, dying of hunger and thirst, in despair at so many setbacks and humiliations, reached the top of a mountain from which they saw the sea. At once they began to dance, forgetting all their exhaustion and disgust at the spectacle of their past lives. Neither do we wish to separate ourselves from the world. There is only one culture. Not that which feeds off abstractions and capital letters. Not that which condemns. Not that which justifies the abuses and deaths of Ethiopia and legitimizes the taste for brutal conquest. We know that one well and want no part of it. But the one which lives in trees and hills and men.

This is why men of the left are presenting themselves before you today in the service of a cause that at first sight had nothing to do with their opinions. I would hope that, like us, you might now be convinced of the opposite. All that is alive is ours. Politics is made for men, not men for politics. For Mediterranean men, a Mediterranean politics is needed. We do not want to live off fables. In the world of violence and death surrounding us, there is no room for hope. But there is perhaps room for civilization, the true kind, the kind that puts truth before fable, life before dreams. And this civilization has no need for hope. Man lives there off his truths.*

It is to this common effort that men of the West must devote themselves. In the framework of internationalism, the thing is achievable. If each person in their own sphere, land or province agrees to a modest labor, success is not far away. As for us, we know our target, our limitations and our possibilities. We have only to open our eyes to be aware of our task: to make people realize that culture can be understood only when placed at the service of life; that the mind is capable of not being man's enemy. Just as the Mediterranean sun is the same for all men, the effort of human intelligence must be a common patrimony rather than a source of conflict and murder.

Can a new Mediterranean culture compatible with our social ideal be achieved? Yes, but it is up to us and to you to help achieve it.

* I have spoken about a new civilization rather than about progress within civilization. It would be too dangerous to wield that wicked toy called Progress.

Defense of Intelligence

1945

After a gap of four years during the war, Temps présent *began to appear again in late August 1944. On March 15, 1945, under the aegis of the Amitié Française association, the Catholic weekly invited "young intellectuals" to meet at the Mutualité hall in Paris. Albert Camus addressed this assembly, which among other speakers included Stanislas Fumet, editor of* Temps présent, *André Mandouze, Emmanuel Mounier and Maurice Schumann. Published at the end of 1945 in the first issue of the magazine* Variété, *the speech "Defense of Intelligence" was to be reprinted by Camus in the first volume of his* Actuelles *(1950), in a section called "Pessimism and Tyranny."*

If the kind of French friendship which concerns us here were to be merely an effusion of feeling among agreeable people, I would not give much for it. That would be the easiest thing, but the least useful. And I assume the people who took this initiative wanted something else—a more difficult friendship, requiring effort. So that we shall not be tempted to give way to facility and content ourselves with mutual congratulation, in the ten minutes allotted me I should simply like to indicate the difficulties of this undertaking. From that point of view, I can do no better than speak about what always stands in the way of friendship—I mean falsehood and hatred.

For we shall do nothing for French friendship if we do not deliver ourselves from falsehood and hatred. In a certain sense, it is only too true that we have failed to deliver ourselves from them. We have been schooled by them for too long. And perhaps Hitlerism's last and most durable victory has been those shameful scars left in the hearts even of those who fought it with all their strength. How could it be otherwise? For years this world has been given over to an unparalleled flood of hatred. For four years, here at home, we have witnessed the methodical exercise of that hatred. Men like you and me, who of a morning would pat children in the Métro, in the evening would become transformed into meticulous executioners. They would become the functionaries of hatred and torture. For four years, those functionaries made their administration work: villages of orphans were built; men were shot in the face to make them unrecognizable; children's corpses were stamped with heels into coffins too small for them; brothers were tortured in front of sisters; cowards were molded and the proudest of souls destroyed. It seems that such stories were not credited abroad. But for four years they had to be credited here, in our fleshly agony. For four years, each morning, every Frenchman would receive his ration of hatred and his slap in the face as soon as he opened his daily paper. Inevitably, something of all that has been left behind.

It has left us with hatred. It has left us with the impulse which, the other day in Dijon, drove a fourteen-year-old child to hurl himself upon a collaborator being lynched and try to gouge his face. It has left us with that rage that scorches our souls at the memory of certain images and certain faces. The hatred of the executioners is matched by the hatred of the victims. And now that the executioners are gone, the French have been left with their own hatred partially unsated. They still look at each other with a residue of anger.

Well, that is what we first need to conquer. We must heal those poisoned hearts. And tomorrow, the hardest victory we have to achieve over the enemy must be won within ourselves, through the exceptional effort that will transform our appetite for hatred into desire for justice. Not yielding to hatred, conceding nothing to violence, not permitting our passions to become blind—this is what we can still do for friendship and against Hitlerism. Even today, some newspapers give free rein to violence and insult. But that is to surrender once more to the enemy. On the contrary, it is up to us never to allow criticism to descend into insult; to admit that our opponent may be right, and his arguments in any case, however faulty, may be disinterested. In short, it is up to us to remake our political mentality.

What does that mean, if we stop to think about it? It means that we must preserve intelligence. For I am convinced that this is where the problem lies. A few years ago, when the Nazis had just taken power, Göring would give a true idea of their philosophy by declaring: "When people talk to me about intelligence, I take out my revolver."[1] And that philosophy spread beyond Germany. At the same time, throughout civilized Europe, the excesses of intellect and the sins of the intellectual were being denounced. Intellectuals themselves, through a telling reaction, were not slow to join the assault. Everywhere philosophies of instinct triumphed and, along with them, that cheap romanticism which prefers feeling to understanding, as if the two could be separated. Since then, intelligence has constantly been called into question. War came, then defeat. Vichy taught us that the main culprit was intelligence. The peasants had read too much Proust. And everyone knows that *Paris-Soir*,[2] Fernandel[3] and corporate banquets were signs of intelligence. The mediocrity of the elites which was killing France apparently had its source in books.

Intelligence is mistreated even now. This merely proves that the enemy is not yet defeated. And it is enough to strive to understand without any preconceived idea, enough to talk about objectivity, for people to denounce your sophistry and accuse all your pretensions. Well, no! That is just what has to be reformed. For, like everyone, I well know the excesses of intellect; like everyone, I know that intellectuals are dangerous creatures who easily betray. But that is the wrong kind of intelligence. The kind we are speaking about is that which relies on courage; that which, for four years, has paid the necessary price for the right to be respected. Whenever this kind of intelligence is extinguished, the night of dictatorships falls. Which is why we have to uphold it with all its duties and all its rights. It is at this price, at this price alone, that French friendship will have any meaning. For friendship is the knowledge of free men.

And there is no freedom without intelligence and without mutual understanding.

In conclusion, it is you students whom I shall address here. I am not one of those who will preach virtue to you. Too many French people confuse that with weakness of blood. If I had the right to do so, I should instead advocate passions. But on one or two points I should like those who will shape the French intelligence of tomorrow at least to be determined never to yield. I should like them not to yield when people tell them that intelligence is always excessive; when people try to prove to them that lying is all right in order to ensure success. I should like them not to yield to trickery, or violence, or cowardice. Then perhaps a French friendship will be possible that will be something more than empty babble. Then, perhaps, in a free nation passionate about truth, man will begin once more to acquire that taste for man without which the world will never be anything but a vast solitude.

Informal Talk by Monsieur Albert Camus [to the Romanians]

1945

When Albert Camus addressed this message to the Romanians, their country was passing through a serious political crisis. Under communist pressure, the government of national unity—established in August 1944 after the crushing of German and Romanian troops by the Red Army—resigned in October, in favor of a pro-Soviet government led by Petru Groza. After the 1946 elections and the abdication of King Michael I in 1947, Romania became a people's democracy under Moscow tutelage. The conditions under which this message was broadcast are unknown. Pierre Kauffmann and Serge Karski, dispatched successively to Romania by the newspaper Combat *of which Camus was then chief editor,*[1] *may have acted as local contacts for its radio transmission.*

The Frenchman who is speaking to you today has no other claim to be addressing you than having for four years been the citizen of a country enslaved and humiliated as Romania was. So it is not any official way of speaking that I can adopt with you today, nor the authoritative manner that more important personages might allow themselves. But it does seem to me that I can speak to you as one of those seemingly anonymous millions of men who made up the French people under oppression.

Like everyone in my country, I know the ties that have always bound Romania and France. But those ties, translated into the language of chancelleries or of academic lectures, have always struck me as a bit abstract. If it was necessary to speak only about them, I should have nothing to say to you. But for four years there has been a European community in which the French people and the Romanian people have formed other ties, and which is a community of suffering. It is here that I am able to speak.

I have no taste for oratorical warnings. And that is why I shall say, as I think, that Romania and France entered shame at the same time and left it at the same time. This is what makes our resemblance and our common destiny. And it is this that should help us understand each other better. For if it is not shared shame and revolt which bring people closer, then nothing in the world can bring them closer and they are condemned to eternal solitude.

Barely emerged from nights of oppression, Europe is obliged to acknowledge her solidarity. We now know that everything which threatens Romanian freedom threatens French freedom, and that conversely everything which hurts a Frenchman affects at the same time the free men of Romania. We know that we shall save ourselves together, with all the other peoples of Europe, or we shall perish together. And that is fine. What we were unable to do in the days when intelligence was free and happy, we shall perhaps do after all these years in which it was insulted and desperate.

I know that some among you are concerned for France and retain the memory of her greatness. I know that they are asking: "What is she doing? What is she going to do?" It is a question I cannot answer. Frenchmen of my age, when they think about their country, experience an anguish they cannot share with anybody. But I can tell you at least what we do know for sure. We are sure that France, and with her Europe, will not be remade from one day to the next. We know that political greatness is lost more quickly than it is achieved. But we know too that there are forms of greatness which are for all time, even though they are not obtained painlessly.

It is these forms of greatness which motivate us, because they are not based on hatred or oppression. I am referring to justice and freedom. We who have so detested injustice and been fired by the hope of freedom for so many years, we no more desire an unjust country than an oppressed country. It seems to me, Romanian friends, that you and the whole of Europe can freely share these forms of greatness with us.

The Crisis of Man

1946

In spring 1946 Albert Camus was invited by the foreign ministry's French cultural relations department to give a series of lectures in North America. During the sea crossing, he drafted "The Crisis of Man," which he read out in French in public for the first time on March 28, 1946, at an evening event at Columbia University, New York, addressed also by "Vercors" (Jean Bruller) and "Thimerais" (Léon Motchane). Camus gave this lecture again throughout his visit to the United States, in a slightly expanded version, the typescript of which was discovered recently in the archives of Dorothy Norman (Beinecke Library, Yale University). This is the version reproduced in translation here. The chief editor of the journal Twice a Year, *Norman published "The Crisis of Man" at the end of 1946, in a translation by Lionel Abel.*

Ladies and gentlemen,

When it was suggested to me that I should give some lectures in the United States of America, I had scruples and hesitated. I am not the right age for giving lectures, and feel more at ease in reflection than categorical assertion, because I do not claim to possess what is generally called truth. When I expressed my scruples, I was told very politely that the important thing was not for me to have any personal opinion. The important thing was for me to be able to provide those few elements of information about France which would allow my audience to form their own opinion. Whereupon I was advised to inform my listeners about the current state of French theater, literature and even philosophy. I replied that it would perhaps be just as interesting to speak about the extraordinary efforts of French railwaymen, or about how miners in the Nord are now working. It was pointed out to me very pertinently that one should never strain one's talent, and that it was right for special interests to be addressed by people competent to do so. With a long-standing interest in literary matters while I certainly knew nothing about shunting, it was natural that I should be told to talk about literature rather than about railways.

At once I was enlightened. The important thing in fact was to talk about what I knew, and to give some idea of France. This is exactly why I have chosen precisely to speak neither about literature nor about theater. For literature, theater, philosophy, intellectual study and the efforts of an entire people are merely the reflections of a fundamental interrogation, a struggle for life and man, which constitute for us the whole problem of today. The French feel that man is still threatened, and they feel too that they will not be able to go on living if a certain idea of man is not rescued from the crisis with which our world is wrestling. And that is why, out of loyalty to my country, I have chosen to speak about the crisis of man. And as the idea was to talk about what I knew, I thought I could not do better than to retrace as clearly as possible the spiritual experience of men of my generation, since that experience has covered the full extent of the world crisis, and can shed some dim light both upon absurd fate and upon one aspect of today's French sensibility.

I should first like to situate this generation. Men of my age in France and in Europe were born just before or during the first great war, reached adolescence at the time of the world economic crisis and were twenty in the year when Hitler came to power. To complete their education, they were then offered the war in Spain, Munich, the 1939 war, defeat and four years of occupation and clandestine struggle. So I suppose it is what people call an interesting generation, which is why I was right to think it will be more instructive for you if I speak not in my own name, but in that of a certain number of Frenchmen who are thirty today, and whose intelligence and hearts were formed during the terrible years when, along with their country, they fed off shame and lived off rebellion.

Yes, it is an interesting generation, first and foremost because, confronted by the absurd world that its elders were creating for it, it believed in nothing and lived in rebellion. The literature of its age was rebelling against clarity, stories and even sentences. Painting was rebelling against subjects, reality and mere harmony. Music was rejecting melody. As for philosophy, it taught that there was no truth, only phenomena; that there might be Mr. Smith, Monsieur Durand and Herr Vogel, but there could be nothing in common between these three specific phenomena. The moral stance of this generation was still more categorical: nationalism appeared to it like an outworn truth, religion like an exile; twenty-five years of international politics had taught it to doubt all pure creeds, and to think that nobody was ever wrong since everybody could be right. As for the traditional morality of our society, it appeared to us what it still is: that is to say, a monstrous hypocrisy.

So we were thus in negation. Of course, this was not new. Other generations, other countries have lived through this experience in other periods of History. But what is new is that these same men, strangers to all values, had to resolve their personal position regarding murder and terror. It was then that they came to think that there perhaps did exist a Crisis of Man, because they had to live in the most agonizing of contradictions. For basically they entered war as you enter Hell, if it is true that Hell is renunciation. They did not like war or violence, but they had to accept war and inflict violence. They felt hatred only for hatred. Yet they had to learn that difficult knowledge. In total contradiction with themselves, without having any traditional value at their disposal, they had to resolve the most painful of problems ever posed to men. So here you have, on the one hand, a remarkable generation as I have just defined it and, on the other, a crisis embracing the world and human consciousness, which I shall now seek to characterize as clearly as possible.

So what is this crisis? Well, rather than characterizing it in general, I should like to illustrate first by four brief stories from a time that the world has begun to forget, but that still sears our hearts.

1. In the Gestapo building in a European capital, after a night of questioning, two suspects still bleeding have been left tied up and

the building's concierge dutifully clears up around them, her mind at peace since she has doubtless eaten her breakfast. Reproached by one of the victims, she replies indignantly with a phrase which, translated into French, might go more or less like this: "I never interfere with what my tenants do."

2. In Lyon, one of my comrades is dragged from his cell for a third bout of questioning. Since his ears have been torn during an earlier interrogation, he is wearing a bandage around his head. The German officer taking him is the very same one who was already there at the earlier sessions, yet it is he who asks with a trace of affection and concern in his voice: "And how are your ears, then?"

3. In Greece, following a Partisan operation, a German officer is getting ready to have three brothers whom he has taken as hostages shot. Their elderly mother throws herself at his feet and he agrees to spare one of them, provided she herself makes the choice. Since she is unable to decide, aim is taken at them. She picks the eldest, because he is head of the family; but by doing so she condemns the two others, just as the German officer wished.

4. A group of deported women, including one of my comrades, is repatriated to France via Switzerland. Barely have they entered Swiss territory than they notice a civil burial. And the sight alone causes them to break out in hysterical laughter. "Look how they treat the dead here," they say.

If I have chosen these stories, it is not because of their sensational character. I know that the world's feelings must be spared, since it usually prefers to close its eyes in order to keep its peace of mind. But it is because they allow me to reply otherwise than with a conventional "yes" to the question: "Is there a Crisis of Man?" They allow me to reply, as all the men about whom I was speaking replied: yes, there is a Crisis of Man, since the death or torture of a human being can in our world be examined with a feeling of indifference or friendly interest, or experimentation, or mere passivity. Yes, there is a Crisis of Man, since the execution of a human being can be envisaged otherwise than with the horror and shock it ought to provoke; since human pain is accepted as a somewhat tedious chore, on the same level as buying food or queuing for every gram of butter.

It is too easy, in this respect, to blame Hitler alone and say that, since the beast is dead, the poison has disappeared. For we well know that the poison has not disappeared; that we all carry it in our very hearts; and that this can be felt in the way in which nations, parties and individuals still look at each other with a residue of anger. I have always thought that a nation stuck by its traitors along with its heroes. But a civilization too, and white civilization in particular, is as responsible for its perversions as for its successes. From this viewpoint we all stick by Hitlerism, and we need to seek the more general causes which made possible the terrible evil that began to ravage the face of Europe.

So let us attempt, with the help of the four stories I have recounted, to enumerate the clearest symptoms of this crisis. They are, first and foremost:

1. The rise of terror, following a perversion of values such that a man or a historical force is no longer judged in terms of their dignity, but in terms of their success. The modern crisis consists entirely in the fact that no Westerner is certain of his immediate future; we all experience more or less clearly the anguish of being ground down in one way or another by History. If you want that wretched man, that Job of Modern Times, not to perish of his wounds on his dung heap, you must first lift that burden of fear and anguish, so that he will rediscover the freedom of spirit without which he will solve none of the problems posed to modern consciousness.

2. This crisis is next based on the impossibility of persuasion. Men live and are able to live only with the idea that they have something in common, where they can always meet. You always believe that by addressing a man as a human being, you can get human reactions from him. But we have discovered this: there are men you cannot persuade. It was impossible for a concentration-camp victim to hope to explain to the SS who were beating him that they ought not to do it. The Greek mother I spoke of could not persuade the German officer that it was unfitting to impose on her the heartbreak to which he was subjecting her. The fact was that the SS or the German

officer no longer represented a man or men, but an instinct raised to the level of an idea or a theory. Passion, even murderous passion, would have been preferable. Because passion comes to an end, and another passion, another cry coming from flesh or the heart, can persuade it. But the man who is capable of showing friendly concern for ears he has previously torn, that man is not a man of passion, he is a mathematician whom nothing can stop or persuade.

3. It is also replacement of the natural object by the form—in other words, the rise of bureaucracy. More and more, contemporary man interposes between nature and himself an abstract and complicated machine which thrusts him into solitude. It is when there is no bread left that coupons appear. The French get only 1,200 calories of food per day, but they have at least six different documents and a hundred stamps on those documents. And it is the same everywhere in the world, where bureaucracy has continued to proliferate. In order to come from France to America, I used up a lot of paper in both countries. So much paper that doubtless I could even have managed to print this lecture in a sufficient number of copies to distribute it here without needing to come myself. By dint of papers, offices and functionaries, a world is created in which human warmth disappears; in which no man can touch another, other than through the maze of what are called formalities. The German officer who caressed my comrade's torn ears thought he could do so because when he had torn them it was part of his job as a functionary, so it could not be wrong. In short, people no longer die, no longer love and no longer kill except vicariously. That is what, I suppose at least, you might call good organization.

4. It is also replacement of real man by political man. There are no more possible individual passions, but only collective passions—in other words, abstract passions. We are all introduced willingly or forcibly into politics. What counts is no longer respecting or sparing a mother's suffering; what counts is securing the victory of a doctrine. And human pain is no longer an outrage, but just a figure on a bill whose dreadful total is not yet calculable.

5. It is obvious that all these symptoms can be summed up in a single one, involving the worship of both efficiency and abstraction.

This is why in today's Europe man knows only solitude and silence. It is because he cannot meet other men on the basis of shared values. And since he is no longer protected by a respect for man based on his values, the only alternative henceforth offered him is to be victim or executioner.

II[1]

This is what men of my generation have understood, and this is the crisis they found and still find confronting them. And we had to resolve it with the values at our disposal: in other words, with nothing but awareness of the absurdity surrounding us. This is how we had to enter war and terror, with neither consolation nor certainty. We knew only that we could not yield to the beasts emerging in every corner of Europe. But we could not justify this obligation we were under. Moreover, the more aware among us perceived that they did not yet have, in the realm of thought, any principle which might allow them to oppose terror and repudiate murder.

For if you basically believe in nothing, if nothing has any meaning and we can proclaim no value, then everything is allowed and nothing is important. Then there is neither good nor evil, and Hitler was neither wrong nor right. You can send millions of innocent people to the gas chamber just as you can dedicate yourself to caring for lepers. You can tear ears with one hand, only to caress them with the other. You can do your housework in front of torture victims. And you can equally well honor the dead or throw them into the dustbin. That is all equivalent. And since we thought nothing had any meaning, we were obliged to conclude that the person who succeeds must be right. And that is so true that even today plenty of intelligent, skeptical people will tell you that if by chance Hitler had won this war, History would have paid homage to him and consecrated the dreadful pedestal upon which he had perched. And we indeed cannot doubt that History such as we conceive it would have consecrated Mr. Hitler and justified terror and murder, just as we all consecrate and justify them as soon as we venture to think that nothing has any meaning.

Some among us, it is true, believed it possible to think that, in the absence of any higher value, one could at least think that History did have a meaning. At any rate, they often acted as if they thought that. They used to say that this war was necessary because it would liquidate the age of nationalisms and prepare the time of Empires, which would be succeeded—perhaps after conflict—by the universal Society and Paradise on earth.

Thinking that, however, they used to arrive at the same result as if, like us, they had thought that nothing had any meaning. For if History has a meaning, it is a total meaning or it is nothing. Those men thought and acted as if History obeyed a sovereign dialectic, and as if we were all advancing together toward a definitive end. They thought and acted according to Hegel's hateful principle: "Man is made for History and not History for Man."[2] In truth, all the political and moral realism guiding the destinies of the world today obeys, often without knowing it, a German-style philosophy of history according to which the whole of humanity is advancing along rational paths toward a definitive universe. Nihilism has been replaced by absolute rationalism and in both cases the results are the same. For if it is true that History obeys a sovereign and fatal logic, if it is true according to that same German philosophy that the feudal State must inevitably succeed the anarchic state, then nations succeed feudalism and Empires nations, to end up with the universal Society, then everything that serves that inevitable march is good and the accomplishments of History are definitive truths. And as these accomplishments can be served only by the ordinary means of wars, plots and murders both individual and collective, all acts are justified not insofar as they are good or bad, but insofar as they are effective or not.

Thus it is that in today's world the men of my generation have for years been subjected to the twofold temptation of thinking that nothing is true or thinking that the sole truth lies in surrender to historical fatality. This is how many people have succumbed to one or other of these temptations. And this is how the world has remained in thrall to the will for power: in other words, ultimately to terror. For if nothing is true or false, if nothing is good or bad, and if the only value is efficiency, then the rule must be to prove yourself the most efficient—in other words, the strongest. The world is no longer divided between just men and unjust men, but between masters and slaves. The one who is right is the one who enslaves. The cleaning woman is right rather than the torture victims. The German officer who tortures and the one who executes, the SS transformed into gravediggers, those are the rational men of this new world. Just look at things around you and see if that is not still true now. We are in the toils of violence and stifling there. Whether it is within nations or in the world, mistrust, resentment, greed, the race to power are busy manufacturing a grim and desperate universe, where every man finds himself obliged to live in the present, the very word "future" representing for him distress in all its forms; delivered up to abstract powers; wasted and stupefied by a headlong life; separated from natural truths, calm leisure and simple happiness. Will you perhaps, however, in this still happy America not see this, or see it only dimly? But the men I am speaking to you about have seen it for years, felt this evil in their flesh, read it on the faces of those they love; and from the depths of their sick hearts there now arises a terrible revolt that will end by carrying us all away. Too many monstrous images still haunt them for them to imagine it will be easy; but they have felt the horror of these years too deeply to accept prolonging it. It is here that the real problem begins for them.

III

If the features of this crisis are indeed the will to power, terror, the replacement of real man by political and historical man, the reign of abstractions and fatality, futureless solitude—and if we wish to resolve this crisis—these are features we must change. And our generation found itself facing this huge problem, with all its negations. So it was from those very negations that it had to draw the strength to struggle. It was quite useless to tell us, "You must believe in God, or Plato, or Marx," because we precisely did not have that kind of faith. The only question was to know if we were going to accept this world in which it was no longer possible to be anything but victim or executioner. And, of course, we wanted to be neither, since we knew at the bottom of our hearts that this distinction was illusory; and that ultimately there were no longer anything but victims, and that murderers and those they killed were eventually reunited in the same defeat. However, the problem was no longer whether or not to accept this condition and the world, but to know what reason we might have for opposing it.

This is why we sought a reason in our revolt itself, which had led us—for no apparent reason—to opt for the struggle against evil. And we thus understood that we had revolted not just for ourselves, but for something that was common to all men.

How was this?

In this world stripped of values, in this desert of the heart in which we lived, what did our revolt actually mean? It made us into men who said "no." But we were at the same time men who said "yes." We said "no" to that world, to its essential absurdity, to the abstractions which threatened us, to the civilization of death being prepared for us. By saying "no" we affirmed that things had gone on long enough; that there was a limit which could not be crossed. But at the same time we affirmed everything *below* that limit; we affirmed that there was something in us which rejected what was outrageous, and which could no longer be humiliated. And naturally that was a contradiction which could not fail to make us reflect. We thought that the world was living and struggling without real values. But all the same we were struggling against Germany. The Frenchmen of the Resistance whom I knew, and who used to read Montaigne on the train while carrying leaflets, proved that in our country, at least, it was possible to understand skeptics at the same time as having an idea of honor. And consequently, by the very fact of living, hoping and struggling, we were all affirming something.

But did that something have a general value? Did it go beyond an individual opinion? Could it serve as a rule of conduct? The answer is very simple. The men I am referring to were ready to die in the course of their revolt. And that death proved that they were sacrificing themselves for the sake of a virtue which transcended their personal existence and went beyond their individual fate. What we rebels were defending against a hostile fate was a value common to all men. When men were tortured in front of a cleaner, when ears were methodically ripped, when mothers were forced to condemn their own children to death, when decent men were buried like swine, those rebels judged that something in them was being negated, something that did not belong just to them, but was a common good in which men have a ready-made solidarity.

Yes, it was the great lesson of those terrible years that the injury done to a student in Prague affected a worker from the Paris suburbs, and that the blood shed somewhere on the banks of a river in Central Europe would bring a Texas farmer to shed his own on the soil of those Ardennes which he now saw for the first time. And that itself was absurd and crazy—impossible, almost, to imagine. But at the same time, in that absurdity there was this lesson that we were in a collective tragedy, where what was at stake was a common dignity, a shared human communion, which had to be defended and maintained. Thenceforth we knew how to act; and we learned how, in the most absolute moral destitution, man can find values capable of regulating his conduct. For if this shared communication among men, in mutual acknowledgment of their dignity, was truth, then it was that very communication which we had to serve.

And in order to maintain this communication, men had to be free, since there is nothing in common between a master and a slave, and it is impossible to speak and communicate with a man enslaved. Yes, servitude is a silence and the most terrible of all.

And in order to maintain this communication, we had to make injustice disappear, because there is no contact between the oppressed and the profiteer. Envy too belongs to the realm of silence.

And in order to maintain this communication, we had to outlaw lying and violence, for the man who lies shuts himself off from other men, and the one who tortures and coerces imposes definitive silence. Thus from the "no" asserted by the very activity of our revolt we derived an ethics of freedom and sincerity. Yes, it was that very communication with which we had to combat the world of murder. This is what we now knew, and what we must retain today in order to defend ourselves from murder. Which is why, we now know, we must struggle against injustice, servitude and terror, because those three scourges are the ones causing silence to prevail among men, erecting barriers between them, hiding them from one another and preventing them from finding the one value that might save them from this despairing world, which is the long fraternity of men struggling against their fate. After this long night, now and at last we know what we must do, confronted by this world torn apart by its crisis.

What must we do? We must:

1. Call things by their name and face up to the fact that we are killing millions of men whenever we agree to think certain thoughts. A person does not think badly because he is a murderer. He is a murderer because he thinks badly. So he can be a murderer without apparently ever having killed. And so we are all more or less murderers. Hence, the first thing to do is purely and simply to reject by thought and by action every form of realist, fatalist thought.

2. The second thing to do is clear the world of the terror that dominates it and prevents it from thinking well. And since I have heard that the United Nations is holding an important session in this very city,[3] we might suggest that the first written text of that world organization should proclaim solemnly, after the Nuremberg Trials, abolition of the death penalty throughout the Universe.

3. The third thing to do is put politics whenever possible back in its proper place, which is a secondary one. It is not actually a matter of giving this world a gospel, or a political or moral catechism. The great misfortune of our time is precisely that politics claims to provide us simultaneously with a catechism, a complete philosophy, and even sometimes an art of love. But the role of politics is to do the housework, not to settle our domestic problems. For my own part, I do not know if an absolute exists. But I do know it is not one of a

political kind. The absolute is not the business of everybody: it is the business of each individual. And all must regulate their reciprocal relations in such a way that everyone has the inner leisure to ponder on the absolute. Our life does no doubt belong to others, and it is right to give it when that is necessary. But our death belongs only to ourselves. Which is my definition of freedom.

4. The fourth thing to do is seek out and create, on the basis of negation, the positive values which will permit reconciliation of negative thought with the possibilities of positive action. That is the task of philosophers, of which I have given only an outline.

5. The fifth thing to do is understand fully that this attitude amounts to creating a universalism in which all men of goodwill may come together. In order to escape solitude, you must speak; but you must speak plainly and—on every occasion—never lie but speak all the truth that you know. But you can speak the truth only in a world where it is defined and based on values common to all men. It is not Mr. Hitler who can decide that this is true or this is not. No man in the world today or tomorrow will ever be able to decide that his truth is good enough to be able to impose it on others. For only the common consciousness of men can assume that ambition. And it is necessary to rediscover the values which nurture that common consciousness. The freedom we have to win, finally, is the right not to lie. Only on that condition shall we know our reasons for living and dying.

For our part, this is where we are. And doubtless it was perhaps not worth going so far in order to get there. But, after all, the History of men is the history of their mistakes, not of their truth. Truth is probably like happiness: it is quite simple and has no history.

Does this mean that all our problems are thereby solved? Of course not. This world is not better or more reasonable. We have still not escaped from absurdity. But at least we have a reason to strive to change our behavior, and it is that reason which we formerly lacked. The world would still be despairing if man did not exist, but there is man and his passions, his dreams and his community. There are some of us in Europe who in this way combine a pessimistic view of the world and a profound optimism about man. We do not claim to escape History, for we are in History.

We claim only to struggle in History in order to preserve that Human share of History which does not belong to it. We wish only to rediscover the paths of that civilization where man, without turning away from History, will no longer be enslaved to it; where the service that every man owes to all men will find itself balanced by meditation, leisure and the share of happiness that everyone owes to himself.

I think I can safely say that we shall always refuse to worship events, facts, wealth, power, History as it is made and the world as it goes. We wish to see the human condition as it is. And what it is, we know. It is that terrible condition which demands truckloads of blood and centuries of history to achieve an imperceptible modification in the fate of men. Such is the law. For years during the eighteenth century heads fell in France like hail, the French Revolution inflamed every heart with enthusiasm and terror. And ultimately, at the beginning of the next century, we achieved the replacement of legitimate monarchy by constitutional monarchy. We French of the twentieth century know that terrible law only too well. There was the war, the occupation, the massacres, thousands of prison walls, a Europe frantic with pain—and all that in order for some of us finally to gain the two or three slight differences which will help them despair less. It is optimism which would be the outrage here. We know that those who are dead today were the best, since it was they who selected themselves. And we who are still alive are obliged to tell ourselves that we are alive only because we did less than others.

This is the reason why we continue to live in contradiction. The only difference is that this generation can now combine that contradiction with an immense hope in man. Since I have wished to inform you about an aspect of French sensibility, it will suffice for you not to forget this: in France and in Europe today there is a generation which thinks, basically, that the person who places hope in the human condition is a madman, but that the one who despairs of events is a coward. It rejects absolute explanations and the sway of political philosophies, but is willing to affirm man in his flesh and his pursuit of freedom. It does not believe it possible to realize universal happiness and satisfaction, but it does believe it possible to diminish the pain of men. It is because the world is unhappy in its essence that we must, this generation thinks, do something for happiness; because it is unjust that we must strive for justice; finally, because it is absurd that we must give it all these reasons.

To conclude, what does this mean? It means one must be modest in one's thoughts and action, keep one's place and do one's job well. It means we all have to create, outside parties and governments, communities of reflection that will initiate dialogue between nations and affirm through their lives and their conversations that this world must stop being one of policemen, soldiers and money to become one of men and women, fruitful work and thoughtful leisure.

That is where I think we shall have to direct our effort, reflection and, if necessary, sacrifice. The decadence of the Greek world began with the assassination of Socrates. And many a Socrates has been killed in Europe in the past few years. This is an indication. It indicates that only the Socratic spirit of leniency toward others and strictness toward oneself is dangerous for civilizations of murder. So it indicates that this spirit alone can regenerate the world. Any other effort, however admirable, directed toward power and domination can only mutilate man even more seriously. In any case, this is the modest revolution we French and Europeans are living through at this time.

Conclusion

Perhaps you will have been surprised that a French writer on an official visit to America should not have felt obliged to present you with an idyllic picture of his country; and, moreover, should so far have made no effort at what is conventionally called propaganda. But perhaps when you reflect on the problem I have outlined to you, you will find this more natural. Propaganda is made, I suppose, to provoke feelings in people which they have not yet known. But the Frenchmen who have shared our experience are actually asking to be neither pitied nor loved to order. The only national problem which they confronted did not depend on the world's opinion. For five years, the question for us was to know if we could save our honor; in other words, retain the right to speak when our turn came after the war was over. And we did not need anyone else to acknowledge that right; we needed only to acknowledge it ourselves. That was not easy, but if we did eventually acknowledge that right, it was because we know—and alone know—the real scale of our sacrifices.

But that right for us is not the right to give lessons. It is only the right to escape the humiliating silence of those who were beaten and defeated for having too long despised man. Beyond that, I beg you to believe that we shall know how to keep our place. Perhaps, as people say, there is a possibility that the history of the next fifty years may be made partly by nations other than France. I know nothing about that personally. But what I do know is that this nation which lost 1,620,000 men twenty-five years ago, and has just lost several hundreds of thousands of volunteers, must acknowledge that it, or someone, perhaps overtaxed its strength. That is a fact. And the opinion of the world, its respect or its scorn, can change nothing about that fact. Which is why it strikes me as ridiculous to solicit or persuade that opinion. But it does not strike me as ridiculous to emphasize before that opinion how much the crisis of the world depends precisely on these disputes over precedence and power.

To summarize this evening's debates and, speaking for the first time in my own name, I should like to say just this: whenever anyone judges France or any other country, or any other question, in terms of power, they will introduce a bit further into the world a conception of man culminating in his mutilation; they will reinforce the thirst for domination and ultimately side with murder. Everything is interconnected in the world, as in ideas. And the person who says or writes that the end justifies the means, the person who says and writes that greatness is measured by strength, that person is absolutely responsible for the hideous piles of crimes disfiguring contemporary Europe.

There you have a clear definition, I think, of the entire meaning of what I felt I needed to tell you. And it was indeed my duty, I suppose, to remain faithful to the voice and experience of our comrades in Europe, so that you would not be tempted to judge them too hastily. For they no longer judge anyone, apart from murderers. And they look at all nations with the hope and the certainty to find in them the human truth that each of them contains.

Regarding in particular you young Americans listening to me this evening, I can tell you that the men about whom I have been speaking respect the humanity in you, and the taste for freedom and happiness that was discernible in the faces of the great Americans. Yes, they expect from you what they expect from all men of goodwill: a sincere contribution to the spirit of dialogue that they intend to establish in the world. Seen from afar, our struggles, our hopes and our demands must perhaps strike you as confused or futile. And it is true that, on the path of wisdom and truth, if there is one, these men have not chosen the straightest and simplest way. But the fact is that the world, and History, have offered them nothing straight or simple. The secret they could not find in their condition, they tried to forge with their own hands. And they will perhaps fail. But I am convinced that their failure will be that of the world itself. In this Europe still poisoned by mute violence and hatred, in this world rent by terror, they are striving to save what can still be saved of man. And that is their sole ambition. But the fact that this final effort has succeeded in finding one of its expressions again in France, and if I have been able this evening to give you some faint idea of the passion for justice inspiring all Frenchmen, that is our sole consolation and will be my simplest pride.

Are We Pessimists?

1946

A month after giving his lecture "The Crisis of Man" at Columbia University (see p. 18), Albert Camus concluded his American tour on May 1, 1946, with an address at Brooklyn College in New York. This lecture, delivered in French, ranks as a complement to "The Crisis of Man," to whose main theme it returns. The text of "Are We Pessimists?" was first published in July 1946 in the American magazine Vogue, *in English, with the title "The Crisis of Man: Inertia Is the Strongest Temptation." The conclusion of this translated version had two additional paragraphs not contained in the typescript found in the author's archives, but which have been included here, translated back into English from the French edition on which the current volume is based. On his return from the United States, Camus reproduced the text in a more condensed form, with the new title "Murderers Ourselves," which appeared in the third (November–December 1946) issue of the French journal* Franchise.

When a European has neatly postulated that life is tragic, he thinks he has become as clever as can be. Absurd, of course. Yet it seems to me that when an American has quite convinced himself that life is a good thing and pain does not exist, he thinks he has shown himself to be as sensible as possible. A serious mistake, naturally. So I find that confronted with a common condition, America and Europe suffer from opposite ills. It seems to me as irrational to say one should not be pessimistic as to say one should not be optimistic. The ancient Greeks knew that life has a face of darkness and a face of light, and they knew that man must keep his eyes fixed simultaneously on this light and on this shadow in order to remain true to his condition. And a civilization is always judged by the way in which it has managed to overcome this contradiction in a higher synthesis. Whatever may be thought in Europe and in America, we are all advancing toward that synthesis, and we all have something to say on the matter. If one fails the others will perish, and once again mud and blood will replace sunlight and darkness. And it is perhaps true that, in this great adventure of the Western spirit, many things do not depend upon us. But what always does depend upon us is the possibility of affirming, maintaining and never betraying what we believe to be the truth.

And the truth is that today's world is neither one of happiness nor of unhappiness. It is a battleground between the need for happiness that is in all men's hearts and a historical fatality wherein the crisis of man has reached its apex. So on the one hand we need to have a proper idea of that crisis, on the other a precise sense of the happiness for which every man can wish. So we need to have lucidity.

The crisis of man is at least half made up of the inertia and weariness of individuals confronted by the stupid principles or bad actions that continue to be heaped on the world. For man's strongest temptation is the temptation of inertia. And because the world is no longer filled by the victims' cries, many people may think it will go on as usual for a few generations more. And because it is easier to do one's daily work and wait peacefully for death to come one day, people believe that they have done enough for the good of man by not killing anyone directly, and by trying to lie as little as possible. But actually no man can die peacefully if he has not at least once risked his own life and that of others, and if he has not done what is necessary for the overall human condition to be made as peaceful as possible.

Thus it is that people who do not want to dwell too long upon human misery prefer to speak about it in a very general way. Thus it is that some people have asked me if I was quite sure there was a crisis of man, and whether this crisis was not, after all, something that had always existed. All this is at once true and false. And if it is true, it is in any case the kind of truth that cannot be spoken to concentration-camp inmates. And I think it impossible that those who have known torture might, while being dealt with, have told themselves calmly that, after all, things had always been this way and they should take comfort from that. Yes, I do indeed think that for them there was a crisis of man. And for all men of my genera-tion this crisis has not ended. To those who ask me that question, I have always replied that I did not know everything, and that I had no general explanation of the world. But I do know at least that for a long time we have not felt good about ourselves, and that we are not sure of our future, and that this is basically not a normal state for men presumed to be civilized. This is what wrongly or rightly we call a crisis of man. After which I said, and now repeat since we have to repeat ourselves, that there is a crisis because there is terror. And there is terror because people believe that nothing has any meaning, or else that historical success alone has one; because human values have been replaced by the values of contempt and efficiency, the will to be free replaced by the will to dominate. You are no longer right because you have justice on your side, but because you succeed. And the more you succeed, the more right you are. Ultimately, that justifies murder. And it is why men are right to be afraid, because in such a world it is always by chance or by some arbitrary benevolence that their life or that of their children is saved. And it is why men are right too to be ashamed, because those who live in such a world without condemning it with all their strength (which means almost all of them) are in their own way as murderous as the rest. This too is true.

But it is also true that we have another strength at our disposal, which is man's will when it is applied to happiness and justice. There too it is enough first to know what we want. And what we want, pre-cisely, is never again to justify force, never again to bow down before the power of arms or money. This, of course, is the kind of assertion which makes realists laugh. Because realists know, for their part, that it is an endless task; consequently they see no good reason to persist with it. They are willing to undertake only tasks that suc-ceed. And this is why they undertake none that is really important or really human; this is why, even without knowing it, they sanction the world of murder; this is why they do not see that, even if that task is endless, we are there to persist with it. I do not subscribe sufficiently to reason to believe in absolute progress, nor in any philosophy of history; but I do believe at least that men have never stopped advancing in the awareness they acquired of their destiny. We have not overcome our condition, but we know it better. We thus know that we are in contradiction, but that we must reject the contradiction and do what we have to in order to reduce it. So our task as men is to find the few formulae which will soothe the infinite anguish of free souls. We have to reconcile what is being torn apart, make justice imaginable in a world so evidently unjust, make happiness meaningful for peoples poisoned by the century's unhappiness. This, of course, is a superhuman task. But people call superhuman the tasks which men take a long time to accomplish. From this point of view, there is nothing superhuman in man's condition.

Is this pessimism? No, it is lucidity endeavoring to define in advance what it wants and what it does not want. If you are ill, you first need to know what malady you are suffering from, then you seek and apply cures. Since we are suffering from abstraction and terror, it is better to know this, in order to decide resolutely what we must do. We young Frenchmen call pessimists rather those who say that all is going well and nothing has changed in the world. For it is from such people that we can expect nothing. It is because of them that the world will indeed continue as usual, but amid prisons and chains. And it is because there are enough men among us who are lucid that there are at the same time enough men who are determined—and more determined than people in America think—to do what is in their power to cure themselves and cure the world of its current malady.

I am often asked here how much the young people of Europe are worth today. I have no answer to that, unaccustomed as I am to passing general judgments. But as for those young people with whom I am acquainted, I know that they live without illusions, and that this has nevertheless only strengthened their determination and their courage. And when I am told it is not good for young people to live without illusions, I say that the question is not to know what is desirable or what is not. The question is to know what is real. And what is real is that those young people have been obliged to live without illusions, in direct contact with the most direct realities of existence, and have nevertheless not perished. For they still manage today to identify the problems confronting the world, and to retain the will to resolve them. This is the proof that energy can be reconciled with lucidity, and passion be united with calm courage. Such is the experience which unfolds today in the hearts of some Europeans, and which involves the future of our civilization as much—neither more nor less—as scientific discoveries or the ingenious invention of the right of veto. This experience can basically be summed up in the maxim of one of our great revolutionaries, Saint-Just, who said: "So I think we must be radical. That excludes neither common sense nor wisdom."[1]

We know the kind of civilization that we want and the horror of what we do not want. But what can we expect? For a time, we can expect the world to continue in the grip of those who have no imagination; those who wish to preserve what can no longer be preserved, who wish to destroy what can never be destroyed. In the grip of those who lie and those who oblige others to lie; in the grip of officials and policemen. And if this continues, one day all will be swept away by those who kill and find it easy to be killers. That is logical. But it is also logical for us to continue to defend, against the attacks of the blind and the grasping, those things that are worth defending for man. We shall continue to do so, because we have agreed that in order to persevere it is not necessary to succeed, and because we know that it is the dogged persistence of some men that alone has ended by changing the world. The first Christians used to call the great movement sustaining them "the Folly of the Cross."[2]

What we need today is a folly of man. A great folly, which thinks ahead, solid and built upon the immense hope, the silent determination, which in the past has sustained and will continue to sustain European spirits in a world they have confronted without the benefit of illusion. When one knows this, it is perhaps easier to answer the question: "Are we pessimists?"

[The Individual and Freedom]

Interventions at the Civilization *Round Table*
1946

At the beginning of 1946, the French pioneer of industrial design Jacques
Viénot founded the Civilization association, around which gravitated
notably Jacques Heurgon, a former teacher of Albert Camus at the Algiers
faculty of letters, and Roger Caillois, with whom the author rubbed shoulders at the reading committee of Éditions Gallimard. On October 22, 1946,
Civilization invited Camus, Georges Friedmann, Maurice de Gandillac,
Pierre de Lanux, Maurice Merleau-Ponty[1] and Jean Wahl to debate "the
fate of the individual in today's world," theme of the third issue of its journal Chemins du monde, which would publish a verbatim record of the
round table. The interventions by Camus are reproduced integrally here,
while those of the other participants have been summarized and placed in
square brackets.

[The Nazi ideology, according to Maurice de Gandillac, based on a tech-
nocratic point of view, sees individuals as "so many creative forces" living
in a "coexistence of struggle" dominated by "the individualism of leaders."
What, by contrast, is the role of individualism in American civilization?
Can there be a free individual and what is his place in liberal capitalist
civilization and in the communist world? Is this a "transitory phase" ini-
tiating "a real liberation of man"? For his part, Jean Wahl refuses to see in
national socialism a form of individualism, while Georges Friedmann recognizes in "technicist civilization" a "denominator," common to America,
the USSR and Germany, whose societies live in an urban "new milieu"
opposed to the rural "natural milieu." The mechanization of life, which

is not limited to these countries alone, generates, "through the presence of ever-denser technology, substitutes for the presence of man." This action of technologies upon the individual "is psychic and transforms us"; it leads to social alienation. Among American soldiers, Friedmann observes "an intimate connivance with technology," but also "the absence of certain feelings which among us are common." If he hastens to add that "a socialist state is far better armed than a capitalist state to resolve most of these problems," he acknowledges that since the nineteenth century the growing statism of modern democracies threatens the freedom of the individual. The task today is "not to regret the past, but to see how to aid blossoming of the individual in the civilizations now being prepared." Pierre de Lanux aims to correct the cliché of American standardization. He detects, from the 1929 economic crisis onward, "a return to individual values," a rebirth of Jeffersonian values. "The problem is not how to conquer freedom, but how to use freedom."]

[To the question "What can and must be saved?," Camus replies:]

I am rather uneasy because I think we should be talking about nuances far more than categorical assertions, which is what we are obliged to make when we speak. It is for nuances that millions of men fought for five years, however extraordinary that may seem. If we pose the problem of the individual, assuming that we know what this is, we must ask categorically: "What is the fate of the individual?" We all know and have all felt vaguely that he is going to be killed.

If this individual is going to be killed, if we feel this, we first have to ask ourselves the following: do we think the individual is something that must be saved? Or do we not want that? [. . .]

It is possible that the bundle of values constituting the individual may appear to certain minds something outworn and not worth saving. In that case, all there is to do is wait for the end of history.

If we do wish to save him, two questions are posed. First: What are the principles of weakness which, in today's individual, impel him sooner or later to be sacrificed? And secondly: What are the external factors, historical or ideological, which threaten this individual and will sooner or later sacrifice him?

Regarding the first question, it seems to me that we might say the following, which goes in the same direction as what Friedmann said: anarchic individualism is outdated, overtaken by history. But within ourselves we carry an anarchic individual and must settle our account with him: he is a bad individual. For my own part, I think he presupposes man's solitude in a certain way, and I am deeply convinced that man is not alone. We have learned over the past few years that whenever an officer was slapped in Prague, sooner or later a Belleville worker was going to get himself killed.

The liberal individualism we spoke about—we have it also within ourselves. It seems to me also doomed, and from this point of view I agree with Friedmann: the analysis of mystified consciousness in Marx remains wholly valid.[2]

In the second place, what is it that threatens the individual from outside? Let us not go in for concrete psychology either, but for concrete sociology. What causes us to have this feeling of fear? Undoubtedly, it is first of all silence. What we have learned during these past years is that we can live only in a world where we think that by making human arguments to someone, we shall receive human actions from him. But we have learned that there are some kinds of men with whom it is useless to make human arguments. It would not have occurred to any concentration-camp inmate to persuade the SS dealing with him that they should not be doing that. From this point of view, we are in the world of silence: in other words, the world of violence.

The second point concurs with Friedmann on another level: abstraction. It is true, on the level of technology, that the human presence, human contact, is increasingly replaced by the intermediary of the mechanical instrument. This is true also on the level of society, for there is an international phenomenon called bureaucracy which ensures that at every rung of relations with the State you never come across a human person.

A third feature of the present epoch is the progressive and inevitable replacement of real man, everyday man, concrete man, by historical man. We are increasingly politicized. You can read it everywhere and you can ask yourself about it. You know that politics increasingly interferes with your reactions and your way of looking at the world.

The fourth feature which it seems to me one might detect is the will for power.

This combination of features represents terror. It strikes me as incontestable that we are living in the world of terror, and with the more or less vague and more or less precise sense of terror. What does it stem from? I think, without philosophizing, that one might all the same say the following: insofar as a man believes in inexorable progress, insofar as a man believes in an inexorable historical logic—believes, for example, that feudal society must inevitably succeed primal anarchy, that nations must emerge from that feudal state, then internationalism or if you will the League of Nations, and then classless society—basing oneself on this absolute rationalism, these historical values which have to be achieved are placed above the values we are accustomed by education or prejudice to consider valid.

So if we base ourselves on absolute rationalism, or on the idea of any kind of progress, we accept the principle that the end justifies the means: if it is inevitable that we must arrive at that classless society, we are not going to hesitate over the choice of means; and lying, violence or killing people will be something perhaps regrettable in the ways of men, but certainly not to be rejected if one's aim represents something inevitable, historical and desirable.

If we think the individual, on the one hand, has his mistakes within him and, on the other, those coercive phenomena before him, then we must tell ourselves that this fate must be opposed as much as possible. But we are living in contradiction because, if we take the average European or even the average intellectual, what principles does he have to set against those principles when he does not believe in them?

Christian minds will grant me that eighty percent of Europeans live outside grace, and that among the remaining twenty the number of authentic Christians is fairly limited.

43

So there is no question of religious, traditional values to set against these values weighing upon the world today. We have no well-grounded Value to set against these values, and if we have no Value, we are—and I confine myself to observing a factual reality—in nihilism. And the problem posed today, as it was posed during the war, is of knowing how the great mass of European men might oppose coercive enterprises without themselves having specific values at their disposal.

The people who believed in nothing during the war had nothing to say to Hitler, because absolute nihilism has the same effect at that level as absolute rationalism. We have to realize that we are in contradiction, and realize that we must overcome it. This, in my view, is exactly where the historical problem facing us lies. In order to overcome this contradiction, it is necessary to think in a certain way, with hands or head. The business of thought, reconstruction, reconciliation of contradictory points of view, cannot take place in a climate of fear.

The individual, if he cares about saving himself, must first harden himself against fear and even demand abolition of the death penalty, which at the judicial level might perhaps reduce tensions. If this can be done, I think we shall succeed, and that is the one initiative which might today save the individual.

People who do not have absolute Truth do not want to kill anyone, so demand that they not be killed. They demand to search for truth, so they need a certain number of historical conditions permitting that search. Which is what I call the conditions for modest thinking. We can define these conditions, and we can act for these conditions to be achieved. As I see it, this action might have around one chance in a thousand. This is not a reason not to attempt it. Of course, this action must draw its principles, if you will, from the little analysis I have ventured to set before you: since the politics of this world, whatever they may be, are based on the will for power, on realism, and on principles that are consequently false, we shall have to reject them totally and withdraw confidence totally from all governments of any kind.

Today, if we want to go further on this level, we must be aware that it is necessary to say things clearly. To cite just one example, I would think—much like Socrates—that a person does not think badly because he is a criminal, but is a criminal because he thinks badly. And if, in the case that concerns us, the world is ruled according to principles which are false, crime and murder are automatically produced. All those who, directly or indirectly, approve principles of this kind should consider themselves murderers, admit that up until today they have been murderers of a kind, indirectly or sometimes directly.

Having put it like this, we must go on to say that if we condemn this society inasmuch as it is governed and based on these principles, we shall have to create within society a new social contract between individuals. And from this viewpoint I see nothing better—given that the question cannot be posed on the national level, and that there are only international problems—than to create internationally that kind of society with individuals who will begin by paying personally. What I have against liberal individualism is that it has only the advantages of freedom. So people will have to pay personally, for example by refusing honors and all that this society can give them; by restraining themselves; by accepting a certain monetary level—refusing to have money above a certain level and disposing of the rest for things that should be defined. They must pay personally, otherwise we are still in mystification. On the other hand, these individuals will have to practice sermonizing. We still have newspapers, speech, a certain number of elements of action which are not murder. This is one provisional and modest element that we absolutely must bring into play, in order to save all that may remain of the individual. This is just a framework, giving a few suggestions to stimulate people's minds.

The fate of the individual lies in this decision to be taken: in the historical analysis we must make and, on the other hand, in decisions. In other words, it is not a matter of agreeing, then just going back to reading your newspaper and not sympathizing in certain respects with the murders drenching Europe in blood today. It is a matter of taking a stand. And by that decision, at that very moment, if exemplary values can be proposed in opposition to those values of power, I say that there will be one chance in a thousand for the individual to be able still to keep his place in a world threatening to suppress him wholly. Without seeking to make a comparison, there was a movement of this kind at the end of the ancient world, when everything was going badly, which was called the society of Stoics—likewise international, insofar as it was then possible to be—and which paved the way for a civilizational turning point, the new civilization being Christianity.

We are at a turning point, and it will be death or a new civilization. It is our generation, I mean the people living today, which must prepare it. This generation is inevitably sacrificed, the question is to know whether its sacrifice will be barren or fruitful, and that is up to us to choose.

[*Merleau-Ponty asks whether Camus, the modesty of whose suggestions he appreciates, really provides a solution, or whether by recommending an apolitical stance he does not instead revert to the kind of individualism he is seeking to banish. Withdrawing into ourselves does not prevent the government from imposing upon us "the ravages we fear." Similarly, the Stoics brought a new civilization into being only by becoming Christians, by ceasing through this external commitment to "seek inner purity." If one does not try to find a form of organized State, one falls "into pure ethics."*]

[*Camus replies:*]

That is true, in one sense; but I have naturally thought about this objection and here is what I have told myself. Does one wish to save the individual or not? If one does wish to do so, in my opinion one rejects murder. But today I find myself in a dilemma, obliged to choose between two ideas equally noble at first, but both ultimately ignoble. The Marxist analysis of mystified consciousness can be applied to Marxist ideology, insofar as it is ideology.

We do not at the outset have the necessary criterion to choose, but we do so ultimately. And the gravity, the distortion from which this worldwide human effort can see itself suffering, strikes me as a lesser gravity than the one that is before our eyes, which is the politics of realism and power—whether of right or left—and which culminates in murder. For all the men who for six years have lived in the hell where we have lived, for all these men there is something which has become physiologically impossible, which is the idea that one might accept murder.

Possibly the solution I am proposing may come to be distorted, but initially the likelihood is less. I think that in any case it will do less harm to man than the other choice.

I shall now reply to the idea that it is purely a matter of ethics. You tell me that the Stoics created a Church. That is just what I mean. I do not maintain that we should live quietly in our country cottages studying the Ancients. I maintain that we should remain in life and politics, that we should testify everywhere, but that this testimony should, at the same as our own, be that of many people. And if I used the word "sermonizing," it was not for no reason.

[Gandillac wonders whether the idea of progress and the conviction of holding a truth must necessarily lead to murder. Violence also expresses an uncertainty, "a not wholly determined anguish of freedom." Uncertainty and certainty can both trigger protest.]

[Camus replies:]

I think the following (and in this I am not a Marxist): I believe that if there is an Absolute, it is the concern of each one of us and not the concern of all; and that consequently an action like the one I confined myself to describing from on high would consist in assembling a certain number of men around values which I would call provisional or intermediate, values sufficient to define a world that would become bearable for them. I think, for example, that a certain justice—I do not say Justice with a capital "J"—or a certain freedom are values which are indispensable for us to be able to live together, on the one hand, and for us to be able to go on with this quest, this conciliation, which seems to me to be one of the tasks of the epoch.

If this action we were discussing needs absolute values in order to be set in motion, it will never be taken, seeing that this world suffers from nihilism. So we must reverse the question: not ask it as you have done, but ask it by saying that the only thing left to do is for us to have the energy, determination and lucidity sufficient to rally a certain number of men around provisional aims. The issue today is to prepare a sequel and a future, and I return to my favorite Stoic society, that stance characteristic of men maintaining a certain order of things here within the world. I once said, at a time when I was involved in journalism, "truth is commercial"—in other words, it sells. And if we tell a certain number of men, "The main thing is not to give you anything resembling an absolute truth, but to give you an aim so that you can pursue it on your own," those men will perhaps find the capacity needed. If we had to choose between something that would give us, say, a seventy-five percent chance of success, there would be no merit in it. If the epoch has something tragic about it, it is because there is actually little chance of succeeding.

[*A long intervention by Friedmann criticizes Camus's political skepticism. After the war, does humanity not "need a rational organization of its means of production and distribution [. . .] need a social action"? Arthur Koestler's book* The Yogi and the Commissar *brings out well the opposition between the person who believes in only internal reform and the one who relies wholly on institutions. This, however, is a "false dilemma," the true problem being "that of the interaction between the ineluctable revolution of institutions and an effort by man upon himself." Similarly, we must avoid giving a mechanistic reading of Marx. Hegel's dialectic, centered upon the "reciprocal action of cause and effect," is at the heart of the problem and allows us "to find how to realize concretely this interaction of political effort and ethics." Squeezed between the two great political blocs, France is particularly well placed to integrate "permanent human values" into political work. The fate of the modern individual depends upon the resolution of this problem.*]

[*Camus replies:*]

To take only the Yogi branch would be to give a wrong idea of my position. Koestler says himself a little further on that what is needed for tomorrow is for the Yogi and the Commissar to be combined within the same men [. . .] There is a community—which has been widely and in my view wrongly mocked in the newspapers—called the Barbu community.[3] There you have the perfect example of one hundred and fifty individuals who, tired of waiting until the fourth generation for the triumph of history, banded together and all hundred and fifty of them created a state of affairs in which they led a worthwhile life, one that they themselves recognized as worthwhile. The statute of the Barbu community says that the community recognizes as laws imposed by the provisional framework in which it finds itself only those that conform with the principles laid down by its rules. This is a striking sign of the will of individuals dissociating themselves from what is wrong and continuing to associate with what is good. It is a position that strives to preserve what is valid.

I am not so pessimistic. I would have to analyze almost all the examples that my friend Friedmann chose at the beginning [. . .] Similarly, the idea of freedom must be closely examined, because people are always talking about it: we need to know what freedom is. Freedom of thought will never be taken away from us; so it is the freedom of expression that needs to be analyzed [. . .] You were talking about the individual being squeezed, and about freedom being squeezed as a result. That is quite a good thing. Not that it should be squeezed! [. . .] But there is true freedom only when there is some kind of squeezing: there are freedom, liberation and struggle. It is the human condition not to possess a ready-made freedom.

[Knowledge Is Universal]

Message Read Out by Jean Amrouche at the
Maison de la Chimie
1946

On November 18, 1946, the delegation to Paris of the Istiqlal (Indepen-
dence) Party celebrated at the Maison de la Chimie the nineteenth anni-
versary of Moroccan sultan Sidi Mohammed Ben Youssef's accession to
the throne. Prominent Arab and French figures were invited to speak at the
event, presented "beneath the sign of the friendship and spiritual affinities
that bind together Eastern and Western thought." In his absence, Albert
Camus entrusted the reading of the following text to Jean Amrouche, a
Christian from Kabylia whom he had come to know through Éditions
Charlot¹ and the journal L'Arche.² The text of this speech, together with
those of the other participants, was published by the Istiqlal documenta-
tion and information office.

"For years we lived anyhow with one another in the naked desert,
under the indifferent heaven . . ."³ Thus begins the great book of
a man who lived and often fought with the Arabs, and who never
recovered from the disillusion that his own country inflicted upon
him by later treating as bargaining chips a people among whom he
himself had found only comrades in arms.

On a different scale, I experience the same feeling of communion and solitude when I think of my Arab friends. And having
often joined them in sorrow, I should like to be able to join them
in happiness and pride. But the opportunities for doing so are rare.

Which is why I am delighted to seize that which is furnished today to demonstrate such solidarity. Since you are all assembled here to fête your sovereign and offer him what is his due, it will not be hard for me, in the name of a number of French writers, to address to His Majesty Sidi Mohammed Ben Youssef, sultan of Morocco, congratulations and good wishes which are not at all official, but simply the free expression of the respectful friendship that free men feel for the person who today represents the hope, and therefore the dignity, of millions of Moroccans.

There is perhaps a more specific reason for the respect and friendship that free writers may feel for your sovereign today. We are not unaware that his greatest concern is to spread education among his people as much as he can. And that is well conceived. For knowledge is always universal: it is what unites, whereas ignorance separates. Murder, hatred and violence do not come from a wicked heart, but from an ignorant soul. The one who knows, by contrast, will always refuse to dominate and do violence. He will always choose example over power.

That is why this sovereign, wise enough—and despite so many obstacles—to give such importance to education, as he works for his people is working for all men. I shall probably never be a Muslim, and I doubt whether any of you assembled here could ever become that strange, unstable and immoderate creature—eager to know and savor everything, living off his contradictions and crazy about an impossible wisdom—called a European. But at a certain degree of knowledge, these differences appear necessary and even fruitful, on condition that they are accompanied by mutual respect. On the day that Europeans cease to view Arabs as a picturesque, incomprehensible people, on the day that Arabs cease to confuse Europeans with the policemen who sometimes represent them, on that day the world will be a happier place to live in.

Perhaps that day is still far off. Today Western nations are wearing themselves out in power struggles, and nothing will be settled until the thirst for power has been slaked. Increasingly, however, men are being brought up with an understanding of this. They may be Moroccan or French or from any other country. What is certain is that they are together, and that they are waging the same fight together. Their duty is to work for knowledge and thereby create the universal values that will allow us to live with our hearts at peace in a world at peace. This is why the respect we feel for your sovereign is tinged with gratitude, for having understood that.

Moroccan friends, the only language appropriate for this anniversary is that of truth. So let us say that it is true that our hearts are not at peace; and that we crave the accord that will finally make of us the equal brothers we are. Let us also say that we are aware of the obstacles which egoism and self-interest still erect on our path today. But let us also say—each of us for our own part, and never in a spirit of hatred—that we shall go on doing whatever is necessary for the barriers finally to fall. Until then, be sure that under the indifferent heaven of power, and in this naked desert of Africa where I have lived and which has endowed me with a soul somewhat resembling yours, we shall continue to fight side by side for a greater and better idea of man.

The Unbeliever and Christians

Lecture at the Latour-Maubourg Monastery
1946

In response to the invitation of Reverend Father Jean Maydieu, whom he had met under the Occupation, Albert Camus took part on December 1, 1946, in a meeting with Christians at the Latour-Maubourg monastery in the 7th arrondissement of Paris. On that occasion he gave a lecture that appeared in Actuelles *with the title "The Unbeliever and Christians." However, a record of the same meeting published in April 1949 in the Dominican journal* La Vie intellectuelle *quotes statements made by Camus, repeating passages from "The Crisis of Man" (see p. 18), that do not appear in the* Actuelles *version. Since no clue enables us to situate those statements in the original exposition by Camus, they have here been placed at the end of the version printed in* Actuelles.

Since you have been so good as to ask a man who does not share your convictions to come and reply to the very general question which you are posing during these deliberations—and before I tell you what it seems to me that unbelievers expect of Christians—I would like at once to recognize your generosity of spirit by proclaiming a few principles.

There is first of all a secular Pharisaism to which I shall endeavor not to yield. I call a secular Pharisee the person who pretends to believe that Christianity is an easy thing, and who appears to ask of the Christian, in the name of a Christianity seen from outside, more than he asks of himself. For I think the Christian does have many obligations, but it is not up to the person who himself rejects these to recall their existence to someone who has already acknowledged them. If anyone can ask something of the Christian, it is the Christian himself. The conclusion is that if, at the end of this talk, I were to allow myself to demand certain duties of you, these could only be ones which must be required of any man today, whether he is a Christian or not.

In the second place, I would also like to say that, since I do not feel I possess any absolute truth or any message, I shall never start off from the principle that Christian truth is illusory, but merely from the fact that I have been unable to enter it. To illustrate this position, I shall willingly confess the following. Three years ago a dispute pitted me against one of you, and not one of the least.[1] The frenzy of those years, the painful memory of two or three murdered friends, had given me that vanity. I can testify, however, that despite a few linguistic excesses uttered by François Mauriac, I never stopped reflecting on what he was saying. Following that reflection—and in this way I am giving you my opinion of the usefulness of believer–unbeliever dialogue—I came to recognize in my heart, and do so publicly here, that basically and on the precise point of our dispute Monsieur François Mauriac was right to oppose me.

That said, it will be easier for me to lay down my third and final principle. It is simple and clear. I shall not try to modify anything of what I think or anything of what you think (insofar as I can judge that) in order to achieve a reconciliation that would be nice for all of us. On the contrary, what I would like to tell you today is that the world needs real dialogue, that the opposite of dialogue is lying as much as silence, and that dialogue is therefore possible only between people who remain what they are and who speak the truth. This amounts to saying that today's world demands of Christians that they should remain Christians. The other day at the Sorbonne, addressing a Marxist lecturer, a Catholic priest said in public that he too was anti-clerical. Well, I do not like priests who are anti-clerical any more than philosophers who are ashamed of themselves. So I shall not for my part try to make myself a Christian in your eyes. I share with you the same horror of evil. But I do not share your hope and I continue to struggle against this universe where children suffer and die.

And why should I not say this here, as I have written it elsewhere? I waited for a long time during those terrible years for a great voice to be raised in Rome. I, an unbeliever? Just so. For I knew that the spirit would fade if, confronted by force, it did not utter a cry of condemnation. Apparently this voice was raised. But I swear to you that, like me, millions of men did not hear it; and there was then a loneliness in every heart, believing or unbelieving, which did not stop spreading as the days passed and the executioners multiplied.

It has since been explained to me that the condemnation had undoubtedly been pronounced. But it had been done in the parlance of encyclicals, which is far from clear. The condemnation had been pronounced, but had not been understood! Who would not sense where the true condemnation lies here? And who would not see that this example in itself provides one of the elements of the reply, perhaps the whole reply, that you are asking from me? What the world expects of Christians is that Christians should speak loudly and clearly, and that they should pronounce their condemnation in such a way that no single doubt could ever arise in the heart of the simplest of men. It is that they should quit abstraction and confront the bloody face that history has assumed today. The alliance we need is an alliance of men determined to speak clearly and to pay in person. When a Spanish bishop blesses a political execution, he is no longer a bishop or a Christian or even a man, he is a dog, just like the person who from the height of an ideology orders that execution without doing the job himself. We expect and I expect an alliance of those who do not wish to be dogs, and who are determined to pay the price that must be paid for a man to be something more than a dog.

And now what can Christians do for us? First of all, put an end to pointless squabbles, the first of which concerns pessimism. I think, for example, that Monsieur Gabriel Marcel would do well to leave in peace forms of thought that excite him and lead him astray. Monsieur Marcel cannot call himself a democrat and at the same time ask for Sartre's play to be banned.[2] It is a tiresome position for everyone. The fact is Monsieur Marcel is seeking to defend absolute values, like modesty and man's divine truth, whereas the point is to defend the few provisional values that will allow Monsieur Marcel to go on struggling one day, and at ease, for those absolute values.

By what right, moreover, would a Christian or a Marxist accuse me of pessimism? I was not the one to invent the wretchedness of creatures, or the terrible curses of God's wrath. I was not the one to proclaim *Nemo bonus*[3] or the damnation of unbaptized children. I was not the one to say that man was incapable of saving himself on his own, and that from the depths of his abasement his only hope lay in God's grace. As for the notorious Marxist optimism! Nobody went further in distrust of man, and ultimately the economic inevitabilities of this universe seem more terrible than the whims of God.

Christians and communists will tell me that their optimism is longer-term. That it is superior to all the rest and that God or history, depending on the case, are the satisfactory outcomes of their dialectic. I have the same argument to make. If Christianity is pessimistic about man, it is optimistic about human destiny. Well, I shall say that being pessimistic about human destiny, I am optimistic about man. And not in the name of a humanism that has always struck me as limited, but in the name of an ignorance that tries to deny nothing.

So this means that the words pessimism and optimism need to be clarified, and that while waiting to be able to do that, we must recognize what unites us rather than what separates us.

I think that is all I had to say. We are confronted by evil. And for me it is true that I feel myself rather like Augustine before he became a Christian, who used to say: "I was looking for the source of evil and could never see the way."[4] But it is also true that, like some others, I know what must be done if not to diminish evil, at least not to increase it. We perhaps cannot prevent this creation being one in which children are tortured. But we can diminish the number of tortured children. And if you do not help us do so, who on earth will?

Between the forces of terror and those of dialogue, a great unequal battle has begun. I have only moderate illusions on the outcome of this battle. But I do believe it must be waged and know that some men at least have decided on that. I merely fear that they sometimes feel rather on their own, that they indeed are on their own, and that after an interval of two millennia we risk seeing the sacrifice of Socrates several times over. The program for tomorrow is the realm of dialogue, or the solemn and ceremonious putting to death of the witnesses of dialogue. After having given my reply, the question I ask in turn of Christians is the following: "Will Socrates still be alone, and is there nothing in him and in your doctrine that urges you to join us?"

I am well aware that Christianity may reply negatively. Oh! not through your mouths, to be sure. But it may be—which is still most likely—that it will persist in compromise, or in delivering its condemnations in the obscure form of the encyclical. Perhaps it will persist in letting itself be stripped forever of the virtue of revolt and indignation which has long belonged to it. Then Christians will live and Christianity will die. Then it will basically be others who will make the sacrifice. It is in any case a future which is not up to me to decide, despite all the hope and anguish it awakens in me. I can speak only about what I know. And what I do know, which sometimes fills me with longing, is that if Christians were to make up their minds to it, millions of voices, millions, I repeat, throughout the world would be added to the cry of a handful of lonely individuals who today, fearing neither God nor man, intercede tirelessly almost everywhere for children and for men.

[*Albert Camus's arguments, which repeat passages from "The Crisis of Man" (see p. 18), as reproduced in* La Vie intellectuelle *(April 1949), begin here.*]

[. . .] since you have been so good as to ask a man who does not share your convictions to come and reply to the question. But I do not share your hope when I see this universe where children are suffering and dying.

That said, how to answer your question: what do we expect from the Catholics of France? I shall broaden that by saying: what does the world expect of Christians?

One should perhaps ask oneself: what does the world expect? By asking ourselves what the world expects, we might perhaps ask ourselves what this world of today is.

Today, you will doubtless concede, the world lives outside grace, and eighty percent of Europeans today live and die bereft of values permitting an action to be grounded or a death to be appeased. I have been and still am one of those, and the men of my generation, provided they have a clear conscience, are good examples of what the world suffers and expects. And it is in speaking of them that I shall be most scrupulous, since I know them, and that I have the greatest chance of answering your question.

I shall say it at once, the great problem troubling today's world is the problem of evil, and this is how I define the interest which Christianity can take in it. It seems to me it will be more educative for all of us if I retain its historical character, by trying to summarize the experience of men of my generation, and by asking myself what Christianity can do for those men at the precise point they have reached.

Frenchmen of my generation were born just before the Great War; they reached adulthood at the time of the economic crisis; they were twenty in the year when Hitler took power; they knew the Spanish war, Munich, then the war of 1939, then defeat and four years of occupation and clandestine struggle. It really is an interesting generation, because it is a generation which has lived in revolt against the absurd world that its elders were making for it.

If you wished to think seriously about it, you would acknowledge that everything in this generation has been a sign of revolt. Literature was in revolt against the sentence, meaning, clarity itself; painting was in revolt against form, subject, reality; music against melody. Philosophy taught us there was no truth, but phenomena; that there might be Mr. Smith, Monsieur Durand, Herr

Vogel, but between these three partial entities there was nothing in common.

The moral attitude of this generation was yet more extreme. Nationalism seemed an outworn truth, religion an exile, twenty-five years of international politics had taught us to doubt every truth, and everybody could be right because nobody was wrong. The ethics of our society had not ceased being a monstrous hypocrisy.

So we were thus in negation. And, of course, what was true for this generation was not new. Many other generations in history found themselves likewise in negation. But what is new is that this generation has been obliged, in the absence of values that could have helped it, to come to terms with murder and terror. In other words, this generation has found itself empty-handed, cast into a crisis of man that we should try to define briefly before being able to appreciate the problem facing us.

How to define this crisis? I have looked for the quickest and most concrete means. It seemed to me that if I recounted to you two short anecdotes, I would achieve my aim most speedily.

One of my comrades had been arrested by the Gestapo. He found himself one morning in the building on Rue de la Pompe, in a room with two other comrades likewise tortured. The concierge of the building had come up to do the housework, and since the individuals she found there reproached her with doing her housework in such circumstances, she replied: "I never concern myself with what my tenants do!"

Another of these anecdotes happened to one of my comrades. He had been dragged from his cell to be interrogated rather brutally; he was wearing a bandage around his ears. Returning to fetch him a second time, a German officer, the same one who had interrogated him before, said to him with a trace of affection and even concern: "How are those ears of yours?"

If I tell you these stories, it is not because of their sensational nature. It is because they seem to me to portray well the state of mind confronting us. They portray well what I call the crisis of man, since they have allowed us to reply ourselves in a non-abstract way to the following question: is there a crisis of man? They have allowed us to reply that there was assuredly a crisis of man, if someone could envisage pain or torture with these normal feelings, with these everyday, banal emotional reactions, signifying that these phenomena of pain were part of everyday life and seen as a rather tedious imposition, like having to queue for coupons.

It was perhaps possible for us to accuse the other: I mean, say it was all Hitler's fault and, since the monster was dead, the poison was going to disappear. But we know well that the poison has not disappeared, that we all carry it in our hearts, and that this can still be felt in the way in which men, parties and nations look at each other with a trace—or a great deal—of anger. I have always thought that a nation was united with its traitors as well as its heroes. And a civilization too: white, Western civilization seems to me responsible for both its successes and its perversions. It seems to me that we are all united with Hitlerism, still are, but are starting to be united with something else, another experience that is starting to unfold across the world and in several nations.

Well, what was that ideology, that crisis I have tried to concretize through these stories?

People of my age have been a bit knocked off balance, and they are scared. I suppose some have then tried to reflect. It has been easy to see that, for them, this crisis was the rise of terror—I shall not dwell on this—and this rise of terror was due to a series of judgments on the values, or the non-values, that consist in no longer judging a man in terms of his dignity or what his individual life was worth, but in terms of other ideas such as success or efficacy. The concierge certainly had a heart like everybody else. But there was a fact, which was the German occupation. This German occupation meant the victory of a certain order. And since this order was victorious, it inevitably—this was a nuisance, but resistance was impossible—involved exercising a certain number of freedoms, including the freedom to torture. So the simplest thing was to get on with one's housework and let things pass.

If I specify that this rise of terror was based on the absence of values, it is because we had to try to make some diagnosis, in order to try to imagine cures.

We attempted to make others too. It seems to me that this terror, this state of anguish, was based on the impossibility of persuasion. Men live and are able to live only in the belief that if you speak to a man in human terms you get human reactions from him. But there are men you cannot persuade. I even imagine that, in concentration camps, the SS man torturing might have been persuaded that what he was doing was fine and this was the right way to proceed. Could the comrade whose ears had been torn be persuaded that the German officer was on the side of truth in doing what he did? There was an absence of common values, which will be the refrain of this brief talk.

There was absence of common values in the sense that anyone, you or I, would have spoken in the name of a certain number of values, vague but upon which one could agree. Whereas for the German officer there was no common value. In his office, he had the impression of being the representative of his ideology and an official. But when he was no longer an official, he found it natural to be human—otherwise he had to defend the values on which his State was based. This is what made Himmler come in by the back door every evening, so as not to wake up his favorite canary.

I think too that this terror was constituted by replacement of the natural object by abstraction and bureaucracy. I shall not dwell on the problem of coupons—you will have understood.

By dint of paper, offices and officials; by dint of placing stairways between men, and forms to be filled; by dint of forbidding all human communication—you succeed in creating this abstract world, where people no longer judge men by what they are, but by what they are relative to the doctrine governing the organization of this bureaucracy. I think, for example, that today a person dies, loves and kills only by proxy. And this is good organization. The problem of the death penalty would be settled in a quite different way if the people pronouncing the death sentence were obliged to do what I shall call "the job" themselves.

This amounts to saying that we were, and still are, in a world where real man is replaced by political man. There is no longer individual passion, just collective—in other words, abstract—passions.

If we are all willingly or forcibly introduced into politics, we are obliged to say that what counts is not whether we respect the suffering of a man or a woman, what counts is securing the victory of a doctrine.

All these symptoms are summed up in the cult of efficiency, based itself on the suppression of common and traditional values, and also in the cult of abstraction and ideology. This is why the men of Europe now know only solitude, and cannot come together with all other men in shared values. And as we are no longer protected, you and I, by a respect for man based on such values, the only alternative given to these men is to be, as I have said elsewhere, either victims or executioners.[5]

This is what men of my generation have understood. They have understood it in a less clear and less detached way than I have been able to convey to you. They have understood it in an obscure way, and sometimes far more in their bones than in their minds. But they have told themselves that it was necessary to regulate their relations with this state of things. This is where the problem began. We had to regulate it with the values at our disposal: in other words, with nothing. This is how we had to enter this war and this terror, at once without solace and without certainty, like blind people looking for the way out. We vaguely knew by a bodily reaction that we would not be able to surrender to a certain order of things; but we did not know how to justify it. The more far-sighted perceived that, in themselves, they had no principle for opposing terror; and if they did it, they did so gratuitously.

For if you believe in nothing, if nothing has a meaning, if you cannot affirm or deny any value, everything is allowed and nothing matters. Doing one's housework or torturing men and women, it all makes no great difference. Nobody is wrong or right. One can send millions of innocent people to the gas chamber as one can devote oneself to caring for lepers. It is all exactly the same. And since we thought that nothing had any meaning, in order not to be fooled in that universe where nothing could be justified we had to conclude that the person who is right is the one who succeeds. Plenty of intelligent and skeptical people say that if Hitler had won the war, History would have consecrated his rule and said that he was a great statesman. And there is no doubt that then many of the men who opposed him would have ended up saying and writing, so that it would become part of History, that in a certain way his means could be justified, since his aim had been achieved.

Some among us, recoiling all the same from such extremes, believed it possible to think that, even without any higher value, one could still believe that History had a meaning. In any case, they acted as if they thought so. They said the war was necessary, because it would liquidate the age of nationalisms and prepare the age of Empires, which would be followed by paradise on earth.

They thus arrived at the same result as if they had thought that nothing had any meaning. For History has a total meaning or it is nothing. They acted as if we were all advancing together toward a definitive end. They thought and acted in accordance with a principle of Hegel's that I take the liberty to find hateful: "Man is made for History, not History for man."[6] Actually, all the realism guiding the destinies of our world seems to me to derive from a Germanic political philosophy, according to which the universe proceeds along rational paths toward a definitive universe. The results are the same. If it is true that History obeys a logic and a fatality—if it is true that the anarchic State must be succeeded by the feudal State, then feudalism by nations, nations by empires, and empires by the Universal Society—then everything that serves this march of History is good and the achievements of History are definitive truths. All one has to do is wait for them to arrive.

Since they can arrive only by the normal means—wars, lies, tricks and individual or collective murders—all acts are justified not insofar as they are good or bad, but insofar as they are effective or not.

That is how in today's world, and for the past decade, men of my generation have for years been subjected to the twofold temptation of thinking that nothing had a meaning or else that only yielding to historical fatality had a meaning. Accordingly, many of them succumbed to one or other of these temptations, and the world has remained subjected to the urge for power—in other words, terror.

Look at things around you and tell me if this picture is exaggerated. We are truly in the chains of violence and power, and we are suffocating in them. Whether it is within nations or across frontiers, greed, resentment, trickery, mistrust, deceit and ulterior motives are in the process of manufacturing a pretty appalling universe for us, where man finds himself stripped of the part of himself which does not belong to History: reflection, leisure, a certain future. I do not ask for much of this; just the cult of happiness and the simplest leisure.

As for settling this problem, I do not need to tell you that it has not been granted to us. Problems of this kind, which are on the level of History, are doubtless not settled either by the work of a few individuals or even by the work of a generation. Time is needed, and it is perhaps part of the logic of History that many sacrifices should be needed, sometimes gratuitous sacrifices.

However, I think I can say that it seemed to us we were justified— we who thought that nothing or little had any meaning—in struggling against that order and that universe. If I do not retrace the reasoning, not philosophical but ethical, which led us to this conclusion, it is because it would take me rather a long way.

So I shall summarize it. Given that we found ourselves confronted by this world, and something had to be done in order not to accept it, since we had nothing with which to stand up to it, we had to find in our revolt itself the means and the reasons to oppose it.

Whether this be a sophistry or Gospel truth, I have no idea, but we succeeded. I would like to emphasize this. When we rejected a certain order of things, a certain order of values, there was perhaps a "no" in this rejection, but there was perhaps also a "yes." I mean that, in a certain way, we were affirming that there was a certain order which we did not want; but also that there was within us something which was worth more than that. And we could say that, insofar as the people who struggled and fought on this level and in this direction were ready to die for that truth which they glimpsed, they proved by this very fact that it was a truth which transcended them. In practical terms, it was not because they were themselves victims of that oppression that they entered that struggle, but because many people for whom they were ready to die were victims of that oppression.

It would not be difficult to find in this the foundations of a theory of mutual communication among men which could give us the two or three provisional values we need.

This is what we could not accept, that men should be separated by terror, or harshness, or bureaucracy. We could not accept that fundamental split between men holding a certain number of values in common.

It was easy for us to think, and this is my one conviction today, that it is this communication which we must defend. It is not difficult to derive values of sincerity, justice and freedom which would make it possible to provide the rule of a provisional action. If we wish to maintain a certain communication among us, we are obliged to demand justice among men. Between oppressed and oppressors, there is only silence; between masters and slaves likewise. And in the same way we are obliged to demand sincerity, for what separates men is as much deceit as avarice.

That is where I am personally, and where many men perhaps still are. And now we can perhaps ask ourselves what Christianity can do for us.

And if this is what we think, and I do indeed think it, what should we do? I shall first say: "What should I do?," which will lead on to: "What should Christians do?"

I shall say that we must call things by their name and recognize fully that we are killing millions of men, or that we are subscribing to the murder of millions of men, whenever we agree to think certain thoughts. One does not think badly when one is a murderer. One is a murderer because one thinks badly. One can be a murderer without apparently having killed. And that is how we are all murderers here, more or less. The first thing to do is purely and simply to reject in thought and action all forms of realist and fatalist thought.

The second thing to do is decongest the world from the terror prevailing in it. If the evil prevailing in the world today consists partly in the absence of values, perhaps we need to reflect on those values, push our reflection to the point where we will be able to find the things which unite us. But we shall not find these in terror. And for reasons of pure realism, I think that abolishing capital punishment can be a means of decongestion.

The third thing to do is put politics back in its true place. It is an anachronistic language. The task is not to give this world a gospel, or a political or moral catechism. The great misfortune of our age is that it claims to provide us with a catechism, a gospel, and even an art of love. The role of politics is to do the housework. I do not know if an absolute exists, but I do know that there is not one of a political kind. The absolute is not the concern of all, but the concern of each individual. And all must settle their mutual relations in such a way that each person can concern himself with the absolute when he so wishes. I think that our life belongs to others, but I think too that our death belongs wholly to ourselves. And that is my definition of freedom.

The fourth thing to do, it seems to me, is to seek and create—on the basis of negation for those who are not Christians, on the basis of certainty for people who are Christians—the provisional values that will allow men of goodwill, whatever their beliefs, to unite on this intermediate level, on this common level. That is the work of philosophers, and I shall not labor it.

The fifth thing, it seems to me, is properly to understand that this attitude amounts to creating an average universalism—in other words, a universalism at the average level of man. In order to escape solitude, I think it is necessary to speak—speak openly, without ever lying—and tell the whole truth as one knows it. And in particular I think it is impossible to realize that universalism without taking personality into account. This amounts to saying that no man can on his own define the destiny of a people, provide the words to explain it or the doctrine everybody needs. This strikes me as utterly impossible to achieve if it is not based on a common morality.

This amounts to saying that we have to create communities, among you Christians, among us so-called solitary individuals, and among other people who are in parties and consequently not solitary. These communities will be dedicated to doing this work of speculation and defending the values we need in daily life, in daily politics, whenever that is necessary. And here is where the role of Christians comes in.

What can Christians do for us? This means that pessimism and optimism, like many other words, are words which need to be defined and revised, and which underlie disputes that we must try to ward off a little in order to settle the most important and most urgent problems.

The second thing to say to a Christian audience is that the situation today allows no compromise, and that Christians have no use for compromise. This for me represents condemnation of the MRP.[7] The Christian must shout out. We have no need of his smile: there are plenty of those around Saint-Sulpice![8] We need his shout. I can never say that strongly enough.

In the third place, the Christian must define those provisional values. He must play his role in that. And I simply think that we must define—and the Christian must define properly for himself— what quality of work we may be able to ask of him today. For Christianity, that consists in remaining itself: in other words, rejecting absolutely all modern ideologies unconditionally. There is a work of adaptation which has often been the richness and effectiveness of Christianity, but which can become deadly to it if it cannot stand firm on its moral and traditional foundations, which are its own. It must be able fully to grasp that today I do not think the world needs a morality of heroes and saints; what has done it most harm is certainly heroism. The first thing to do should be to make a formal critique of heroism. My opinion would not be that Monsieur Duhamel should be the one to make it, but that it could be someone who has proved himself capable of considering these problems at, dare I say, a similar level.[9]

The final task for the Christian—which is where I am likely to end—is to adopt clearly his own language. In Christian metaphysics and in the Christian stance in general there is something that has made its richness and should continue to do so. To my knowledge, it is one of the rare philosophies to be coherent, capable of acting at once on the historical and on the eternal plane. Unfortunately this has sometimes led to certain excesses. The historical sense has been transformed into realism, and the eternal sense into virtual indifference toward social problems and immediate problems. I believe, on the contrary, that Christians in their thought and in their action should strive to use their historical sense to recognize the urgency of the problem that is posed, but also of the eternal problem, in order to reject utterly its degradation. This requires clear language.

And I do not see why I should not say it here, as I have written it elsewhere, hoping not to shock you too much. I waited for a long while during those terrible war years for a loud voice to be raised in Rome. When a Spanish bishop blesses political executions—forgive me for what I am about to say—he is neither a bishop nor a Christian, not even a man: he is a murderer. And I think the duty of the Christian—and God knows that some did uphold it—this duty is to say that the bishop is indeed a murderer. And all men have no other task than to do what is needed for the fewest people possible to be murderers, and for the role of man to be raised above the role of murderer.

This is all I had to say. What I know, and what sometimes causes me to yearn, is that if Christians throughout the world so decided, millions of voices would join a handful of solitary individuals who, more or less everywhere, are tirelessly appealing today on behalf of children and on behalf of men.

"Spain? I don't think I can speak about it anymore . . ."

1946–1947

A "second fatherland" for Albert Camus, whose maternal grandparents came originally from Majorca, Spain, occupied a special place in the author's life, work and political commitment. From the 1934 miners' revolts, which were the subject of the play Revolt in the Asturias *(1936), of which he was one of the coauthors, up to his protest against the entry of Franco's Spain into UNESCO, via the fate of exiles fleeing Francoism, Camus never ceased to multiply appeals, articles and interventions in favor of the Spanish republicans. The text that follows seems to have been drafted in late 1946 or early 1947. Although nothing indicates that its author delivered it in public, since its style suggests that such was its purpose, the decision was taken to include it in the present volume.*

Spain? I don't think I can speak about it anymore. In 1938, men of my blood and my age shared the revolt and the despair of the Spanish Republic. In 1944, we shared its immense hope, and I spoke on its behalf to the extent that I could. Since we had taken part in the same defeat, my belief was that we should take part in the same victory. But apparently my belief was not reasonable. And we spoke in vain. And there is no victory for anyone today, since there is no justice for Spain. Justice is like democracy: it is total or it does not exist. Who will dare tell me that I am free, when the proudest of my friends are still in Spanish prisons? No, all that remains is to hold one's tongue and be loyal.

Spanish comrades, we now know that the world is cowardly. You thought you were an example, but you were only a bargaining chip. The story is an old one and a mockery which we all share. Blood, struggle, exile, rage, all this is useless for the moment. When all you have for yourself is justice, nobility and right, you may as well say you have nothing in the eyes of the realists. And the realists today rule the world and are tearing each other apart. You thought your land was that of Cervantes, Calderón, Goya and Machado.[1] You are shown daily that in the eyes of the realists it is only the land of mercury[2] and a few ports of interest to soldiers.

But a day will perhaps come when greatness will no longer be measured by numbers of cannon and scale of destruction; when civilization, already on its deathbed, will wish to go back to its spiritual sources and rediscover the art of living. This time, this time of truth, will first and foremost be that of Spain, last land of true civilization. Yes, it is this time for which I am waiting among all of you, with the same invincible, blind hope, the same determination to live, which ends up forcing through victories, compensating for pain and restoring justice. On that day, and for the first time after eight years, a vast weight of shame and bitterness will be lifted and I shall finally be able to breathe freely. On that day, your freedom will be ours. As is ours your harsh silence of today.

I Reply . . .

1948

On May 25, 1948, the stage actor and former pilot Garry Davis renounced his American nationality and proclaimed himself a "citizen of the world." In September he sought asylum at the United Nations, whose general assembly was meeting in Paris, and called for the creation of a world government. Camus joined the committee of solidarity with Davis that was then established. After a first article on the subject appearing on November 20 in Le Franc-Tireur, *he took part in a meeting on December 3 at the Salle Pleyel in Paris. He made a speech there that was reproduced in the form of an interview in the first issue of* La Patrie mondiale, *an ephemeral journal launched by the Davis solidarity committee, then reprinted on December 9 in* Combat.[1]

Q: What are you doing, then?

R: What we can.

Q: What's the use of that?

R: What's the use of the UN?

Q: Why doesn't Davis go and speak in Soviet Russia?

R: Because he isn't allowed in there. Meanwhile, he's speaking to the Soviet envoy along with the rest.

Q: Why doesn't Davis go and speak in the USA?

R: Let's be logical. You daily label the UN an American colony.

Q: Why don't you give up French nationality?

R: That's a good objection, a bit treacherous, which is natural since it comes to us from your friends. Here's my reply:

Davis has given up very many privileges in giving up American nationality. Being French, however, today implies more burdens than privileges. If you have demands, it's quite hard to renounce your country when it's in distress.

Q: Doesn't Davis's gesture strike you as theatrical, hence suspect?

R: It's not his fault if what's merely obvious is seen as theatrical today. On a different scale, Socrates too used to stage non-stop shows on the marketplaces. And nobody managed to prove him wrong, except by condemning him to death. That's just the kind of refutation which is most commonly resorted to in contemporary political society. But it's also the most ordinary means society has of admitting its degradation and impotence.

Q: Don't you see that Davis is useful to American imperialism?

R: Davis, by giving up American nationality, is parting ways with that particular imperialism along with the rest. This gives him the right to condemn that imperialism, a right that strikes me as hard to grant to those who want to limit all sovereignties apart from the Soviet kind.

Q: Don't you see that Davis is useful to Soviet imperialism?

R: Same reply as to the last question, only in reverse. I'd add the following: imperialisms are like twins: they grow up together and cannot do without one another.

Q: Sovereignties are a reality—don't you see that one must take such a reality into account?

R: Cancer is also a reality. Yet we seek to cure it and nobody has yet had the audacity to say that, in order to cure a cancer which has added to an excessively sanguine temperament, it's necessary to eat more and more beefsteaks. It's true that doctors have never seen themselves as Church leaders holding all truth. That's the advantage they have over our politicians.

Q: Does this prevent limitation of sovereignties from being a Utopia in the present historical circumstances? (Objection presented by *Le Rassemblement*,[2] in an unsigned article.)

R: It's General de Gaulle who'll provide the answer to *Le Rassemblement*. For he said, in relation to the Ruhr,[3] that we were not obliged to have a good solution ready in order to recognize and reject a bad solution. Besides, Davis is proposing a solution and it's you who call it utopian. You remind us of those patriarchs who, precisely in the name of reality, warn their offspring against the spirit of adventure. Eventually it turns out that the offspring honor their family insofar as they disobey their father and leave the family grocery. History is always only a Utopia made flesh.

Q: Don't you see that the United States is the only obstacle to the establishment of socialism in the world? (This question is sometimes formulated in another way: don't you see that the USSR is the only obstacle to world freedom?)

R: If you get the war you predict with an obstinacy that could be better applied elsewhere, the amount of destruction and suffering that will descend upon the world, of which the Second World War gives only a faint idea, will make any historical future unforeseeable. I wouldn't give much for either freedom or socialism in a Europe reduced to ruins, in which men will no longer even have the strength to express their pain.

Q: Does this mean that you'll choose capitulation rather than war?

R: I know that some of you grant a free choice between hanging and shooting. That's their idea of human freedom. As for us, we do what we can for this choice not to become inevitable. For your part, you do what's needed for this choice to become inevitable.

Q: But if it is inevitable, what will you do?

R: If you do succeed in making it inevitable, which I don't believe, we'll have no choice other than the death agony of the world. All else is journalism, of the worst kind.

I've finished, and in conclusion I'll ask a question of our critics. It's certainly my turn. Are they sure, in their heart of hearts, that the political conviction or the doctrine that inspires them is sufficiently infallible for them to reject unthinkingly the warnings of those who remind them of the distress of millions of their fellow creatures, the cry of innocence, the simplest happiness, and who ask them to weigh these poor truths against their albeit legitimate hopes? Are they sure they are right enough to risk even one chance in a thousand of bringing still closer the danger of nuclear war? Indeed, are they so sure of themselves, and so prodigiously infallible, that they have to overlook all else? This is a question that we put to them, that has already been put to them, and to which we're still waiting for their reply.

Witness for Freedom

1948

At the end of 1947, David Rousset, Jean-Paul Sartre and Georges Altman, among others, established the Rassemblement Démocratique Révolution-naire (RDR), a political movement proposing a third-way alternative to the division of the left between the Atlantic and Soviet blocs. Without being a member of this, Albert Camus was a sympathizer of the RDR and its journal La Gauche, *in which he published two texts in the course of 1948. On December 13, Camus made a speech to more than four thousand people at the Salle Pleyel in Paris, on the occasion of an RDR meeting in which André Breton, Jean-Paul Sartre, Richard Wright and Carlo Levi also took part. The text of Camus's speech was published in issue 10 of* La Gauche *on December 20, 1948, and then in the first issue of the journal* Empédocle[1] *(April 1949), with the title "The Artist Is a Witness for Freedom."*

We are in a period where, driven by mediocre, ferocious ideologies, men are growing accustomed to being ashamed of everything. Ashamed of themselves, ashamed of being happy, of loving or creating. A period in which Racine would blush for *Bérénice* and Rembrandt, to gain forgiveness for having painted *The Night Watch*, would rush off to join the local guard. So today's writers and artists have a sickly conscience, and we are accustomed to apologize for our calling. To be honest, people are only too eager to help us do so. From every corner of our political society, a great outcry is raised against us, urging us to justify ourselves. We must justify ourselves for being useless at the same time as, by our very uselessness, serving ugly causes. And when we reply that it is very hard to absolve ourselves of such contradictory accusations, people tell us that it is not possible to justify oneself in the eyes of everybody, but that we can gain the generous forgiveness of some by taking their side, which is anyway the only true one, if they are to be believed. If this kind of argument hangs fire, they go on to tell the artist: "Look at the wretched state of the world. What are you doing about it?" To this cynical blackmail, the artist might reply: "The wretched state of the world? I'm not adding to it. Who among you can say as much?" But it still remains true that not one of us, if he is serious, can remain indifferent to the appeal raised by a despairing human-ity. So at all costs we have to feel guilty. There we are, dragged into the lay confessional, the worst of all.

And yet it is not so simple. The choice we are asked to make is not automatic: it is determined by other choices, made earlier. And the first choice an artist makes is precisely to be an artist. And if he has chosen to be an artist, this relates to what he himself is, and has to do with a certain way he has of thinking about art. And if these reasons have seemed good enough to him to justify his choice, there is a fair chance that they will continue to be good enough to help him define his position toward history. This is what I think, at least, and I should like to single myself out a bit this evening by stressing—since we are speaking freely here and in our own names—not a guilty conscience, which I do not have, but the two feelings which, confronted by and on account of the wretched state of the world, I do entertain toward our vocation: to wit, gratitude and pride. Since one has to justify oneself, I should like to say why there is a justification for practicing, to the extent of our strengths and talents, a vocation that in the midst of a world wasted by hatred allows each of us to say calmly that he is nobody's mortal enemy. But this requires explanation, and I can explain only by talking a bit about the world in which we live, and about what we artists and writers are destined to do in it.

The world around us is in distress, and people ask us to do some-thing to change it. But what is this distress? At first sight, it is easily defined: there has been a lot of killing in the world over the past few years, and some people foresee that there will be more killing. Such a large number of deaths ends up dampening the atmosphere. Of course, this is not new. Official history has always been the history of great murderers. Cain has been killing Abel before today! But only today is Cain killing Abel in the name of logic and then laying claim to the Légion d'Honneur. I shall take an example, in order to explain myself better.

During the great November 1947 strikes, the newspapers announced that the Paris executioner too would be stopping work. Not enough attention, in my view, has been paid to this decision by our compatriot. His demands were clear. He naturally asked for a bonus for each execution, which is normal in every firm. But above all he vigorously laid claim to the rank of office manager. He basically wanted to receive from the State, which he was sure he served well, the sole consecration, the one tangible honor, that a modern nation could offer to its good servants: by which I mean an administrative rank. In this way, one of our last liberal professions was expiring under the weight of history. For it really was indeed under the weight of history. In the days of barbarism, a dreadful aura kept the executioner apart from the world. He was the one who, by vocation, violated the mystery of life and the flesh. He was and knew himself to be an object of horror. And this horror at the same time consecrated the price of human life. Today he is merely an object of shame. And in these conditions, I find that he is right to no longer wish to be the poor relative kept in the kitchen because he does not have clean fingernails. In a civilization where murder and violence are already doctrines and on the way to becoming institutions, executioners have every right to join the civil service. To be honest, we French are a bit behind. Almost everywhere in the world, executioners are already occupying ministerial chairs. They have simply replaced the ax with the rubber stamp.

When death becomes a business of statistics and administration, it actually means that the business of the world is going badly. But if death becomes abstract, it means that life is abstract too. And everyone's life cannot be other than abstract once they decide to submit it to an ideology. The trouble is that we live at a time of ideologies, and totalitarian ideologies: in other words, ideologies sufficiently sure of themselves, their idiotic reasoning or their fleeting truth to see the salvation of the world only in their own domination. And wishing to dominate someone or something means wanting someone's impotence, silence or death. To confirm this, it is enough to look around us.

There is no life without dialogue. And across most of the world, dialogue is today replaced by polemic. The twentieth century is the century of polemic and insult. Between nations and individuals, and even at the level of formerly disinterested disciplines, polemic holds the place which was traditionally held by considered dialogue. Day and night thousands of voices, each pursuing from its own corner a noisy monologue, unleash on people a torrent of mystifying words, attacks, defenses, passions. But what is the mechanism of polemic? It consists in viewing the opponent as an enemy, consequently simplifying him and refusing to see him. When I insult a person, I no longer know the color of his gaze, nor if he sometimes smiles and how. Grown three-quarters blind thanks to polemic, we no longer live among men but in a world of shapes.

There is no life without persuasion. And today's history knows only intimidation. Men live—and are able to live—only in the belief that they have something in common, where they can always meet. But we have discovered the following: there are men who cannot be persuaded. It was and is impossible for a victim of the concentration camps to explain to the people debasing him that they should not do so. For the latter no longer represent men, but an idea tempered to the most inflexible of wills. The person who seeks to dominate is deaf. Faced with him, you must fight or die. This is why the men of today live in terror. In the *Book of the Dead*, it is written that the just Egyptian, in order to deserve his pardon, must be able to say: "I have inspired fear in no man." In these circumstances, on the day of the Last Judgment our great contemporaries will be sought in vain in the cohort of the blessed.

Is it any surprise that those shapes, now deaf and blind, terrorized, fed on coupons and their whole lives summarized in police dossiers, should then be treated as anonymous abstractions? It is noteworthy that the regimes which have emerged from these ideologies are precisely those which proceed systematically to uproot populations, parading them across the breadth of Europe like livid symbols that take on a pathetic life only as statistical numbers. Since these fine philosophies entered history, vast masses of men, each of whom once had his own way of shaking hands, are buried forever beneath the two initials[2] denoting displaced persons that a very logical world has invented for them.

Yes, all this is logical. When you want to unite the whole world in the name of a theory, there is no other way but to make this world as emaciated, blind and deaf as the theory itself. There is no other way but to cut the very roots attaching men to life and nature. And it is no accident if in great European literature since Dostoyevsky you find no landscapes. It is no accident if the significant books of today, instead of being concerned with the subtleties of the heart and the truths of love, are interested only in judges, trials and the machinery of accusation; if, instead of opening windows onto the beauty of the world, they are carefully closed upon the anguish of isolated individuals. It is no accident if the philosopher who today inspires all European thought is the one who has written that only the modern city allows the mind to become aware of itself, and who has gone so far as to say that nature is abstract and reason alone concrete. Such indeed is the stance of Hegel,[3] and it is the starting point of a vast adventure of intelligence that ends up killing everything. In the great spectacle of nature, these drunken minds no longer see anything but themselves. This is the final blindness.

Why continue? Those who have seen the ruined cities of Europe know what I am talking about. They furnish the image of this emaciated world, ravaged by pride, where throughout a dreary apocalypse phantoms roam in search of a lost friendship with nature and with human beings. The great drama of Western man is that between him and his historical future neither the forces of nature nor those of friendship are any longer interposed. His roots cut, his arms withered, he is already merging with the gallows that awaits him. But at least, having arrived at that height of unreason, nothing must stop us denouncing the fraud of this century, which feigns to pursue the empire of reason while seeking only the reasons to love that it has lost. And our writers are well aware of it, who all end up invoking that wretched, bloodless substitute for love that is called morality. The men of today can perhaps control everything within them, and that is their greatness. But there is at least one thing that most of them will never be able to rediscover, which is the strength of love that has been taken from them. This is basically why they are ashamed. And it is quite right that artists share this shame, since they have contributed to it. But they should at least be capable of saying that they are ashamed of themselves, not of their vocation.

For everything that makes the dignity of art is opposed to such a world and challenges it. The work of art, by the very fact that it exists, denies the conquests of ideology. One of the meanings of tomorrow's history is the struggle, already begun, between conquerors and artists. Yet both propose the same end. Political action and creation are the two faces of a single revolt against the disorders of the world. In both cases, the aim is to give the world its unity. And for a long time the cause of the artist and that of the political innovator were merged. The ambition of Bonaparte is the same as that of Goethe. But Bonaparte left our schools the drum and Goethe *The Roman Elegies*. But since ideologies of efficiency, based on technology, have intervened, since through a subtle movement the revolutionary has become a conqueror, the two currents of thought are diverging. For what the conqueror of right or left seeks is not the unity which above all is harmony of opposites; it is totality, which is the crushing of differences. The artist distinguishes where the conqueror evens out. The artist who lives and creates at the level of the flesh and passion knows that nothing is simple and the other exists. The conqueror wants the other not to exist; his world is a world of masters and slaves, the very one in which we are living. The world of the artist is that of living debate and of understanding. I do not know a single great work which is built on hatred alone, whereas we are familiar with the empires of hatred. In a time in which the conqueror, through the very logic of his stance, becomes an executioner and policeman, the artist is forced into resistance. Confronted with contemporary political society, the only coherent stance for the artist—otherwise he must renounce art—is unconditional rejection. Even if he would like to, he cannot be in league with those who use the language or the means of contemporary ideologies.

This is why it is pointless and absurd to demand of us justification and commitment. We are indeed committed, albeit involuntarily. And ultimately it is not combat which makes artists of us, but art which obliges us to be combatants. Through his very function, the artist is freedom's witness; and this is a justification for which he sometimes pays dearly. Through his very function, he is involved in the most inextricable density of history, where man's very flesh is stifled. The world being what it is, even if we have guts, we are involved in it; and by nature we are enemies of the abstract idols riding high in it today, be they national or partisan. Not in the name of morality and virtue, as people try to make us believe through an additional deception. We are not virtuous people— and in view of the anthropometric air virtue assumes among our reformers, there is no reason to regret this. It is in the name of man's passion for what is unique in man that we shall always reject these movements which cloak themselves in the most wretched form of reason.

But this at the same time defines our solidarity with everybody. It is because we have to defend the right to solitude of everyone that we shall never again be solitary. We are in a hurry, we cannot work all alone. Tolstoy was able, for his part, to write the greatest novel in all literature about a war in which he had not served. Our own wars do not leave us time to write about anything other than themselves, and at the same time they kill Péguy and thousands of young poets.[4] This is why I find, beyond our differences, which may be great, that the coming together of these men, on this evening, means something. Across frontiers, sometimes without knowing it, they are working together on the thousand faces of a single work which will rise up against the totalitarian creation. All together, yes, and with them, those thousands of men who are seeking to erect the silent forms of their creations in the tumult of cities. And with them even those who are not here, but who will inevitably rejoin us one day. And those others too who think they can work for the totalitarian ideology by means of their art, whereas in the very heart of their work the power of art shatters propaganda, invokes the unity of which they are the true servants, and dooms them to our inevitable brotherhood as well as to the mistrust of those provisionally employing them.

True artists do not make good political victors, for they are incapable of accepting lightly, as I know only too well, the death of their enemy. They are on the side of life, not of death. They are witnesses of the flesh, not of the law. By their vocation, they are condemned to understand even what is inimical to them. This does not mean, however, that they are incapable of judging good and evil. But even with the worst criminal, the ability of artists to live another's life allows them to recognize men's constant justification, which is pain. This is what will always prevent us from pronouncing the absolute sentence, and consequently from ratifying the absolute punishment. In the world of the death sentence that is our own, artists bear witness to the part of man which refuses to die. Enemies of nobody, except executioners! And this is what will always doom them, as eternal Girondins, to the threats and the blows of our cotton-oversleeved Montagnards.[5] That awkward position, after all, through its very discomfort creates their greatness. A day will come when all will recognize it and, respectful of our differences, the worthiest among us will then stop tearing each other apart as they do now. They will recognize that their deepest vocation is to defend to the bitter end the right of their adversaries not to share their opinions. They will proclaim, depending on their condition, that it is better to be mistaken without killing anyone, and while letting people speak, than to be right in the midst of silence and mass graves. They will try to demonstrate that, if revolutions can succeed through violence, they cannot be maintained except by dialogue. And they will then know that this singular vocation creates for them the most upsetting fraternity of all: that of uncertain battles and threatened glories; that which, throughout all the ages of intelligence, has never stopped struggling to affirm, against the abstractions of history, that which transcends all history and which is the flesh, whether suffering or joyful. The whole of today's Europe, stiff in its arrogance, cries out to them that this undertaking is absurd and pointless. But we are all in the world to prove the opposite.

Time of the Murderers

1949

During the summer of 1949, Albert Camus was invited by the cultural relations department of the foreign ministry to give a series of lectures in South America, mainly in Brazil but also in Chile. (He made a brief stay in Argentina, moreover, and passed through Uruguay, but without making any public appearances there.) It was in the course of this journey that he delivered on several occasions the following lecture in French, the type-script of which, preserved in the author's archives, bears the title "Time of the Murderers." The themes explored by Camus are in continuity with those of his 1946 North American lectures, and indeed passages from "The Crisis of Man" (see p. 18) are repeated here, as well as parts of "Witness for Freedom" (see p. 75). They also prefigure L'Homme révolté (The Rebel), a book-length essay published in 1951, for which "Time of the Murderers" represents one of the preparatory works.

Ladies and gentlemen,

Some of you are so generous as to take an interest in Europe. And I am aware there is merit in this. That old continent bears many scars that give it a sinister air. It is frequently ill-tempered, and has an unfounded inclination to believe that nothing exists outside its borders, though these are no wider than those of Brazil alone. But it does after all have a past: centuries of glory, which is nothing, and of culture, which is worth more. And in the great desert of a world made barren by the spirit of power, in an age when men driven by ferocious second-rate ideologies grow accustomed to be ashamed of everything and of happiness itself, it does happen that here or there men scattered across the continents still turn toward unhappy Europe and worry about her future, well aware that Europe's enslavement or despair cannot fail to entail the eclipse of the two or three values which no citizen of any country will ever be able to forgo, without renouncing the appellation of man.

I share that anxiety and should like to respond to it. I do not have the gift of prophecy and am not qualified to decide if Europe still has a future. It is also very likely that Europe needs to refresh herself through contact with free peoples. But I can say this at least: Europe, in order to be useful again to the world, must be cured of a certain number of illnesses. Among these ills, some are entirely outside my competence. Other men today are striving to name and cure these. But there is at least one of Europe's illnesses which I have shared with the men of my generation, and about which I have happened to reflect. So it seems to me, coming here and in response to our common anxiety, that I can do nothing better than say as simply as I can what I know about this illness and contribute to the diagnosis which must always precede any eventual cure.

By doing so, it seems to me, I shall at the same time help to round out the way people think about Europe. For Europe is viewed as the land of humanism, and in a sense that is right. But for the past few years, she has been something else: the land of concentration camps and cold, scientific destruction. How did the land of humanism produce the concentration camps? And once it was done, how did the humanists themselves come to terms with the concentration camps? Those are the questions which men of my generation can deal with, and which I should like to tackle, leaving to others more qualified the task of talking to you about humanism and the Europe of brethren.

Europe is today in distress. What is this distress? At first sight it is easily defined: there has been a lot of killing over the past few years and some people even foresee that there will be more killing. Such a large number of deaths ends up dampening the atmosphere. This is not new, of course. Official history has always been the history of great murderers. Cain has been killing Abel before today! But only today is Cain killing Abel in the name of logic and then laying claim to the Légion d'Honneur. I shall give an example in order to explain myself better.

During the strikes of 1947, the newspapers announced that the Paris executioner too would be stopping work. Not enough attention, in my view, has been paid to this decision by our compatriot. His demands were clear. He naturally asked for a bonus for each execution, which is normal in every occupation. But above all he laid vigorous claim to the rank of office manager. He basically wanted to receive from the State, which he was sure he served well, the sole consecration—the one tangible honor—that a modern nation could offer to its good servants: I mean an administrative rank. In this way one of our last liberal professions was expiring under the weight of history. For it really was indeed under the weight of history. In the days of barbarism, a dreadful aura kept the executioner apart from the world. He was the one who, by vocation, violated the mystery of life and the flesh. He was and knew himself to be an object of horror. And that horror at the same time consecrated the price of human life. Today he is merely an object of shame. And in these conditions I find that he is right to no longer wish to be the poor relative kept in the kitchen because he does not have clean fingernails. In a civilization where murder and violence are already doctrines and on the way to becoming institutions, executioners have every right to join the civil service. To be honest, we French are a bit behind. Almost everywhere in the world, executioners are already occupying ministerial chairs. They have simply replaced the ax with the rubber stamp.

When death becomes a matter of statistics and administration, that really means that something is not right. [*Train anecdote.*[1]] Europe is sick, since putting a human being to death can be envisaged there otherwise than with the horror and outrage it ought to provoke; since torturing men is accepted as a rather tiresome chore, like shopping and having to queue for every gram of butter. Europe suffers in this way from murder and abstraction. My opinion is that these are the same sickness. I am merely proposing to you, in the two parts of my talk, to examine how we have got into this and how we can get out.

I

The answer to the first question is simple. We got into it through thought. And it is a sickness that in a way we wanted.

Exceptions apart, none of us of course has ever actually performed the job of executioner. But we have found ourselves and still find ourselves confronted by historical projects of large-scale extermination. It is even possible that we have fought them, for example, with courage and tenacity. But with what arguments were we able to support the condemnation we delivered against them? Had we never entertained thoughts or doctrines which ultimately vindicated the mass graves? So far as men of my generation are concerned, the answer unfortunately is "yes." One does not think badly because one is a murderer, but one is a murderer because one thinks badly. This is the first reflection I should like to share with you.

Many of us were carried along in fact by the nihilism of the interwar period. And so far as they are concerned, the question is not to know whether they had excuses for living in negation. They did have some. What matters is to know whether they did live in it. Men of my age in France and in Europe, for example, were born just before or during the first great war, reached adolescence at the moment of the world economic crisis and were twenty in the year when Hitler took power. To complete their education, they were then offered the war in Spain, Munich, the 1939 war, defeat and four years of occupation and clandestine struggle. Eventually they were promised the atomic firework. So I suppose this is what one would call an interesting generation. But all the more interesting, in that it went into that interminable experience with the force of revolt alone, since it believed in nothing. The literature of its day was in revolt against clarity, narrative and even sentences. Painting was in revolt against the subject, reality and simple harmony. Music rejected melody. As for philosophy, it taught that there was no truth, just phenomena; that Mr. Smith, Monsieur Durand and Herr Vogel might exist, but there was nothing in common between these three particular phenomena. The moral stance of this generation was even more categorical: nationalism struck it as an outworn truth, religion as an exile; twenty years of international politics had taught it to doubt all pure creeds, and to think that no one was ever wrong since everyone reckoned they were right. As for society's traditional morality, that struck it as what it has always been: in other words, an abdication or a monstrous hypocrisy.

So this generation lived in nihilism. Of course, that was not new either. Other generations, other countries have lived this experience at other periods in history. But what is new is that these same men, foreign to all values, had to decide on their individual positions in relation to murder and terror. For they went into war, for example, as one goes into hell, if it is true that hell is renunciation. They loved neither war nor violence. They had to accept war and exercise violence. They felt hatred only for hatred. Yet they had to learn that difficult knowledge. In order to fight, it is necessary to believe in something. These men seemingly believed in nothing. So they could not fight. But if you do not fight, then you adopt the enemy's values, even if they are contemptible values, since you allow them to triumph.

We knew instinctively we could not surrender to the monsters which were emerging throughout Europe. But we were unable to justify that obligation we were under. That was the sickness of Europe, which can still be defined like this: not so long ago, it was bad actions that needed to be justified, and today it is good ones. And they were not easy to justify, since the most aware among us could see that they did not yet have any principle in thought which might allow them to oppose terror and repudiate murder.

For if in fact one believes in nothing, if nothing has any meaning and we cannot affirm any value, then everything is allowed and nothing matters. Then there is neither good nor evil, and Hitler, for example, was neither wrong nor right. Malice and virtue are chance or whim. You can send thousands of innocents to the gas chamber as you can devote yourself to caring for lepers. You can just as well honor the dead as throw them into the dustbin. It all amounts to the same. [*Four illegible words.*] "A pair of boots," wrote the nihilist Pisarev, "is worth more than Shakespeare."[2]

And when we think that nothing has any meaning, the only conclusion is that the person who is right is the one who succeeds. The only rule is to prove oneself most effective, meaning strongest. The world is no longer shared between the just and unjust, but between masters and slaves. And that is so true that still today plenty of intelligent, skeptical people will tell you that if by chance Hitler had won this war, History would have paid homage to him, and would have consecrated the horrific pedestal upon which he had perched. What is so surprising about that! As Simone Weil said, "Official history consists in taking murderers at their word."[3] And truly we cannot doubt that History, such as we conceive of it, would have consecrated Hitler and justified terror and murder, just as we all consecrate and justify them at times when we venture to think that nothing has any meaning.

So wherever one turns, murder—and scientific, *useful* murder—occupies a special place at the heart of negation and nihilism. This way of thinking led ultimately, in the most natural way, to the C[*oncentration*] C[*amps*]. So if we thought it legitimate to ensconce ourselves in total negation, we had to be prepared to kill and to kill scientifically. Of course, certain arrangements were needed for that. But basically fewer than people think, judging by experience, without counting the fact that it is always possible to have the killing done for you, as normally occurs. In any case, nothing in what we thought enabled us to refute what we were seeing, even if it was a question of Dachau. And that is why so many men of my generation found themselves cast almost at random into that wretched adventure without any spiritual resource that could prevent murder or legitimize it; swept along by a whole epoch of impassioned nihilism, yet in solitude; bearing arms, but with heavy hearts.

It is because they were keenly aware of this abandonment that a certain number of other men seemingly repudiated nihilism and, while still rejecting higher principles of explanation, opted for the values of History. Historical materialism in particular was there, which they saw as a refuge in which they thought they could find a rule for action without renouncing any part of their revolt. It was enough to act in the direction of History. Those men used to say, for example, that this war and many other things were necessary, because it would liquidate the age of nationalisms and prepare the time of Empires, which—after new conflicts or not—would be succeeded by the universal society.

Thinking like this, however, they arrived at the same result as if they had thought nothing had any meaning. For if History has a meaning, it is a total meaning or it is nothing. Those men thought and acted as if History obeyed a sovereign dialectic, and as if we were all advancing together toward a definitive goal. They thought and acted according to Hegel's principle: "Man is made for History, not History for man."[4] In truth, all the political and moral realism which guided and still guides the world's destiny obeys, often without knowing it and with a hundred years of delay, a philosophy of History born in Germany, according to which the whole of humanity is advancing along rational paths toward a definitive universe. Nihilism was replaced by a naive rationalism, and in both cases the results are the same. For if it is true that History obeys a sovereign logic, and if it is true, according to that same philosophy, that the state of anarchy must inevitably be succeeded by the feudal state, feudalism by nations, and nations by Empires, finally culminating in the universal Society, then everything which serves this inevitable progress is good and the accomplishments of History are definitive truths.

And since these accomplishments cannot be served other than by the normal means of wars, plots and murders, both individual and collective, all acts are justified not insofar as they are good or bad, but insofar as they are effective or not. This line of argument leads no less naturally to the C[*oncentration*] C[*amp*] and scientific murder. In their consequences, there are no differences between the two attitudes about which I have been speaking. Both are situated at the end of that long adventure of the modern mind which, since what Nietzsche called the death of God, has not ceased to write the tragedy of European pride in the blood of History. Every false idea ends in bloodshed, which is the justice of this land. But it is always the blood of others, which is the injustice of our condition.

II

So it is really these false ideas which have made Europe sick. They have given her the virus of efficiency, and made murder necessary. Being efficient is today's great slogan, and insofar as despair or logic have made us want efficiency, to the same extent we are all responsible for the murders of History. Because wishing for efficiency means wishing for domination. Wanting to dominate someone or something means wishing for someone's impotence, silence or death. This is why we are living rather like phantoms, in a world henceforth abstract, silenced by shrieking and threatened with ruin. For philosophies placing efficiency at the summit of all values are philosophies of death. It is under their influence that the forces of life have deserted Europe, and that the continent's civilization today presents signs of decline. Civilizations have their own kind of scurvy, which in this case is the evil of abstraction.

[*Illegible words.*] I shall give just a few examples. And first polemic. There is no life without dialogue. And across most of the world, dialogue is today replaced by polemic, the language of efficiency. The twentieth century in our lands is the century of polemic and insult. Between nations and individuals, and even at the level of formerly disinterested disciplines, polemic holds the place which was traditionally held by considered dialogue. Day and night, thousands of voices, each pursuing from its own corner a noisy monologue, unleash on our peoples a torrent of mystifying words. But what is the mechanism of polemic? It consists in viewing the opponent as an enemy, consequently simplifying him and refusing to see him. When I insult a person, I no longer know the color of his gaze. Thanks to polemic, we no longer live in a world of men, but in a world of shapes.

Nor is there any life without persuasion. And today's history knows only intimidation, the politics of effectiveness. Men live—and can live—only in the belief that they have something in common, where they can always meet. But we have discovered the following: there are men who cannot be persuaded. It was and is impossible for a victim of the concentration camps to explain to the people debasing him that they should not do so. For the latter no longer represent men, but an idea tempered to the most inflexible will. The person who seeks to dominate is deaf. Faced by him, you must fight or die. This is why today's men live in terror. In the *Book of the Dead* it is written that the just Egyptian, in order to deserve his pardon, must be able to say: "I have inspired fear in no man." In these circumstances, on the day of the Last Judgment our great contemporaries will be sought in vain in the cohort of the blessed.

Is it any surprise that these shapes now deaf and blind, terrorized, fed on coupons, and their whole life summarized in police dossiers, should then be treated as anonymous abstractions? It is noteworthy that the regimes which have emerged from the ideologies about which I am speaking are precisely those which proceed systematically to uproot populations, parading them across the breadth of Europe like livid symbols that take on a pathetic life only as statistical numbers. Since these fine philosophies entered history, vast masses of men, each of whom once had his own way of shaking hands, are buried forever beneath the two initials[5] denoting displaced persons that a very logical world has invented for them.

For all this is logical. When you want to unite the whole world in the name of a theory, by means of efficiency, there is no other way but to make that world as emaciated, blind and deaf as the theory itself, as cold as reason, as cruel as [*illegible word*]. There is no other way but to sever the very roots attaching man to life and nature. Nature is what escapes history and reason. So it is nature which must be [*illegible word*]. And it is no accident if, since Dostoyevsky, one finds no landscapes in great European literature. It is no accident if the significant books of today, instead of being concerned with the subtleties of the heart and the truths of love, are interested only in judges, trials and the machinery of accusations; if, instead of opening windows onto the beauty of the world, they are carefully closed upon the anguish of solitary individuals. [*Seven illegible words.*] Characters are a literature of landscapes. It is no accident if the philosopher who today inspires much of European thought is the one who has written that only the modern city allows the mind to become aware of itself, and who has gone so far as to say that nature is abstract and reason alone concrete. Such indeed is the stance of Hegel,[6] and it is the starting point of a vast adventure of intelligence that ends up killing everything. In the great spectacle of nature, these drunken minds no longer see anything but themselves. This is the final blindness.

Why continue? Those who know the ruined cities of Europe know what I am talking about. They furnish the image of this emaciated world, ravaged by pride, where throughout a dreary apocalypse phantoms roam in search of a lost friendship with nature and with human beings. The great drama of Western man is that between him and his historical future neither the forces of nature nor those of friendship are any longer interposed. His roots cut, his arms withered, he is already merging with the gallows to which his murders and his ideologies condemn him.

III

I shall halt this description here, though it is incomplete. Too many human beings in Europe today are wretched witnesses of its reality for any pleasure to be taken in it. What interests me is knowing how to emerge from this state and, precisely, whether we are capable of emerging from it. There was a time when divine commandments gave everyone their rulebook, and I quite understand that this was a solution. But those times are gone and eighty percent of Europeans today live outside grace.

The only practical conclusion is that Europe can no longer draw the strength for a rebirth except from what she has at her disposal: I mean, her negations and her revolt. But after all, you will say, it is her philosophers of revolt who have brought her to where she is. She first of all revolted against a world that had no meaning, and she derived from that the notion that it was necessary to dominate that world through the paths of power. She chose efficiency. She has what she wished for. And it is true that most Europeans, without knowing it, chose to live as they are living. In this case, there would be no other outcome than cloisters and deserts. The future of the world could then be abandoned to those childlike peoples laughing atop their machines.

My answer is different, however, and I give it for what it is worth. Revolt does not lead to domination, and it is through a perversion of intellectual pride that so many dreadful consequences have been drawn from it. Nothing justifies that destructive fury other than the blindness of an indignation which no longer even sees its own causes. Suppressing the higher justification, nihilism rejects every limit and ends up reckoning that it does not matter killing what is already fated to die.

But this is madness. And revolt can still give us, precisely at its own level, a rule of action that lessens men's pain instead of increasing it. In this world devoid of values, in this desert of the heart where we have lived, what did this revolt really mean? It made us into men who said "no." But at the same time we were men who said "yes." We said "no" to that world, to its essential absurdity, to the abstractions threatening us, to the civilization of death being prepared for us. By saying "no," we were affirming that things had gone on long enough and there was a limit that could not be crossed. But at the same time we were affirming everything which fell short of that limit; we were affirming that there was something in us which rejected the outrage, and which could not be humiliated for too long. And, of course, this was a contradiction which could not fail to make us reflect. We thought that this world was living and struggling without real values. And yet we were struggling against Germany, for example. And consequently, through the very fact of rejecting and struggling, we were all affirming something.

[*German anecdote.*[7]]

But did this something have a general value? Did it go beyond the opinion of an individual? Could it serve as a rule for behavior? The answer has already been given. The men I am talking about were ready to die in the course of their revolt. And their death proved they were sacrificing themselves for the sake of a truth which transcended their personal existence, which went beyond their individual fate. What our rebels were defending against a hostile destiny was a value common to all. When men were being tortured assiduously, when mothers saw themselves obliged to condemn their children to death, when the just were being buried like swine, those rebels reckoned that something in them was denied which did not belong just to them, but was a common space where men have a ready-made solidarity. But in this absurdity there was at the same time the following lesson: that we were in a collective tragedy, whose stake was a shared dignity, a communion of men among themselves, that had to be defended and maintained before anything else was known about it.

Yes, it is the great lesson of these terrible years that the affront done to a Prague student affected a worker from the Paris suburbs, and that the blood shed somewhere on the banks of a European river would lead a Scottish crofter to shed his own blood on those Ardennes which he was seeing for the first time. And even that was absurd and crazy, impossible—or almost—to conceive.

On that basis, we knew how to act and we learned how, in the most absolute moral destitution, man can rediscover values sufficient to regulate his behavior. For if this communion of men among themselves, in mutual recognition of their flesh and their dignity, was truth, it is this very communication, this dialogue, which had to be served.

And in order to maintain this communication, men had to be free, since there is nothing in common between a master and a slave, nor can one talk and communicate with a man in bondage. Bondage is a silence, and the most terrible of all.

And in order to maintain this communication, we also needed to ensure that injustice would disappear, because there is no dialogue between the oppressed man and the profiteer. Envy too belongs to the domain of silence.

And in order to maintain this communication, we need lastly to proscribe lying and violence, for the man who lies closes himself off from other men, and the one who tortures and constrains imposes definitive silence.

So on the basis of negation, and through the mere action of our revolt, it was possible to rediscover an ethics of freedom and sincerity, an ethics of dialogue.

In order to heal Europe, in order to serve the future of the world, it is this ethics of dialogue with which we must provisionally counter the ethics of murder. We must struggle against injustice, against bondage and terror, because these three scourges are the ones which cause silence to hold sway among men, which raise barriers between them, which conceal them from one another and prevent them from coming together in the one value that could save them from this despairing world: the long brotherhood of men struggling against their destiny. At the end of this endless night, now and at last, we know what we must do.

What does this mean in practical terms? It means that Europe will not heal if we do not call things by their name; if we do not accept the idea that we are killing men, whenever we take pleasure in certain thoughts. So the first thing to do, quite simply, is to reject in thought and action every cynical philosophy. We shall not be saying by this that we are rejecting all violence, which would be utopian, but that we are rejecting comfortable violence: I mean, violence legitimized by *raison d'État* or by some philosophy. No violence can be exercised by proxy, none justified in general. Each violent act must call everything into question for the man who commits it. Abolition of the death penalty and the condemnation of concentration-camp systems ought, in any case, to be the first article of the international Code whose creation we are all awaiting. The death penalty is imaginable only on the basis of men who think they possess absolute truth. That is not the case with us. And we are therefore obliged to conclude that we can describe no one as absolutely guilty. So it is impossible to impose an absolute punishment.

Europe will not heal unless we deny political philosophies the right to regulate everything. It is not really a matter of giving this world a political and ethical catechism. The great misfortune of our time is precisely that politics claims to arm us simultaneously with a catechism, a complete philosophy and even sometimes an art of love. But the role of politics is to do the housework, not to regulate our inner problems. For my own part, I do not know if an absolute exists. But I do know that it is not part of the political order. The absolute is not everybody's business, but the business of each one of us. And everybody must regulate their relations with one another in such a way that each of us has the inner leisure to question himself about the absolute. Our life doubtless belongs to others and it is right to give it when that is necessary. But our death belongs only to ourselves—that is my definition of freedom.

Europe will not heal if she does not seek to create, on the basis of negation, the provisional values which will allow reconciliation of negative thought with the possibilities of positive action. That is the task for philosophers, of which I have given merely an outline. But it would at least allow us to call into question a certain number of falsified values with which our contemporaries are living, the first of which is heroism. It must be calmly stated, there is a charge to be brought against heroism and the charge will be usurpation. For this value is falsified in the sense that our philosophies of exaltation too often accord it a place that is not its own: by which I mean the foremost. "Courage," Schopenhauer would say, "merely a subaltern's virtue."[8] Let us not go so far. But let us at least say that we do not want any old heroes. Many among us can testify that the German SS were courageous. That does not prove they were right when they organized concentration camps. So heroism is a secondary virtue, which depends on other virtues in order to retain any meaning. The person who dies for injustice is not thereby justified. There would also be courage, but of another kind, in being able to recognize that the foremost virtue is not heroism, but honor, without which courage loses its meaning and heroism is debased.

To conclude, Europe will not heal without reinventing a universalism in which all men of goodwill may come together. In order to emerge from solitude and abstraction, it is necessary to talk. But it is necessary to be frank, and on every occasion to speak all the truth one knows. But one can speak the truth only in a world where this is defined and based on values common to all men. No man in the world, today or tomorrow, can ever decide that his truth is good enough to be able to impose it on others. For only the common conscience of men can assume that ambition. And it is necessary to rediscover the values which sustain that conscience, destroyed today by terror. This means that, outside political parties, we all have to create communities of reflection which will initiate dialogue, across frontiers; and which will assert—through their lives and their conversations—that this world must cease being one of policemen, soldiers and money to become one of men and women, productive work and considered leisure. The freedom we must win, finally, is the right not to lie. Only on that condition shall we know our reasons for living and for dying. Only on that condition shall we be able, amid the general complicity wherein we live, to try at least to be innocent murderers.

Conclusion

I am now done with the few reflections I wished to offer you. You will perhaps think the rather limited stance I have spoken about has only modest chances against the forces of murder. But I shall conclude by saying that this is not my view. For what is involved is a well-calculated prudence, in any case provisional, requiring strength and determination. More simply, it requires one to love life more than any idea. This is perhaps what makes it difficult, in a Europe which has forgotten how to love life, and which pretends to love the future above all else only to sacrifice everything to it. But if Europe wishes to regain the taste for life, she will have to replace values of efficiency by values of example.

And, in truth, if she does not do so, nobody in the world will do so in her place. She has been involved in the same murderous undertakings as the other powers which today pretend to lead the world. But those powers have merely followed the lessons of Europe. And the latter [*two illegible words*] is capable of shaping a solution, and capable of shaping the thoughts on which our common salvation henceforth depends.

Someone in the ancient world precisely gave us the example of—and the path to—this salvation. He knew that life contains a part of shadow and a part of light; that man could not claim to regulate everything and it was necessary to show him his vanity. He knew that there are things one does not know, and that if one claims to know everything, then one ends up killing everything. With a premonition of what Montaigne was to say—"It is putting a very high price on one's conjectures to have someone roasted alive on their account"[9]—he used to preach in the streets of Athens the value of ignorance [*illegible words*] in order for men to become tolerable to men. Eventually, of course, they put him to death. With Socrates dead, then the decline of the Greek world began. And many a Socrates has been killed in Europe in the past few years. This is a sign. It is a sign that only the Socratic spirit of tolerance toward others and severity toward oneself is dangerous at this time for our civilization of murder. Nietzsche knew this well, having managed to identify Socrates as the worst enemy of the will to power. So it is a sign that this spirit alone can do good to the world. Any other effort, however admirable, aimed at domination cannot but mutilate man still more gravely. Socrates was right: there is no man without dialogue. And it seems that, for Europe and the world, the moment has come to bring the forces of dialogue together against the ideologies of power.

And here I shall recall that I am a writer. For one of the meanings of today's history—and even more of tomorrow's—is the struggle between artists and conquerors, and, however ridiculous it may seem, between words and bullets. Conquerors and artists want the same thing and live by the same revolt. But modern conquerors want a united world, and can obtain this only by passing through war and violence. They have just one rival, and soon just one enemy, which is art. For artists too want that unity, but they look for it and sometimes find it in beauty, after a long inner asceticism. "Poets," said Shelley, "are the unacknowledged legislators of the world."[10] But he thereby at the same time defined the great responsibility of contemporary artists, who must acknowledge what they are and, for example, that they are on the side of life not death. They are witnesses of the flesh, not the law. By their vocation, they are condemned to an understanding precisely of what is antagonistic to them. Which does not mean, however, that they are incapable of judging good and evil. But even with the worst criminal, the ability of artists to live another person's life allows them to recognize man's constant justification, which is pain. It is this compassion, in the strongest sense of the word, which in history has in the past already made them [*illegible words*]. Rather than evading this risk and this responsibility, artists must accept them [*illegible words*]. And struggle in their own way, which can only be [*illegible word*].

Europe will not heal if she does not reject adoration of events, facts, wealth, power, history as it is made and the world as it goes on; if she does not agree to see the human condition as it is. And what it is we all know. It is that terrible condition which requires truckloads of blood and centuries of history to achieve an imperceptible modification in the fate of men. Such is the law. In the eighteenth century, for years heads in France fell like hail. The French Revolution fired every heart with enthusiasm and terror. And eventually, at the start of the following century, people managed to replace legitimate monarchy by constitutional monarchy. We French of the twentieth century know this terrible law only too well. There was the war, the occupation, the massacres, thousands of prison walls, a Europe frantic with pain—and all of it so that, in the devastated world, the two or three slight differences would become perceptible which will help us to despair less. It is the optimism of the sated which would be shocking here. Europe must relearn modesty. For the person who puts his hope in the human condition is perhaps a madman. But the one who despairs of events is certainly a coward.

Through their work and through their example, all that remains for artists from now on is to prove that compassion too is a strength; that it is better to be wrong, while murdering no one and letting others speak, than to be right amid silence and mass graves. It remains for them to proclaim that if revolutions can succeed through violence, they can be maintained only in dialogue. A part of the European future is in the hands of our thinkers and artists, who thus simultaneously know misery and glory. But it has always been thus, and this itself is exciting. History today places in the foreground the eternal vocation of intelligence, that which through centuries of uncertain battles and threatened glories has never ceased struggling to affirm, against the abstractions of history, what transcends all history and which is the flesh, whether suffering or joyful. All Europe today, standing in her pomp, cries out to us that this undertaking is ridiculous and pointless. But we are all in the world to prove the opposite.

The Europe of Loyalty

1951

On April 12, 1951, the Association of Friends of the Spanish Republic, whose moving spirits included Édouard Herriot, René Cassin and also Pierre Mendès France, organized a meeting at the Salle Saulnier in Paris. Invited to speak, Albert Camus reaffirmed that Europe could be constructed only with a Spain liberated from Francoism, at the very moment when the United States, England and France were renewing diplomatic relations with Franco. The text of Camus's speech was published as early as May 1951, in the fiftieth issue of Pierre Monatte's revolutionary syndicalist journal La Révolution prolétarienne.[1]

The democracies of the West seem to make a habit of betraying their friends. The regimes of the East feel obliged to devour them. Between the two, we have to make a Europe neither of liars nor of slaves. For some Europe must surely be made, as they are right to tell us in the American Senate. We simply do not want any old Europe. Accepting to build a Europe with the criminal generals of Germany and the rebel general Franco would mean accepting a Europe of renegades. And, after all, if it is that kind of Europe which the Western democracies want, it was easy for them to have it. Hitler tried to build it and almost succeeded; it was necessary only to kneel and the ideal Europe would have been built on the bones and ashes of murdered free men. Men of the West did not want that. They fought from 1936 until 1945 and millions died, or lay dying in prison darkness, for Europe and her culture to remain a hope and retain a meaning. If some people have forgotten that today, we have not forgotten it. Europe is first and foremost a loyalty. That is why we are here this evening.

If I am to believe the Francoist papers, Marshal Pétain called Franco the brightest sword of Europe. These are military courtesies, of no consequence. But we precisely do not want a Europe defended by that kind of sword. Serrano Suñer,[2] servant of the chief Nazis, has just written an article where he calls for an aristocratic Europe. I have nothing against the aristocracy. On the contrary, I think the problem European civilization faces is to create new elites, its own having been dishonored. But Suñer's aristocracy is too much like Hitler's lords. It is the aristocracy of a gang, the royalty of crime, the cruel lordship of mediocrity. For my part, I know only two kinds of aristocracy: those of intelligence and work. These are oppressed, insulted, or cynically exploited in today's world by a tribe of lackeys and officials at the disposal of power. Freed and reconciled, above all reconciled, they will make the only Europe that could last: not that of forced labor, and intelligence enslaved to doctrine; nor the one in which we live, of hypocrisy and the ethics of shopkeepers; but the living Europe of municipalities and trade unions that will prepare the rebirth for which we are waiting. In this immense undertaking, it is my conviction that we cannot do without Spain.

Europe has in fact become this inhuman land where everyone talks nevertheless about humanism, this slave encampment and this world of shadows and ruins, only because she has shamelessly given herself over to the grossest doctrines; because she has dreamed of being a land of gods, and in order to deify man has chosen to enslave all men to the means of power. The philosophies of the North have assisted and advised her in this fine undertaking. And today, in the Europe of Nietzsche, Hegel and Marx, we are culling the fruits of that madness. If man has become God, we are surely obliged to say that he has not become much: this god looks like a helot or a prosecutor. Never have such petty gods ruled the world. Who, seeing them on the front page of the papers or on our cinema screens, would be surprised that their Churches are primarily police forces?

Europe was never as great as in the tension she managed to introduce among her peoples, her values and her doctrines. Either she is this balance and this tension, or she is nothing. As soon as she renounced it, and chose to make the abstract unity of a doctrine hold sway through violence, she went into a decline; she became the exhausted mother who now gives birth only to mean, hateful creatures. And it is perhaps right that these creatures should end up hurling themselves upon one another, in order at last to find an impossible peace in a desperate death. But our task and common role is not to serve this terrible justice. It is to re-create a more modest justice in a renascent Europe; consequently, to renounce doctrines claiming to sacrifice everything to history, reason and power. And for that we need to rediscover the path to the world; we need to balance men with nature, evil with beauty, justice with compassion. In short, we need to be reborn in the hard and watchful tension which makes societies productive. It is here that Spain must help us.

For how can we do without that Spanish culture where never, not once in centuries of history, were the flesh and men's anguish sacrificed to pure ideas? That culture which managed to give the world simultaneously Don Juan and Don Quixote, the supreme images of sensuality and mysticism? What culture in its craziest creations does not depart from everyday realism? In short a complete culture which, with its creative strength, covers the entire universe from sunlight to darkness? This is the culture that can help us remake a Europe which will neither exclude any of the world nor mutilate anything human. It still partly contributes today to sustaining our hope. And at the very time when that culture was gagged in Spain, it was still giving its blood, the best of it, to this Europe and to this hope. The Spanish dead of the German camps, of the Glières,[3] of the Leclerc Division and the twenty-five thousand killed in the deserts of Libya,[4] were this culture and this Europe. It is to them that we are loyal. And if they are able to live again somewhere, today and in their own country, it is among those students and workers of Barcelona who have just told the astonished world that the true Spain is not dead, but is once again claiming its place.[5]

But if the Europe of tomorrow cannot do without Spain, she cannot for the same reasons put up with Franco's Spain. Europe is an expression of contrasts, unable to tolerate doctrines stupid enough and cruel enough to forbid any expression apart from their own. A few months ago, at the same time as a Spanish minister was hoping that the elites of France and Spain might increasingly interpenetrate, his censorship was banning Anouilh[6] and Marcel Aymé.[7] Since these writers had never passed for implacable revolutionaries, you can guess how much of Sartre, Malraux or Gide can penetrate Spain. As for us, we readily agree to read Monsieur Benavente.[8] The only problem is that Monsieur Benavente's books are unreadable. Recent Francoist articles have claimed that censorship had been relaxed. After examining the texts, we can be reassured. The relaxation consists in asserting that everything is allowed, except what is forbidden. Franco, who willingly draws inspiration from one of our great writers—I mean Joseph Prudhomme[9]—has declared that "the Spain of the Toledo Alcázar was attached to the seat of Saint Peter." But he censors the Pope himself when the latter argues for freedom of the press. In our own Europe, the Pope has the right to speak, as do also those who think he uses that right badly.

The Europe we want is also an order. And when anybody can arrest anybody, when informing is encouraged, when pregnant women in prisons are generously allowed off work but only in their ninth month, then we are in disorder. And Franco is proving to the whole world that he is far more dangerous an anarchist than our friends in the CNT,[10] who for their part do want a certain order. And for me at least, the disorder is at its utmost in that hideous confusion where religion mingles with executions and the priest is silhouetted behind the executioner. Execution orders end in Franco's Spain with this pious wish, addressed to the prison director: "May God grant you a long life." Prisoners are also given subscriptions to the weekly *Redención*. This Europe where God is reserved for the particular use of prison directors—is this the civilization for which we must fight and die? No! Fortunately a redemption exists to which we have no need to subscribe, and which consists in the judgment of free men. If there is a Christ in Spain, he is indeed in the prisons, but on pallets in the cells; he is with those Catholics who refuse communion because the executioner priest has made it obligatory in certain prisons. Those are our brothers, and the sons of free Europe.

Our Europe is also that of true culture. And—I regret having to say this—I see no sign of culture in Franco's Spain. I have recently read the philosophy of history that is personal to the Caudillo. It is summed up in the following (and I quote): "the free-masonry concealed in the Trojan Horse of the *Encyclopédie* was introduced into Spain by the Bourbons." At the same time, I read that a Catholic pilgrim from America, received by Franco, found him "extraordinarily intelligent." A pilgrim is always an enthusiast. He does not want to have taken all that trouble for nothing. But actually I find Franco's utterance and the pilgrim's a bit incompatible. And my conviction is strengthened that culture and today's official Spain have merely polite relations when I read that "Franco must with his sword cut the Gordian knots of age-old problems whose solution was reserved for his genius"; or again that "It seems that God has placed Franco's destiny under the sign of these dazzling historical apparitions by isolating that haloed head on the horizon of our century." No, idolatry is not culture. Culture at least dies from ridicule. For Franco, demanding his place in the concert of nations and claiming the right (which we claim with him) for Spain to have the government it pleases, sums up his doctrine in the following formula upon which, as you will easily understand, I cannot stop reflecting: "It is not that we were going in a different direction . . . It is that we are going faster than the rest and are already on the way back, whereas the rest are still going toward the goal." This audacious metaphor is in fact enough to explain everything, and to justify why for our own culture we prefer the Europe of Unamuno to that of Monsieur Rocamora.[11]

Our Europe, in short—and this sums up everything—cannot do without peace. Franco's Spain, for its part, lives and keeps going only because war is threatening us, while the Spanish Republic is strengthened whenever peace sees its chances grow. If Europe, in order to exist, has to pass through war, it will be a Europe of policemen and ruins. So it is understandable that Franco should be seen as indispensable, thanks to the inopportune absence of Hitler and Mussolini. This is precisely the assessment of those whose idea of Europe fills us with such horror. Franco was judged severely until the moment when people realized he had thirty divisions. That is when he entered truth. For his use, Pascal's quip was refashioned, becoming: "Error on this side of the thirtieth division, truth on the other."[12] Under these conditions, why wage war against Russia? She is truer than truth, since she has one hundred and seventy-five divisions. But she is the enemy, and everything which can combat her is good. In order to win, it is first necessary to betray truth. Well, this is the time to say that the Europe we want will never be one where the justice of a cause is evaluated by the number of its big guns. It is already stupid to calculate the strength of an army by the number of its officers. By that reckoning, the Spanish army is really the strongest in the world.

But it is also the weakest. You would have to be a State Department expert to imagine that the Spanish people will fight in the name of a freedom it does not possess. But being stupid is nothing. What is more serious is the betrayal of a sacred cause, that of the only Europe we wanted. By signing the restoration of relations with Franco, official America and its allies have signed their break with a certain Europe that is our own—and which we shall continue to defend and to serve together. And we shall serve her well only by distinguishing ourselves precisely from all those who have no moral right to serve her: from those who, with the help of a police provocation, are allowing irreproachable militants of the CNT like José Peirats[13] to be tortured in our country; from those who are allowing the Algerian elections to be rigged; from those too who are washing their hands of the blood of those shot in Prague and insulting the prisoners in the Russian concentration camps. Those people strip themselves of the right to speak about Europe and to denounce Franco. Who will speak, then? Who will denounce him? Spanish friends, the answer is simple: the calm voice of loyalty. But is loyalty not isolated? No, across the world we—the loyal— are millions preparing for the day we meet again. Three hundred thousand inhabitants of Barcelona have just shouted it out to you. It is up to us to unite and to do nothing that might separate us. Yes, let us simply unite, and do you too unite, I beg of you. Exiled Spain finds its justification here, in this finally accomplished union, in this patient and unbending struggle. A day will come when Europe will triumph over her miseries and her crimes, when she will finally live again.

But that day will be the very same—and this is what I have been trying to tell you—as the one when the Spain of loyalty, arriving from the four corners of the earth, will assemble on the summit of the Pyrenees and see stretching out before her the ancient, wounded land that so many of you have awaited in vain, and that has been silently awaiting you for so long. On that day, we other Europeans will rediscover with you an additional fatherland.

[Spain and War]

Lecture at the Casal de Catalunya
1951

On July 19, 1951, at the premises of the Education League in Rue Récamier in Paris, the Casal de Catalunya celebrated the fifteenth anniversary of the social and libertarian revolution of July 19, 1936, in Spain. Invited to speak alongside Octavio Paz, Jean-Paul Sartre and Jean Cassou, Albert Camus delivered this speech, the text of which appeared on August 4, 1951, in Soli-daridad obrera, *weekly of the Spanish CNT.*[1] *It was republished three years later, in the fifth (spring 1954) issue of the journal* Témoins, *accompanied by the speech made by Albert Camus at the Mutualité in Paris on June 30, 1953, following the East Berlin workers' risings (see p. 139). The two texts combined appeared under the single title "Calendar of Freedom."*

On July 19, 1936, the Second World War began in Spain. We are commemorating the event today. That war has ended everywhere today, except precisely in Spain. The pretext for not ending it is the obligation to prepare ourselves for the third world war. This sums up the tragedy of Republican Spain, which saw a civil and a foreign war imposed on her by rebel military leaders, and who today sees the same leaders imposed on her in the name of a foreign war. For fifteen years one of the most righteous causes that can be encountered in a man's lifetime has found itself constantly distorted—and on occasion betrayed—for the larger interests of a world given over to power struggles. The republic's cause found itself and still does find itself always identified with that of peace, and that is no doubt its justification. Unfortunately the world has not stopped being at war since July 19, 1936, and the Spanish Republic has consequently not stopped being betrayed or cynically exploited. This is why it is perhaps pointless to address ourselves, as we have so often done, to the spirit of justice and freedom, to the conscience of governments. A government, by definition, has no conscience. It sometimes has a policy, and that is all. And perhaps the surest way of speaking up for the Spanish Republic is no longer to say that it is unworthy for a democracy to kill for the second time those who have fought and died for the freedom of us all. That language is the language of truth, so it echoes in the desert. The right way will rather be to say that if maintaining Franco is justified only by the necessity to ensure the defense of the West, it is justified by nothing. People should know that defense of the West will lose its justification and its best warriors if it authorizes maintaining a regime of usurpation and tyranny.

Since Western governments have decided to take account only of realities, one might as well tell them that the convictions of a considerable part of Europe are also part of reality, and it will not be possible to deny them to the end. Twentieth-century governments have an unfortunate tendency to believe that public opinion and conscience can be ruled like forces from the physical world. And it is true that, through propaganda techniques or terror, they have managed to give opinion and conscience a distressing elasticity. There is a limit to everything, however, and particularly to the flexibility of opinion. It has been possible to dupe the revolutionary conscience to the point of making it praise the wretched exploits of tyranny. The very immoderation of that tyranny, however, renders this dupery obvious, and in mid-century we see the revolutionary conscience awakening once more and turning back toward its origins. On the other hand, it has been possible to dupe the ideal of freedom for which peoples and individuals have managed to fight even as their governments were capitulating. It has been possible to make those peoples wait, and make them agree to ever-graver compromises. But a limit has now been reached which must be clearly declared, and beyond which it will no longer be possible to exploit free consciences: on the contrary, they too will have to be fought.

This limit, for us Europeans who became aware of our destiny and our truths on July 19, 1936, is Spain and its liberties.

The worst mistake that Western governments could commit would be to ignore the reality of this limit. Our worst cowardice would be to let them ignore it. I have read, in the very odd articles devoted to what it calls the Spanish problem by a newspaper which had accustomed us to more neutrality, that the Spanish republican leaders hardly believe any longer in the Republic.[2] If that were true, it would justify the worst initiatives against that republic. But the author of these articles, Monsieur Créach, speaking of those republican leaders, added: "those at least who live in Spain." Unfortunately for Monsieur Créach—and fortunately for the freedom of Europe—the republican leaders do not live in Spain. Or, if they do live there, Monsieur Créach cannot meet them in the ministries and salons of Madrid. Those whom he knows and whom he calls republicans have indeed stopped believing in the Republic. But they stopped believing in it from the moment they agreed to subject it for a second time to its murderers. The true and only republican leaders who live in Spain have such a categorical opinion that I fear it cannot please Monsieur Créach, or any of those who in order to serve Franco never stop invoking the danger of war and the requirements of Western defense. It is the opinion of these underground fighters which must be made known, for it alone can indicate the limit to which we must all keep and which, for our own part, we shall not allow to be crossed. That is why I wish my voice were stronger than it is, and would reach directly those whose task it is to define Western policy in terms of reality, in order to bring them some unambiguous statements by the spokesman of Spain's strongest underground movement. Those statements, whose origin and authenticity I guarantee, are brief. Here they are: "By customs, culture and civilization we belong to the Western world. But while Franco remains in power, we shall do all that is necessary to prevent any man in our country ever taking up arms for the West. We are organized for this."

This is a reality which the realists of the West will do well to meditate. And not just in relation to Spain. For the fighter who speaks here, and whose life today is in perpetual danger, is the brother-in-arms of hundreds of thousands of Europeans resembling him, who are determined to fight for their freedoms and certain Western values; who know too that every fight entails a minimum of realism, but will never confuse realism with cynicism or take up arms to defend the West with Franco's Moors[3] and freedom with the admirers of Hitler. For there is a limit there that will not be crossed. For almost ten years we have eaten the bread of shame and defeat. On the day of deliverance, at the peak of our greatest hope, we learned into the bargain that our victory too had been betrayed and we had to give up some of our illusions. Some of them? Of course! After all, we are not children. But certainly not all of them, certainly not our most essential loyalty. On this clearly drawn limit at all events stands Spain, which once again helps us to see clearly. No battle will be just if it is actually fought against the Spanish people. And if it is fought against that people, it will be fought without us. No Europe, no culture will be free if it is built on the enslavement of the Spanish people. And if it is built on that enslavement, it will be done against us. The intelligent realism of Western policies will ultimately culminate in winning to their cause five aerodromes and three thousand Spanish officers, and in definitively alienating hundreds of thousands of Europeans. After which, those political geniuses will congratulate themselves amid the ruins. Unless the realists do really come to understand the language of realism, grasping finally that the Kremlin's best ally today is not Spanish communism but General Franco himself and his Western props.

These warnings will perhaps be useless. But for the moment, and despite everything, some space is left for hope. The fact that these warnings are uttered, the fact that a Spanish fighter has been able to adopt the language I have cited—these things prove at least that no defeat will be definitive as long as the Spanish people, as it has just proved,[4] retains its fighting strength. Paradoxically, it is this starved, enslaved people, exiled from the community of nations, which is today the guardian and the witness of our hope. This people at least—quite different therein from Monsieur Créach's leaders—is alive, suffering and struggling. To such an extent that it embarrasses the theorists of realism, who used to assert that this people was mainly thinking about its own peace of mind. But so little was that the case that those theorists are now making concessions. The newspapers in which what claims to be the European elite painstakingly expresses itself today have striven to explain the phenomenon of the Spanish strikes in a way that left intact the true strengths of the Franco regime. Their last brainwave is that these strikes were encouraged by the bourgeoisie and the army. But the truth is that these strikes were first and foremost carried out by those who were working and suffering. And if, as is possible, Spanish bosses and bishops saw in them an opportunity to express their opposition without paying for it in person, then they are only more contemptible for having counted on the torment and bloodshed of the Spanish people to say what they were incapable of shouting out themselves. Those actions were spontaneous, and their spirit guarantees the reality of our comrade's statements and underpins the only hope which we can entertain.

Let us beware of believing that the Republican cause is wavering! Let us beware of believing that Europe is dying! What are dying, from East to West, are ideologies. And perhaps Europe, with which Spain is interdependent, is so wretched only because she has turned away entirely, even in her revolutionary thought, from a generous source of life; from a thought in which justice and freedom met in a physical unity equally distant from bourgeois philosophies and from Caesarist socialism. The peoples of Spain, Italy and France preserve the secret of that thought, and will continue to preserve it so that it may serve at the time of rebirth. Then July 19, 1936, too will be one of the dates of the century's second revolution, that which finds its source in the Paris Commune, which still flows beneath semblances of defeat, but which has not yet finished shaking the world and will eventually carry man further than the revolution of 1917 succeeded in doing. Fed by Spain and in general by the libertarian genius, it will one day give us back a Spain and a Europe, and with them new tasks and with battles finally out in the open. This at least provides our hope and our reasons for fighting.

Spanish comrades, in saying this I do not, believe me, forget that if fifteen years are a small thing in historical terms, the fifteen years that we have just gone through have weighed with a dreadful weight on many of you, in the silence of exile. There is something about which I no longer know how to speak, because I have said it too often, which is my own passionate desire to see you recover the only land that is worthy of you. Once again this evening I feel the bitterness there may be in speaking to you only about struggles and renewed battles, instead of about the deserved happiness to which you have a right. But all we can do to justify so much suffering and so many deaths is to carry their hopes within us, and not allow this suffering to have been in vain or these deaths to have been alone. These implacable fifteen years which have exhausted so many men in the task have forged a few others whose destiny is to justify the former. Harsh as that may be, it is how peoples and civilizations arise. And after all, it is from you, from Spain in part, that some of us have learned to stand upright and accept unflaggingly the hard duty of freedom. For Europe and for us, often without knowing it, you have been and you are the masters of freedom. This hard duty that never ends, it is now our turn to share it with you, without flagging or compromise. Therein lies your justification. Since becoming an adult, I have encountered in history many conquerors whose face I have found hideous. Because I have read in them hatred and solitude. For they were nothing when they were not conquerors. In order simply to exist, they had to kill and enslave. But there is another order of men, who help us to breathe, who have found existence and freedom only in the freedom and happiness of all, and who consequently even from defeats draw reasons to live and love. Such people, even in defeat, will never be solitary.

Albert Camus Talks About the General Election in Britain

1951

From the end of 1947 on, the BBC invited French intellectuals to express themselves through a monthly report called "Letter from Paris," broadcast on its Third Programme. Albert Camus agreed to comment in that context on the snap general election called in October 1951, when Clement Attlee's Labour Party, despite winning a majority of votes, ended up with fewer parliamentary seats than the Conservatives. Six years after his unexpected defeat in the 1945 election, Churchill once again became prime minister. Camus's talk, translated here, was probably recorded in Paris rather than London, and was first broadcast on November 8, 1951, with this title. It was rebroadcast on November 10 in an English translation, and for a third time on the thirtieth of the same month, accompanied on that occasion by a contribution from Raymond Aron reacting to Camus's comments.

I am not going to follow convention by saying that England's domestic politics does not concern me. On the contrary, I have the impression that it does concern me, just as directly or indirectly it concerns millions of Europeans. I can readily admit, however, that my English listeners may consider my opinion, like that of any Frenchman without political responsibility, of no immediate significance to them. This is precisely why I shall speak both sincerely and freely about your latest elections. Sincerely, because I am acutely aware of their significance. Freely, because I am committing only myself here and have no need to disguise my thinking. Also, I am addressing free men.

First and foremost, I think it would be dishonest to hide my preferences. Although I am not really a socialist, since my sympathies lie with libertarian forms of syndicalism, I did hope that Labour would win these elections. Were I to be asked why, I should confess of course that I argue primarily by analogy: I would rather see labor governments than conservative ministries in continental Europe. The reason for this is simple. Those of my English listeners who know the revolting disproportion on display in the towns of the continent, between the destitution of the suburbs and the overwhelming luxury of the few, will understand that simple decency dictates the wish for a set of measures to raise the living standard of workers, through a proportionate reduction of ostentatious fortunes, some of which make no pretence of not having been built on fraud. I am well aware that the English have paid for the relative social justice in which they live with a great deal of austerity, and I have no personal bias in favor of austerity. When all is said and done, however, we can observe about us daily that austerity is a far lesser evil than injustice.

I am also interested in Labour as the example of a socialism devoid of philosophy, or almost so. For a century, European socialism has given priority to the philosophy of its leaders over the concrete interests of its working-class troops. Since this philosophy, effective in its critical aspect, is unrealistic in positive terms, it has constantly clashed with reality; and the continent's socialists have had no choice other than opportunism, which condemns them to defeat, or terror, whose ultimate aim is to bend human and economic reality to principles that do not suit it. When it enters history, philosophy can take us very far. In Europe, at any rate, it has produced liars and executioners, whereas socialism was aiming to create a city of free and generous men. On the other hand, it seems to me that English Labour, like Scandinavian socialism, has remained more or less true to its origins, albeit sometimes tainted by opportunism; and that it has managed to achieve a minimum of justice with a maximum of political freedom. The example that

England has given us in this respect should shame many European governments.

This example is instructive, in any case, for a European from the continent. So much so that it strikes me as impossible to judge the English elections and their international importance without precisely taking account of the problems posed by social justice, both for you and on the continent. I mean by this that there are not two problems: social justice as a domestic issue and peace as an external problem. There is only one, rendering peace dependent on social justice within, while justice within is bound up with the fate of peace and war. Europe, we may be sure, will not have peace without social justice. We are told, for example, that Mr. Churchill has strengthened all the departments involved in defense, and that in any new tragic circumstances he will seize the helm with a firm hand. I can easily believe that. Throughout the war years I admired Mr. Churchill's language. It conveyed the hope and pride not of your country alone, but also our own hope and pride, gagged as we were. Those are things which some people at least, of whom I am one, will never forget, despite all that separates them from Mr. Churchill. But we are also told that your prime minister wishes to complete his great life as a statesman by consolidating peace. This fills me with unreserved joy. I am convinced, however, that Mr. Churchill will not be able to confine himself to meeting Stalin— whom, if memory serves me, he already met at Yalta. He will also in many respects have to continue the same domestic policy as Mr. Attlee. In short, it seems to me that, under the pressure of international circumstances, Labour has not emerged from your recent elections utterly defeated, since Mr. Churchill to a considerable extent will be obliged by his very desire for peace to become a Labourite. Let me explain.

There can be no doubt, in fact, that peace depends on how the Western democracies will win the cold war without casting themselves into the flames of actual war. England is the only one of all the European democracies already to have won that cold war, for its own part, by virtue of the fact that communism has virtually disappeared there. We cannot claim as much. When in Italy and

France one-quarter of the electoral body votes for the designated enemy, it is clear that despite all our rearmament measures we are not capable of resisting that adversary effectively. Those who deny this are lying. And what constitutes the strength of the communist party in continental Europe is not that party's absurd propaganda, nor of course the example of the Russian concentration camps; it is the permanent scandal all around us with respect to social justice. What are we to think of a nation in struggle against a communist power which allows the perpetuation at home of disorder that is able to create communists just as humidity helps propagate plants? We can think only one thing, which is that such a nation is rendering itself hostage to every kind of adventure, with the risk of unleashing the final adventure that will set everything ablaze.

Our European democracies all have a real desire for peace. They know if nothing else—and we French know better than anyone—that war is no longer a good bargain, and that nuclear war would be absurd and suicidal. But even if we are all aware of this, we do not all have the same means to offer peace. What is the use of a defeated man offering peace to one who stands over him fully armed? Even supposing that two fully armed men confront one another, what is the use of one offering peace to the other if behind the former stands a family member ready to strangle his adversary? This is why—and I say it weighing my words well—the continental democracies can no longer really serve peace in the present state of affairs. All we can do, in the first place, is try to recover from the cancer devouring us; or, which comes to the same, try to restore harmony in our own family. England, by contrast, is the country which in these last years of cold war has pledged most to peace, while letting it be clearly understood that it would not yield to the spirit of aggression. Perhaps we still breathe freely today only thanks to the wisdom that your government has on various occasions been able to display. But your country was able to enjoy the luxury of maintaining peace after securing victory only because it deliberately renounced a certain domestic luxury. For social injustice is an extravagant luxury, to be enjoyed only by nations which have a lot of money to compensate for its ravages or a lot of policemen to silence the revolts against it. England, which lacks funds but not freedom, has managed to renounce that luxury, which is why it has provisionally won the cold war that continental Europe is in the process of losing, thanks to the greed and imprudence of its elites.

These are the reasons why it seems to me that a Conservative government, if it wishes to follow a policy of peace while discouraging aggression, will have to leave intact the substance of the social reforms from which England has recently benefited. It is not merely the narrowness of its victory or the increase in votes for Labour which should convince it of this, but the exigencies of the cold war itself. My only worry would be that the Conservatives might imagine they could pursue a foreign policy of peace while breaking with the domestic policy of their rivals. This worry is not that of a political partisan, it is that of a man who lives apart from parties and official circles; a man who has been able to reflect in full independence on the reasons for the weakness currently affecting democratic Europe, and who has found these in the indifference or disaffection of ever-broader masses who rightly consider themselves harmed by the distribution of national income. Dictatorships can allow themselves to wage war with wretched troops: they have ways of persuading them. Democracies, however, need soldiers who have something to defend. When everything is taken from a man, even hope, he has nothing left to defend. Several million Europeans apparently think they have nothing to defend by defending their nation. There you have the most important fact of our history, the tragic evidence that makes your strength and our weakness. But when it comes to you, do at least preserve your most reliable strength by at all costs maintaining justice. To conclude, if Mr. Churchill—as I hope with every fiber of my being—wins peace, he will owe it also to the reforms begun by the coalition government and consolidated by Mr. Attlee. And that will be a powerful symbol, despite any apparent contradictions, of the profound cohesion of a people which, once again in our long history, will have deserved our esteem and gratitude.

But if I may allow myself to speak with the same freedom, I shall add that your country will acquire still greater claims to the gratitude of free men once it ceases to exercise its virtues in isolation. Europe, precisely because of its disorders, needs England; and however wretched the continent may appear, England will certainly not be able to save itself without Europe. The prejudices or indifference that your politicians often foster toward the continent may be legitimate, but they are nevertheless regrettable. Mistrust may be all very well as a method; it is detestable as a principle. A moment always arrives when principle comes up against fact. The facts show that, like it or not, England and Europe stand together. This marriage may seem ill-assorted. But as one of our moralists said: there are good marriages, but no delightful ones.[1] Since ours is not delightful, let us at least ensure that it is good, since divorce is impossible. For divorce is indeed impossible. In vain will England give every last pledge of peace; it will be drawn into war if Europe, incapable of finding its own cohesion, abandons itself irretrievably to one or other of the two blocs. And there will be no European cohesion if our continent fails to find the path of justice. And Europe will not find that path if the forces and men who have always served the cause of peace and justice do not unite. Those forces and those men, in Europe, are mostly socialist: that is a fact. But European socialism, demoralized by its doctrinaire follies and opportunist excesses, cannot do without English trade unionism. The great mistake of the Labour government was to ignore or rebuff that fraternal Europe, thus letting our continent be transformed gradually into the arena of a war currently cold, tomorrow hot, that nobody wants. If the recovery time in opposition that lies ahead of Labour politicians were to lead them to understand this better—if Mr. Churchill, thanks to his realism or inspired by one of those great visions which do sometimes crown long political careers, were to identify both with the reforms of Labour and with working-class Europe, thus showing a supreme ability to defend the interests of justice and peace simultaneously—then Europe, France and individual Frenchmen like me, whatever their preferences, would be able to rejoice at your recent elections, in the name of something transcending party and nation, which depending on the case is called human dignity or happiness.

Appeal for Those Under Sentence of Death

1952

"Franco is still assassinating!" the League for the Rights of Man accused on the poster announcing, for February 22, 1952, at the Salle Wagram in Paris, a grand protest meeting against the Franco regime's death sentence on eleven Spanish trade unionists from the CNT.[1] Many intellectuals were there on the platform, including Georges Altman, André Breton, Albert Béguin, Albert Camus, Louis Guilloux, Jean-Paul Sartre, René Char and Ignazio Silone. It was during this meeting that Camus launched the appeal reproduced below, which would be published by the journal Esprit *in April 1952. Despite this large demonstration, five of the eleven trade unionists (Santiago Amir Gruañas, Pedro Adrover Font, Jorge Pons Argilés, José Pérez Pedrero and Ginés Urrea Piña) were shot dead on March 14, 1952.*

One Paris daily announces today to its avid readers a study on the main orientations of Francoist policy. This evening, we are unfortunately obliged to confine ourselves to examining just one of the directions in which that policy has set out, a direction which has the advantage at least of having been constant and determined.

For almost fifteen years now, actually, Francoism has been aiming at the same target: the face and breast of every free Spaniard.

Let us acknowledge that it has often hit this target, and if despite so many bullets it has not yet disfigured that face perpetually reborn, it now has high hopes of finishing the job thanks to the unexpected complicity of a world that calls itself free.

Well, we shall refuse to the bitter end any share in that complicity! Once again we find ourselves confronting the intolerable scandal of Europe's conscience; once again, tirelessly, we shall denounce it. After so many others, these new victims cry out to us from the depths of their cells that at least on this point mystification cannot last for long.

It is necessary to choose, in fact, between Francoism and democracy. For there is no middle term between these two conceptions. The middle term is precisely this vile confusion in which we find ourselves, where democracies try their hands at being cynical, while Francoism courteously tries its hand at becoming a respecter of laws. So it grants four lawyers to eleven defendants whom a bench of officers judge in a trice, before the lawyers have managed to speak, by virtue of a special law. And similarly Franco is refusing to condemn a sixteen-year-old child to death: this is why he is keeping him in a cell until he reaches adulthood, in order then to have him shot according to the rules. It is time, it is high time, for the representatives of democracies to disown this farce and reject, publicly and definitively, the curious theory which consists in saying: "We'll give arms to a dictator and he'll become a democrat." No! If you give him arms, he will follow his trade by shooting point-blank into the belly of freedom.

It is necessary to choose between Christ and the killer, and it is time, it is high time, for the Catholic hierarchy to denounce, publicly and definitively, that horrible coupling. People have reproached Philip II for tending to believe that God was Spanish. But Philip II was a modest man compared with Franco, who makes people ceaselessly repeat to him, to the sound of execution drumbeats, that God is Falangist. Well, what are they waiting for to condemn that strange religion which, for fifteen years now, has been busy blessing hideous Masses where hosts of lead are distributed by the dozen, in a constant barrage, to consecrate the blood of the righteous?

In any case, if this denunciation is not made without delay, I do not see what reason there would be to choose between hypocrisy and terror, since hypocrisy would have made itself forever the servant of terror. Then the unity of the world would indeed be consecrated, but in infamy. For our part, at least, in the midst of this repugnant outbidding, we shall stand firm, we shall be able to see what remains to be saved this evening as we shall tomorrow. And that which remains to be saved is life, the fragile, precious life of free men. For if we allow these men to be killed, we shall miss them, never doubt. There are not so many of us. On the contrary, we are suffocating in a Europe where human quality is rapidly being degraded day by day. For every free man who falls, ten slaves are born and the future darkens a bit more.

It is that future which we must keep open. It is that chance of life, and with it the chance of greatness, which we have to preserve. And the cry that reaches us, faced with these multiple murders, is first and foremost a horrified protest at the systematic destruction of all those whose very existence still saves this world from dishonor.

Some have said that the Spanish people were the aristocracy of Europe. Who would doubt it, seeing what is all around us? Unfortunately, that aristocracy today is that of sacrifice. It is an elite being killed, whereas we need it to live and help us live. This is why we must act without delay, when each day, each hour, can be counted.

Let each one of us do what he can, but all that he can. Let us not fall asleep, let us not succumb to melancholy or be too easily discouraged. Let us not too easily take our share of the martyrdom of others. Let us above all not yield to the temptation of saying that this martyrdom will not be useless. For if this martyrdom in order to be useful can count only on human memory, it does risk one day being in vain. There are too many victims today, and of all kinds: memory is not enough for them. We do not need the death of these men; we first need their life.

No, let us not allow them to die; the human heart is not sure enough. Whereas their life at least is sure, the warmth of their blood, their pride as free men. It is all this that we must keep among us. But for that, we have to wrench these men away from the executioners, from the bloody Masses, from the contemptible calculations of the chancelleries, from the heads of state who greet democratic presidents after decorating the masters of the Gestapo:

we have to wrench them away, above all, from the world's indifference. For each free man we save, ten future slaves die and the future becomes possible again. This is the meaning of our action this evening. Before the executioners of Spain as before all tyrannies, it is also the meaning of our hope.

Spain and Culture

1952

On November 30, 1952, a big meeting was organized at the Salle Wagram in Paris to protest against the admission to UNESCO some ten days earlier of Franco's Spain. Albert Camus, who from the month of June had registered his refusal to collaborate with the institution for as long as there was any question of admitting Franco's Spain, was present at this rally alongside Jean Cassou, Louis Martin-Chauffier, Émile Kahn, Charles-André Julien, Salvador de Madariaga and Eduardo Santos (see pp. 205 and 181). He delivered this speech there, which was published as early as December in the Spanish anarcho-syndicalist paper Solidaridad obrera,[1] *then in No. 22 of the review* Preuves. *The author would retain the text, moreover, for the "Creation and Freedom" chapter of his* Actuelles II, *which appeared in October 1953.*

We have a new and reassuring victory of democracy to celebrate today. But it is a victory it has won over itself and its own principles. Franco's Spain is stealthily introduced into the well-heated temple of culture and education, while the Spain of Cervantes and Unamuno[2] is once more cast into the street. When you know that in Madrid the current minister of information, henceforth a direct collaborator with UNESCO, is the very one who made Nazi propaganda during Hitler's rule; when you know that the government that has just decorated the Christian poet Paul Claudel is the very one which decorated Himmler's Order of Red Arrows, organizer of the gas chambers—then you are truly justified in saying that it is not Calderón or Lope de Vega[3] whom the democracies have just welcomed into their society of educators, but Joseph Goebbels. Seven years after the end of the war, this superb recantation should warrant our congratulations to the government of Monsieur Pinay.[4] For he at least is not open to reproach for being troubled by scruples where high politics are concerned. Until now everyone believed that the fate of history depended somewhat on the struggle of educators against executioners. But no one thought it was actually enough officially to call the executioners educators. Monsieur Pinay's government thought of that.

Of course, the operation is somewhat awkward and had to be carried out at full speed. So what? School is one thing, the market another! To tell the truth, there is something of the slave market in this story. Victims of the Falange have been exchanged for colonial subjects. As for culture, that will be for later. Besides, it is not the business of governments. Artists make culture, then governments control it and on occasion suppress artists in order to control it better. A day finally comes when a handful of military men and industrialists is able to say "we" when speaking about Molière or Voltaire, or to print a distorted version of the works of a poet they have previously shot.[5] That day—which is where we now are— should prompt in us at least one compassionate thought for poor Hitler. Instead of killing himself out of an excess of romanticism, it would have been enough for him to imitate his friend Franco and just wait. Today he would be a UNESCO delegate for the education of Haut-Niger, and Mussolini himself would be helping to raise the cultural level of those little Ethiopians whose fathers he massacred a bit, not so long ago.[6] Then, in a finally reconciled Europe, we would attend the definitive victory of culture, on the occasion of a huge banquet of generals and marshals, waited on by a bevy of democratic, but determinedly realistic, ministers.

The word disgust would be a very weak word here. But from now on it strikes me as useless to express yet again our indignation. Since our governments are intelligent and realistic enough to do without honor and culture, let us yield nothing to sentiment and endeavor instead to be realistic. Since it is the objective assessment of the historical situation which takes Franco to UNESCO, eight years after the power of the dictatorships collapsed in the ruins of Berlin, let us then be objective and reason coldly about the arguments presented to us to justify maintaining Franco.

The first argument concerns the principle of non-intervention. It can be summarized like this: a country's domestic affairs are the business of that country alone. In other words, a good democrat always stays at home. This principle is unassailable. It has disadvantages, to be sure. The coming to power of Hitler concerned only Germany, and the first concentration-camp victims, whether Jews or communists, were indeed German. But eight years later, Buchenwald, the capital of sorrow, was a European town. No matter, principles are principles, our neighbor is master of his own home. Let us admit it, then, and acknowledge that our next-door neighbor is perfectly free to beat his wife and give his children Calvados to drink. In our society, to be sure, there is a small qualification. If the neighbor goes too far, his children will be taken away and entrusted to a public charitable foundation. Franco, for his part, may go too far. But let us further suppose that the neighbor could take it out without restraint upon the domestic pet. You cannot do anything about that, of course. You have the punishment he deserves at your fingertips, but you put your hands in your pockets because it is none of your business. However, if this neighbor is also a tradesman, you are not compelled to shop from him. Nor does anything oblige you to supply him, lend him money or dine with him. Basically, without interfering in his affairs, you can turn your back on him. And if even enough people in the neighborhood treat him in this way, he will have an opportunity to reflect, to see where his interests lie, and a chance at least to change his whole conception of family love. Without counting the fact that this quarantine may give his wife a point. Let there be no doubt, this would be true non-intervention. But from the moment you dine with him and lend him money, you give him the means and clear conscience necessary to continue; and this time you are carrying out a real intervention, but against his victims. And finally, when you surreptitiously stick the label "vitamins" on the bottle of Calvados with which he comforts his children, above all when you decide in the eyes of the world to entrust him with the education of your own, then you are ultimately more criminal than he is—and doubly criminal since you are encouraging crime and calling it virtue.

Here a second argument comes in, which consists in saying that Franco is being helped, despite his failings, because he is against communism. He is against it first and foremost at home. He is against it also by providing the bases necessary for the strategy of the coming war. Here again, let us not ask if this line of argument is glorious, but if it is intelligent.

Let us note first of all that it absolutely contradicts the previous line of argument. You cannot be for non-intervention and also seek to prevent a political party, whichever it may be, from being victorious in a country that is not your own. But this contradiction does not put off anyone. Because no one, apart perhaps from Pontius Pilate, has ever really believed in non-intervention in foreign policy. So let us be serious, let us suppose we might imagine for just a second an alliance with Franco in order to preserve our freedoms, and let us then ask how he might help the Atlantic strategists in their struggle against the strategists of the East. In the first place, it is a constant experience in contemporary Europe that maintenance of a totalitarian regime in the shorter or longer run means strengthening communism. It is in countries where freedom is a national practice as well as a doctrine that communism does not prosper. Nothing is easier for it, on the other hand, as the example of the East European countries proves, than to follow in the footsteps of fascism. It is certainly in Spain that communism has least chance, because it confronts an authentic popular and libertarian left—and the Spanish character as a whole. In the last free elections in Spain, in 1936, the communists won only fifteen seats out of four hundred and forty-three in the Cortes. And it is absolutely true that nothing less than a conspiracy of international stupidity will be needed to make Spaniards into consistent Marxists. But even supposing, which is absurd, that Franco's regime is indeed the only bulwark against communism, and since we are now being realistic, what are we to think of a policy which, seeking to weaken communism in this regard, would strengthen it in ten other ways? Because for millions of men in Europe nothing will ever be able to prevent the Spanish affair, like anti-Semitism, concentration camps or the technique of basing trials on confessions, from constituting a test allowing us to judge the sincerity of a democratic policy. And the systematic maintenance of Franco will always prevent such men from believing in the sincerity of democratic governments claiming to represent freedom and justice. Such men will never be able to agree to defend freedom alongside the murderers of all freedom. Can a policy placing so many free men in that impasse be called a realistic policy? It is simply a criminal policy, since by consolidating crime it helps only to reduce to despair all those, Spaniards and others, who reject crime whatever its source.

As for the purely strategic value of Spain, I am not competent to talk about that, being an eternal novice in military science. But I would not give much for the Iberian peninsula on the day when the French and Italian parliaments have a few hundred new communist deputies. For having wished to halt communism in Spain by unworthy means, people will give a serious chance to the communization of Europe. And if this is achieved, Spain will be communized into the bargain, and arguments will set off from that strategic peninsula that will convince the theorists in Washington. "So we'll go to war," the latter will say. No doubt, and perhaps they will even win. But I think of Goya and his mutilated corpses. Do you know what he said? "Grande hazaña! Con muertos!"[7] Yet those are the wretched arguments today justifying the outrage which has brought us together. I have made no attempt to pretend to believe, in fact, that any cultural considerations could be involved. What is involved is simply a bargain behind a screen of culture. But even as a bargain it cannot be justified. Perhaps it will eventually enrich a few greengrocers, but it does not help any country or cause; it merely removes the few reasons that men in Europe may still have to struggle. That is why for an intellectual there cannot be two positions when Franco is received into UNESCO. And it is not enough to say that we shall refuse to collaborate in any way with an organization which accepts to cover an operation of this kind. From now on, each in our own place, we shall fight it frontally and with determination, in order to trumpet forth as quickly as possible that it is not what it claims to be, and that rather than an assemblage of intellectuals dedicated to culture it is an association of governments in the service of any old policy.

Yes, from the moment when Franco entered UNESCO, UNESCO left universal culture—and that is what we must say. We are met with the objection that UNESCO is useful. There would be much to say about the relations between offices and culture, but let us at least be sure that nothing of what perpetuates the lie in which we live can be useful. If UNESCO has not been capable of preserving its independence, it is better for it to disappear. After all, cultural societies pass and culture remains. Let us at least be confident that culture will not disappear because an organism of high politics is denounced for what it is. True culture lives from truth and dies from lies. It is still alive in any case, far from the palaces and lifts of UNESCO, far from the prisons of Madrid, on the paths of exile. It still has its society, the only one I recognize, that of creators and free men, which against the cruelty of totalitarians and the cowardice of bourgeois democracies, against the Prague trials and the Barcelona executions, recognizes all members but serves only one of them: freedom. And this is the society into which, for our part, we shall receive the Spain of freedom. Not bringing her in by the back door and avoiding all debate, but openly, ceremoniously, and with the respect and affection we owe her, the admiration we feel for her works and her spirit, and lastly the gratitude we entertain for the great country that has given us and still gives us our noblest lessons.

Bread and Freedom

1953

On May 10, 1953, the local branches of several French trade unions, linked to Spanish trade-union organizations in exile, organized at the Labor Exchange in Saint-Étienne a big meeting entitled "Defense of All Freedoms." After a number of speeches devoted mainly to workers' strikes, to the independence of unions from politics, to colonial repression, to the Franco dictatorship and to the Soviet regime, Albert Camus was the last speaker to take the floor. The text of his address was first published in September 1953, in No. 75 of the review La Révolution prolétarienne, under the title "Restoring the Value of Freedom." It also appeared in the chapter "Creation and Freedom" of his Actuelles II, published in October the same year.

If you add up all the abuses and many acts of violence that have just been denounced here, a time can be envisaged when, in a Europe of camp victims, only prison guards will enjoy freedom, and these will still have to imprison each other. When only one is left, he will be named head guard and we will have the perfect society, in which all problems of opposition, the nightmare of twentieth-century governments, will finally and definitively be settled.

Of course, this is just a prophecy. And though governments and police forces throughout the world are striving with great goodwill to reach that happy ending, we are not there yet. In our own countries, for example, in Western Europe, freedom is officially well regarded. But it reminds me of those poor female cousins to be seen in certain bourgeois families. The cousin has been widowed and so has lost her natural protector. She has then been taken in, given a bedroom on the fifth floor and admitted to the kitchen. She is sometimes paraded in town on Sunday, to prove they are virtuous people not curs. But the rest of the time, and especially on big occasions, she must keep her mouth shut. And even if some distracted policeman happens to rape her in a corner, no fuss is made about it; it has all happened before, especially with the master of the house, and after all it is not worth the trouble of getting on the wrong side of the authorities. In the East, it must be said, they are more honest. Settling accounts with the female cousin once and for all, they have shoved her into a cupboard, with two strong bolts. Supposedly she will get out again in half a century, more or less, when the ideal society has definitively been established. Festivals will be held in her honor at that point in time. But in my opinion she risks being somewhat moth-eaten by then, and I greatly fear she will no longer be of any use. When you then add that these two conceptions of freedom, the cupboard one and the kitchen one, have resolved to impose themselves on one another, and are obliged in all this commotion to restrict the cousin's movements even further, you will easily understand that our history is one of slavery more than freedom; and that the world we live in is the one you have just been told about, which the newspapers make plain to see every morning, turning our days and our weeks into one single day of outrage and disgust.

The simplest and most tempting thing is to accuse governments, or some obscure powers, for these nasty ways. Besides, it is quite true they are guilty; and their guilt is so heavy and long-standing that its origin is no longer even visible. But they are not the only ones responsible. After all, if freedom had only ever had governments to watch over its growth, it most likely would still be in its infancy, or buried for good with the epitaph: "An angel gone to heaven." The society of money and exploitation has never, to my knowledge, been charged with ensuring that freedom and justice hold sway. The police states have never been suspected of opening law schools in the basements where they interrogate their patients. So when they oppress and exploit, they are only doing their job; and whoever hands the disposal of freedom over to them unchecked has no right to be surprised if it is at once dishonored. If freedom today is humiliated or enslaved, it is not because its enemies have resorted to treachery. It is precisely because it has lost its natural protector. Yes, freedom is indeed a widow. But we must admit, because this is true: it is the widow of us all.

Freedom is the concern of the oppressed, and its traditional protectors have always emerged from oppressed peoples. It is the communes which in feudal Europe sustained the ferments of freedom, inhabitants of the towns and cities which caused it to triumph fleetingly in 1789, and from the nineteenth century it has been working-class movements which have taken responsibility for the twofold honor of freedom and justice, which they have never dreamed of calling incompatible. It is manual and intellectual workers who gave substance to freedom, and helped it to progress in the world until it became the very principle of our thought, the air which we can no longer do without and which we breathe without noticing, until the moment when deprived of it we feel ourselves dying. And if it is on the retreat today across so much of the world, this is doubtless because the enslaving projects have never been more cynical and better armed; but it is also because, due to fatigue, despair or a false idea of strategy and efficiency, its true defenders have turned away from it. Yes, the great event of the twentieth century has been the abandonment of the values of freedom by the revolutionary movement; the progressive retreat of libertarian socialism before Caesarist, military socialism. From that moment, a certain hope has disappeared from the world and solitude has invested every free man.

When, after Marx, the rumor began to spread and to be reinforced that freedom was bourgeois claptrap, a single word was misplaced in that dictum, but we are still paying for that wrong place in the convulsions of the century. What should have been said was that bourgeois freedom was claptrap, not all freedom. What should have been said was that bourgeois freedom was precisely not freedom, or in the best case not yet, but that there were freedoms to be won and never again relinquished. It is quite true that no freedom is possible for a man tied all day long to the lathe, who when evening comes is crammed with his family into a single room. But that condemns a class, a society and the servitude it assumes, not freedom itself, which the poorest among us cannot do without. For even should society find itself suddenly transformed and become decent and comfortable for all, if freedom did not prevail in it then it would still be barbaric. And because bourgeois society talks about freedom without practicing it, must working-class society then also refuse to practice it and merely boast of not talking about it? Yet the confusion has done its work and, in the revolutionary movement, freedom has gradually found itself condemned because bourgeois society has made mystifying use of it. From a proper and healthy mistrust toward the forms of prostitution that bourgeois society was wont to inflict on freedom, people have come to distrust freedom itself. At best, it has been dispatched to the end of time, with a request to agree not to talk about it any more until then. It has been declared that justice is needed first and we can see later on about freedom, as if slaves could ever hope to obtain justice. And forceful intellectuals have announced to the worker that bread alone mattered to him, not freedom; as if the worker did not know that his bread depended also on his freedom. And to be sure, faced by the long injustice of bourgeois society, the temptation was strong to resort to such extremes. After all, there is perhaps none among us here who, in action or reflection, has not succumbed to them. But history has advanced and what we have seen must now make us reflect. Revolution made by workers triumphed in 1917, and that truly was the dawn of real freedom and the greatest hope this world has known. But that revolution, encircled, threatened within as without, armed itself and equipped itself with police. Inheriting a dictum and a doctrine that unfortunately made freedom suspect to it, the revolution then gradually lost momentum while the police grew stronger, and the world's greatest hope ossified into the world's most effective dictatorship. Furthermore, the fake freedom of bourgeois society did not feel any the worse for that. That which was killed in the Moscow Trials and incidentally also in the camps of the revolution, that which is murdered when as in Hungary a railwayman is shot for professional misconduct, that is not bourgeois freedom but the freedom of 1917. Bourgeois freedom, for its part, can at the same time proceed with all its mystifications. The trials and perversions of revolutionary society give it both a clear conscience and some arguments.

To conclude, what characterizes the world in which we live is precisely this cynical dialectic, which counters enslavement by injustice and reinforces each with the other. When Franco the friend of Goebbels and Himmler, Franco the true victor of the Second World War, is welcomed into the palace of culture, those who protest—saying that the rights of man inscribed in the UNESCO charter are being ridiculed daily in Franco's prisons—are solemnly told that Poland too is in UNESCO, and that regarding public freedoms there is nothing to choose between the two. Stupid argument, of course! If you have had the misfortune to have married off your elder daughter to a sergeant-major in the Africa battalions, that is no reason to marry off the younger to an inspector in the vice squad:[1] one black sheep in the family is enough. However, the stupid argument is effective, as is proved to us daily. The person pointing to the colonial slave and calling for justice is shown the Russian camp victim, and vice versa. And if you protest against the murder in Prague of an opposition historian like Kalandra,[2] two or three American Negroes are thrown in your face. In this disgusting bidding contest, just one thing never changes: the victim, always the same. Just one value is constantly violated or prostituted— freedom—and it then becomes clear that everywhere, along with it, justice too is debased.

So how can we break this hellish circle? It is quite obvious we can do so only by restoring at once, within ourselves and around us, the value of freedom—and by never again allowing it to be sacrificed even temporarily or separated from our demand for justice. Today's watchword for us all can only be this: without surrendering anything in terms of justice, yield nothing in terms of freedom. In particular, the few democratic freedoms we still enjoy are not unimportant illusions that we could allow to be stripped from us without protest. They represent precisely what is left to us of the great revolutionary conquests of the two last centuries. So they are not, as so many clever demagogues tell us, the negation of true freedom. There is no ideal freedom that will suddenly be given us one day, like getting our pension at the end of our life. There are freedoms to be won, painfully, one at a time, and those we still have are stages, naturally insufficient but nevertheless stages, on the path of a concrete liberation. If we allow them to be suppressed, we do not therefore move forward. On the contrary we retreat, we go backward, and some day will have to retrace the same route; but this new effort will once again be accomplished in human blood and sweat.

No, choosing freedom today does not mean moving, like Kravchenko, from being a profiteer of the Soviet regime to being a profiteer of the bourgeois regime.[3] For that would mean instead twice choosing slavery and—the ultimate condemnation—twice choosing it for others. Opting for freedom is not, as we are told, opting against justice. On the contrary, we choose freedom today at the level of those who everywhere are suffering and struggling, and there alone. We choose it at the same time as justice, and the truth is we can now no longer choose one without the other. If someone takes away your bread, he is at the same time suppressing your freedom. But if someone strips you of your freedom, you may be sure that your bread too is threatened, for it no longer depends on you and your struggle, but on the whim of some master. Poverty increases in the world as freedom retreats, and vice versa. And if this implacable century has taught us anything, it is that economic revolution will be free or will not happen, just as liberation will be economic or will not happen. The oppressed do not want only to be freed from their hunger, they want also to be freed from their masters. They well know that they will truly be released from hunger only when they keep their masters, all their masters, in check.

I shall add in conclusion that to separate freedom from justice amounts to separating culture and labor, which is the archetypal social sin. The disarray of the workers' movement in Europe comes partly from the fact that it has lost its true homeland, wherein it recovered its strength after all defeats, which was its faith in freedom. But likewise the disarray of European intellectuals comes from the fact that a twofold mystification, bourgeois and pseudo-revolutionary, has separated them from their sole source of authenticity: the labor and suffering of all. Has cut them off from their only natural allies, the workers. For my part I have only ever acknowledged two aristocracies, that of labor and that of intelligence; and I now know that it is insane and criminal to want to subordinate one to the other. I know that the two of them form just a single nobility; that their truth and above all their effectiveness lie in their union; that separated they will allow themselves to be reduced one at a time by the forces of tyranny and barbarity, but, on the other hand, that united they will dominate the world. This is why every project which aims to alienate and separate them is a project directed against man and his highest hopes. The first endeavor of every dictatorial project is thus to enslave labor and culture simultaneously. For it is necessary to gag both, otherwise, as tyrants are well aware, one will sooner or later speak for the other. This is why in my view there are two ways today for an intellectual to betray, and in both cases he betrays because he accepts just one thing: this separation of labor and culture. The first way characterizes bourgeois intellectuals who accept their privileges being paid for by enslavement of the workers. These often say they are defending freedom, but they principally defend the privileges that freedom gives them, and these alone.* The second way characterizes intellectuals who consider themselves on the left and who, from mistrust of freedom, accept control of culture—and the freedom it implies—on the pretext of serving some future justice. In both cases, whether you are a profiteer of injustice or a renegade of freedom, you ratify and consecrate the separation of intellectual and manual labor which condemns to impotence both labor and culture. You stifle both freedom and justice.

It is true that freedom, when primarily created by privilege, does insult labor and separate it from culture. But freedom is not primar-

---

* And furthermore most of the time they do not even defend freedom, as soon as there is any risk in doing so.

ily created by privilege; it is created above all by duty. And from the moment when each of us tries to ensure the precedence of freedom's duties over its privileges, from that moment freedom unites labor and culture and unleashes the only force which can serve justice effectively. The rule of our action, the secret of our resistance, can then be formulated simply: all that humiliates labor humiliates intelligence, and vice versa. And the revolutionary struggle, the age-old striving for liberation, is primarily defined as a twofold, constant rejection of humiliation.

To be honest, we have not yet emerged from such humiliation. But the wheel is turning, history is changing, a time is approaching—I am sure—when we shall no longer be alone. For me, our meeting today is already a sign. That trade unionists should assemble and rally around freedoms in order to defend them—yes, that really did warrant everybody hurrying in from all sides to display their unity and their hope. The road to be traversed is long. Yet if war does not come to jumble everything up in its hideous confusion, we shall have time finally to give form to the justice and freedom we all need. But for this we must immediately and clearly reject, without anger but implacably, the lies we have been stuffed with. No, freedom is not built on concentration camps, or on the enslaved peoples of the colonies, or on working-class destitution! No, the doves of peace do not perch on gallows! No, the forces of freedom cannot mix up the sons of the victims with the executioners of Madrid and elsewhere! Of this at least we shall henceforth be quite sure. And we shall be sure that freedom is not a gift you receive from a State or leader, but a possession you win daily, through the effort of each and the union of all.

[The Berlin Events and Us]

Lecture at the Mutualité
1953

On June 16, 1953, a workers' revolt broke out in East Berlin, following the government's decision to increase work rates without compensatory wage increases. Very quickly the movement spread to the rest of the country. On June 17, tens of thousands of people went on strike and gathered in the main towns of the DDR. Overtaken by events, the general secretary of the SED (United Socialist Party of Germany), Walter Ulbricht, called for Soviet troops, whose intervention left some fifty demonstrators dead and many wounded. On June 30, 1953, a meeting of support was organized at the Mutualité hall in Paris. Camus made this speech there, the text of which was published in the fifth issue of the review Témoins (spring 1954), preceded by his July 19, 1951, speech at the Casal de Catalunya in Paris commemorating the fifteenth anniversary of the Spanish social revolution (see p. 109). The two texts together appeared under the same title: "Calendar of Freedom."

Belonging to no political party and very little tempted for the moment to join any, I feel it might help our assembly this evening if in a few sentences I managed to clarify the reasons which brought me onto this platform. In order to put them into the proper context, before anything else it must be said that the Berlin events have in certain milieux aroused a rather shameful delight that we cannot share. At the moment when, after two years of agony, the Rosenbergs were led off to their death,[1] the news that workers were being shot down in East Berlin, far from drawing a veil over the torture of the Rosenbergs—as what is commonly called the bourgeois press attempted to do—merely added for us to the relentless sorrows of a world where, one by one, systematically, all hopes are murdered. When *Le Figaro* talks eloquently about the revolutionary people of Berlin, it would make us laugh if on the same day *L'Humanité*—castigating what, as in the good old days, it calls "agitators"—were not confronting us with the tragedy in which we live and the two-fold mystification that prostitutes our very language.

But if I think it impossible for the Berlin riots to make us forget the Rosenbergs, it seems even more dreadful to me that men calling themselves left-wing should try to hide from sight those Germans gunned down in the shadow of the Rosenbergs. Yet that is what we have seen and what we do see daily, which is precisely why we are here. We are here because, if we were not, there would otherwise appear to be no one from among those whose proclaimed vocation it is to defend workers. We are here because the Berlin workers risk being betrayed after being killed, and being betrayed by those very people whose solidarity they could hope for.

When you claim to be dedicated to the emancipation of labor, did not the uprising of workers who in Germany and Czechoslovakia rejected increased working standards and proceeded logically to demand free elections,[2] thus showing all those dynamic intellectuals who used to preach the opposite to them that justice cannot be separated from freedom—that uprising, and the great lesson it brought with it and the repression that followed it—yes, did that uprising not deserve a pause for thought? Did it not deserve, after so many nonsensical positions had been proclaimed, a firm, clear affirmation of solidarity? When a worker, somewhere in the world, raises his bare fists against a tank and shouts that he is not a slave, what then are we if we remain indifferent? And what then does it mean for us to intervene on behalf of the Rosenbergs, if we keep silent about Goettling?[3]

But what we have witnessed has been an abdication of responsibility, which is why disgust as much as indignation makes us speak out this evening. So far as I am concerned, in any case, it seemed to me we could not acquire a clear conscience at so cheap a price. I naturally admire and envy the fortunate ease with which a certain left-wing press and its collaborators have neutralized—the appropriate word—the Berlin tragedy. I admire the fact that from the first day our progressive organs perceived so spontaneously that the Stalin Allee demonstrations had been inspired by the Russian government.[4] This ingenious explanation found itself somewhat cast into the shade once bullets had mowed down the Kremlin's demonstrators. But it had already succeeded in muddling a few ideas. After which, a bit of typographical doctoring was enough to banish to page three the most important news received for years. I also admire the fact that one journalist was able to conclude a report on the Berlin events, viewed mainly via intermediaries, by warning us that the departure of the Russians, abandoning the Germans to themselves, would leave the field open for atrocities even uglier than those our own liberation witnessed. It is indeed astonishing that the only lesson to be drawn from the Berlin riots is that we should basically have wept over Hitler's departure. It is no longer admiration actually, but a kind of respectful esteem, that I feel for the journalist of a supposedly left-wing weekly who, on the occasion of a report on the same events, managed to write unblushingly that one could not but admire the discipline and composure of the Russian troops.

But ultimately, despite all this admiration, there is at least one argument which I do not think we can accept: the one that consists in saying we do not have enough information. For, after all, we are never more than half informed about what goes on in totalitarian regimes of any kind. And must dictatorship alone then be exempted from the judgment of public opinion, because it alone refuses to inform public opinion? And must we keep silent about all Bastilles on the pretext that their prisoners are not directly connected by a special line to our newspaper editors? Only the fact that the events which concern us took place a few paces away from the Western sector prevented them from being entirely camouflaged. Otherwise we would have known nothing about this riot, or would have learned about it only as we learned about the risings in Czechoslovakia, little by little, through the thick walls of police forces and prisons. But these events took place before the eyes of Berliners, in front of a Dutch camera too, and we can no longer fail to know that what was first and foremost involved—however people from both sides may have sought to exploit it—was a working-class revolt against a government and an army that claimed to serve the workers. And if we were not sufficiently convinced of this, the speeches of the East Berlin government would confirm it to us. Those who after this say publicly that they are not sufficiently informed—I challenge them to tell themselves this, all alone at the hour of truth. This means the fog enveloping certain aspects of the revolt, and our lack of knowledge about the fate of thousands of men—it is unworthy to use these to the detriment of the victims alone. If this lack of knowledge indicts anyone, it is the authors of the repression, not the rebels. For what must be said—and for me is the ultimate condemnation—is basically that even today men are still killed because they have called for workers' freedom, and nevertheless we shall never know their names. But just because these victims will forever remain anonymous, must they be liquidated once again and this time in our memory? We know only that they are workers rising to defend their lot. And because we do not even know their names, people would make this a pretext to render them still more anonymous, to refuse them the condition that is theirs, to question their status as workers and even, whenever possible, to dishonor them by calling them fascist scum?

No, this is a job we refuse to carry out, and it is to compensate a bit for that disgusting brew that we are all here. And in short, just to clarify in one sentence the reasons for our collective presence, we need to declare before the German and Czech workers now reduced to silence that we reject any possibility of being upbraided one day with the words: "They murdered them and, as for you, you buried them shamefully."

I have few things to add before closing this meeting. Many decisive choices have been made by each of us since the Liberation. But today, faced with the most serious event to have occurred since that liberation, in my view we have reached the moment of a definitive choice. It strikes me as impossible for men who say they are attached to the dignity and emancipation of labor to accept by their silence the execution of workers whose only crime is to have risen against intolerable material conditions. We have none of us been able to prevent this tragedy, it is true. But the repression has not halted and we can still, by demonstrating our views, weigh however slightly upon the outcome. When the first signs of anti-Semitism appeared in the East, it was the spontaneous indignation of those in the West who were not simply partisans which, in a certain way, showed the people's governments that they could not allow that perversion to become established. And this is why, with all of you here, I address myself to those who—as we have not forgotten—used to be our comrades, to say: even if we could save just one German worker's life in the coming days, that life would warrant our having assembled here, and would warrant at least those who have kept silent now speaking up and helping us to save it. Do not prefer your arguments and your dreams to that distress which has been calling out to you for two weeks. Do not excuse the blood and pain of today out of consideration for a historic future which will be devoid of meaning at least for those it has killed. Believe us, for the last time, when we tell you that no human dream, however grand, justifies killing someone who works and is poor. No one asks you to repudiate anything of what you believe or wish for. But in the very name of the truth you claim to serve, simply demand with us that commission of inquiry on which all the union federations will be represented, and which will serve at least as mediator in a drama whose stake is not the ideal society you argue about and dream of, for a day not yet discernible, but the dreadful death with which the humble are threatened on this very day, for having believed, like the Marx about whom they were told daily, that equality could not and should not do without freedom.

The Future of European Civilization

1955

In April 1955, Albert Camus visited Greece in the context of Franco-Hellenic exchanges organized by the French embassy in Greece. It was during this three-week stay that on April 28, at the Athens Graeco-French Cultural Union, he took part in this discussion, in French, on the future of European civilization. It was Camus himself, during preparatory exchanges for his visit, who had chosen the theme and asked for it to be developed through questions and answers rather by means of a formal lecture. The text below is based on the transcript of a recording published in 1956 by the French Institute Library in Athens. The interventions by Camus are reproduced integrally here, while the words of the other participants have been summarized and placed in square brackets.

[Mr. Papanoutsos asks the writer to define the essential features of European civilization (of which he himself defined two: on the one hand, the will to base oneself on science and technology, despite the disillusionment this can lead to, and to subject nature to human desires; on the other hand, concern for the dignity of the human individual); to specify the properties that must be preserved at all costs; and to say to what extent these are threatened by the great historical forces of the moment.]

Well, I must say that I am quite intimidated by the wide scope of this question. If this problem was indeed posed as a framework for our discussion this evening, I would nevertheless consider it somewhat ambitious. In particular, I should like first to speak about the impediment I feel to making any definitive pronouncements on this subject.

In the first place, I have great difficulty in situating myself in any future perspective. I have a sense of the present—in quite a strong and intense way, I think—and something of a sense of the past. As for the future, however, I think that my imaginative resources are inadequate. It always takes a real effort on my part to try to imagine the future of a thought or a position.

The second impediment is one of a far more general nature. It seems to me that, in view of the quantity of knowledge of every kind involved in the fate of Europe and civilization, settling these questions would require a culture which I do not possess.

That said, Sir, I think you have established well the distinction which can be introduced into the phenomenon of civilization in general and especially our own. It is true that the answer is different depending on the point of view we may adopt. If we consider that Western civilization is the humanization of nature, in other words technologies and science, not only has Europe triumphed, but the forces threatening her today are forces which have taken from Western Europe her technologies, or her technological ambitions, and in any case her scientific method or her method of reasoning. In such cases, European civilization is not threatened, other than by a general suicide, and in a way by itself.

If, on the contrary, we consider that our civilization is centered around the notion of the human individual, this viewpoint, which can also be defended, leads, as you rightly emphasize, to a wholly different answer. To wit, that probably—I repeat probably—it is hard to find an epoch where the quantity of humiliated people is so great. However, I shall not say that this epoch is particularly contemptuous of the human individual. Alongside those forces which to simplify things we may call those of evil, there can be no doubt in fact that the reaction of collective consciousness, particularly the consciousness of individual rights, has for centuries been spreading more and more. It is simply that two world wars have trampled upon it somewhat, and I think we must reasonably reply that our civilization is threatened precisely insofar as that human individual, which it had succeeded in placing at the center of reflection, is today humiliated more or less everywhere.

What I can add to this useful distinction is that we might ask ourselves (I shall still express myself conditionally)—we might ask ourselves whether precisely the singular success of Western civilization in its scientific aspect is not partly responsible for that civilization's singular moral failure. Put otherwise, whether the absolute and in a sense blind belief in the power of reason (let us call it Cartesian reason, to simplify things, since that is what lies at the center of contemporary knowledge)—whether this absolute belief in rationalist reason is not to a certain extent responsible for a shrinking of human sensibility which, through stages which it would obviously take too long to define, has managed little by little to bring about this degradation of the individual universe. The technological universe in itself is no bad thing, and I am absolutely opposed to all schools of thought which would like to return to the spinning wheel or the hand plow. But technological reason, placed at the center of the Universe, viewed as the most important mechanical agent of a civilization, ends up by provoking a kind of perversion, both in the intellectual domain and in customs, that risks bringing about that failure about which we have been speaking. It would be interesting to investigate how.

It is now necessary to answer the three specific questions you have asked me. First, what are the elements constituting European civilization? I shall answer that I do not know. But every one of us has a privileged and in a sense sentimental perspective (which does not, however, prevent it from being argued and based on observation) that has made him choose one of these elements among others. For my part (and for once I shall be able to answer clearly), European civilization is first and foremost a pluralist civilization. I mean that it is the place of diverse thoughts, contradictions, contrasting values and an unending dialectic. The living dialectic in Europe is that which does not culminate in a kind of ideology at once totalitarian and orthodox. This pluralism which has always been the foundation of the European idea of freedom strikes me as our civilization's most important contribution. This is precisely what is in danger today, and which we must strive to preserve.

The great watchword of Voltaire, I think, who used to say, "I disapprove of what you say, but I will defend to the death your right to say it," is clearly a great watchword of European thought.[1]

There is no doubt that, on the plane of intellectual freedom (though it can be found on other planes), this is the principle which is being questioned today, which is under attack and seems to me must be defended. As for the question of knowing if it will be saved and whether the future belongs to us, as people say, well, I give this kind of question the same answer I give to other questions which I ask myself and in similar situations. In certain circumstances, it seems to me that a man may answer: "This is true, in my view, or probably true. So it must survive. There is no certainty that I can ensure it will survive; there is no certainty that death does not await this thing that strikes me as essential. In any case, the only thing I can do is fight for it to survive."

[*Mr. Papanoutsos wonders whether it will be possible to harmonize developments in science and technology (cybernetics, machines) with the rights of the human individual.*]

On this point, I shall say for once that I am not pessimistic. I mean that one must be patient. There are after all two phenomena characterizing European history. The first is that the world has changed far more from 1800 to 1950, say, than it changed during the long centuries which separated the medieval communities, for instance, from our classical age. In a century, there has been a kind of violent takeoff, an acceleration of history such that it strikes me as hard for man—with the means of intelligence alone, which are means of meditation and reflection, and which consequently require time—for man, then, to have managed to keep pace with the machines he had released.

The second point, which Ortega y Gasset brought out well in his *The Revolt of the Masses*,[2] is contained in a number. From the sixth to the eighteenth century, the population of Europe never exceeded one hundred and eighty million inhabitants. From 1800 to 1914, in other words in scarcely more than a century, it went from one hundred and eighty million inhabitants to four hundred and sixty million. The advent of the masses is highlighted by this number. Accompanied (and naturally these two factors interact) by the acceleration of history, this advent has led us to a situation which very decisively transcends the intellectual and rational frameworks that gave birth to it. Our problem today is first the adaptation of our intelligence to the new realities which the world offers us. The ideologies on which we live are ideologies that are a hundred years behind. And this is why they accept innovations so reluctantly. Nothing is more confident of its own truth than an outdated ideology.

[*The second person to intervene, Mr. Tsatsos, thinks European culture is crossed by two opposing currents, one classical and the other romantic. The former is rational, stressing limits and opposing the limitless; it affirms measure and what is relative in the historical world, rejecting all that is absolute, extreme and Messianic. It is attached to the present, to immanence and to the living individual, to whom it accords an exceptional value. The romantic current affirms what the classical tendency rejects: the irrational and intuition. Totalitarian ideologies, at first sight well organized, in fact sacrifice the present to the future, and Messianism of the hereafter is replaced by the cult of the future. Has not Hellenism, which belongs to the classical humanist current, an essential contribution to make to the social and cultural renewal of Europe?*]

Well, I again feel somewhat intimidated by this question. That said, I find your distinction between romanticism and classicism so seductive that we might extend it to the whole history of civilizations. In this case, it would be reasonable to hope. For since all civilizations have been obliged to come to terms with these two tendencies of human nature, embodied in history, and since history has continued until now, nothing stops us thinking that we might take a few steps forward. But I want to clarify my thought. You are right to think that this world has only negative attitudes to offer;

but I think we would be wrong to consider the notion of measure, which is one of the rare notions about which I have reflected, to be a negative notion. You know that it is not; I do not have to teach you that. But why is it not?

If today in a Paris colloquium you were to evoke the notion of measure, a thousand pairs of romantic arms would be raised toward the ceiling. For our intellectuals, measure is nothing other than diabolical bourgeois moderation. But it is nothing of the sort. Measure is neither rejection of contradiction nor the solution of contradiction. In Hellenism, if my knowledge on this point is adequate, measure has always been recognition of contradiction and the decision to maintain it at all costs. A rule of this kind is not just a rational, humanist and kindly rule. It really implies a kind of heroism. In any case, it might well provide us not with the solution—which is not what we expect—but with a method for tackling study of the problems confronting us and for advancing toward a bearable future.

Let us, if you will, apply this method to contemporary Europe. There is a bourgeois, individualist Europe, the one that thinks about its refrigerators and its gourmet restaurants, which says: "I don't vote, myself." That is bourgeois Europe, it is true. That Europe does not want to live. No doubt it says it wants to live, but it has put life at so low a level that it has no chance of prolonging itself in history; it is vegetating, and no society has vegetated for long. But I see nothing there that is the expression of classical measure. I see only an individualistic nihilism, which consists in saying: "We don't want either romanticism or excess; we don't want to live at the boundaries or experience strife." If you do not want to live at the boundaries or experience strife, you will not live and especially your society will not live.

The great lesson—and I say this because I am formally opposed to the ideology of the people's democracies—the great lesson that comes to us from the East is precisely the sense of participation in a common effort, and there is no reason for us to reject that example.

From this point of view, I have no approval to bestow on bourgeois Europe. But instead I would adopt a position that consists in saying: "We know the extreme, we have lived it, we shall live it when necessary, and we can say that we have lived it because we have passed through events which have allowed us to know it." There really was a French national solidarity, and there was a Greek national solidarity—the solidarity of suffering. This solidarity we can find again at any time, and not just in the guise of suffering. If we were to reflect sufficiently on that experience, I am convinced that we would understand better the notion of measure conceived of as the reconciliation of contradictions, and particularly in the social and political domain as reconciliation of the rights and duties of the individual. The position of bourgeois Europe comes down essentially to claiming solely human rights. Human rights are values that we must defend, but not if those rights mean the denial of duties. And vice versa. The human duties of which they boast to us in the East are not duties we will accept if they mean denial of all that constitutes man's right to be what he is.

It strikes me, then, that in this direction we might define social rules in which that kind of balance, hard to maintain, will be achieved, it being understood of course that the balance in question cannot by definition be a comfort. Today people say of a man that "he is well balanced" with a touch of contempt. Balance actually involves effort and courage at all times. The society that will have courage is the true society of the future. Moreover, in my view it is on the way to appearing in various parts of the world, and here again I shall not be entirely pessimistic. Hope exists. It comes to us from the Hellenism which first defined it and has provided the most moving illustrations of it throughout the centuries. We can hope today that this seed will bear fruit once again and help us find the solution to our problems.

[*Mr. Theotokas, the third person to intervene, observes that the romantic opposition to the world of science and technology is outdated, and that the current problem consists in harmonizing these new forces with human nature. Present-day Europe is condemned by its structure: it is divided among many states and is incapable of mastering the scientific and technological dynamic. Without political unity, is Europe not incapable of ensuring such harmonization?*]

I shall first tell you my total agreement, basically, and then make one small reservation. I think like you that Europe is currently corseted in a score or so of girdles that do not allow her to breathe. At a moment when Athens is six hours away from Paris, when you can go from Rome to Paris in three hours, and when frontiers exist only for customs officials and the passengers subjected to their jurisdiction, we are living in a feudal state. Europe, which thought up every last one of the ideologies dominating the world today, which today sees them turning against her, embodied as they are in larger and industrially more powerful countries—this Europe, which had the ability and the power to think up those ideologies, can also have the power to think up notions which will enable us to control or counterbalance those ideologies. She simply needs a breathing space; she needs leisure and thoughts which are not provincial, as all our thoughts are at present. Parisian ideas are provincial ideas; Athenian ideas are provincial ideas too, in the sense that we all have the greatest difficulty in having enough contacts, and enough knowledge, for the random values isolated in our respective countries to cross-fertilize each other. Well, I think that this ideal at which we are all basically aiming, which we must defend and for which we must do all that can possibly be done—we shall not achieve this ideal immediately. Just now you uttered a fateful word, which was "sovereignty." The word "sovereignty" has for a long while thrown a spanner in all the works of international history. It will continue to do so. The wounds of the recent war are still too fresh, too painful, for us to hope that national collectivities might make that effort of which only superior individuals are capable, and which consists in mastering one's own feelings. So we find ourselves, psychologically, faced with obstacles that will make achieving this hard. That said, I share your opinion: we must struggle to succeed in overcoming these obstacles and making Europe—I mean the Europe in which Paris, Athens, Rome, Berlin will be the nerve centers of a Middle empire, dare I say, which in a certain way will be able to play its part in the history of tomorrow.

The small reservation which I shall introduce is the following. You said we cannot address the problem of Europe's future intellectually, cannot reflect upon it, so long as we do not have that structure to lean upon. My reservation consists in saying: we must tackle the problem all the same, and give some content to European values, even if Europe will not happen tomorrow.

You gave an example just now which struck me. You said: "After all, before its unity had been achieved Germany was not a power." That is quite true. It does not stop us being able to say that a large proportion of contemporary ideologies were formed in the German ideology of the nineteenth century, and that all the German philosophers, especially the greatest one of all, who gave birth to this new form of thought, preceded German unity (if we consider that German unity was accomplished in 1871, of course). There does therefore exist a possibility of influencing a civilization, even in our present derelict and impoverished state. In any case, the role of intellectuals and writers is in a certain way to continue their efforts on their own plane, while pushing at the wheel of history if they can and if they have the time, so that at the right moment the necessary values will be, if not ready, at least already able to leaven the mix.

[*Mr. Vegleris recalls that two elements are essential for European culture: the principle of freedom, and the principle of social justice, which must correct what is destructive in the former. He wonders whether Europe is capable of combining these two principles better.*]

Crudely simplifying things, we might say that today the West claims to put freedom before justice, the East justice before freedom. We shall not examine the question of knowing whether freedom prevails in the West and whether justice prevails in the East, but confine ourselves to registering the pretensions of both societies. It may be that freedom brandishing the atomic bomb and justice brandishing another may destroy themselves mutually on a frontier that is easy to foresee. In that case, I confess to not having enough imagination for what could follow a third world war, nuclear in nature. And for my own part I consider very guilty those State leaders who let their peoples think such a future imaginable after such a war. However, if that nuclear war, that suicide, does not occur, we are still going to find ourselves before the two statues of liberty and justice facing one another with turned-up noses. I think the balance of forces is more or less equivalent today, size of population in the East being made up for in the West by more advanced technological levels. So I think that inevitably history itself, in which so many people place so much confidence, is going to justify this confidence. And the notion of measure and contradiction will actually come into play at this point. For it is inscribed in human nature and in the nature of history. People will arrive, for instance, at the conception that a certain number of minds have already reached: namely, that freedom has a limit and justice too has a limit. That the limit of freedom is to be found in justice, that is to say in the existence and the acknowledgment of others. And that the limit of justice is to be found in freedom—in other words, the right of individuals to exist such as they are within a collectivity.

[*A series of questions follows from various interlocutors.*]

[*European civilization is not one but plural, and rather than about fusion into a single unity should we not speak about harmonious collaboration?*]

I think I can answer that briefly, Sir. Harmony is an excellent thing. Unfortunately, it is not always possible. For example, it can be said that marriage is an excellent institution, on condition that the spouses are in agreement. But it does happen that they are not, so much so that in certain cases—rare, I acknowledge—marriage is a catastrophe. So if we count only upon the goodwill of the European peoples—and we must count upon it, because it is obviously impossible to move forward without it—it will not be sufficient to take us forward. So institutions are needed. Your objection to such institutions, which would of course be common institutions, is that the difference of customs and ways of living between the European peoples runs counter to them. I shall put up the example of France against you. A Marseillais is certainly closer to a Neapolitan than to an inhabitant of Brest. There is a great difference between someone from Perpignan and someone from Roubaix. Despite this, the unity of France is a fait accompli and today Perpignan and Roubaix elect a single government, be it good or bad.

[*What is the contribution to European culture of Jean Genet's work, along with* The Mandarins *and* The Story of O?³]

Contribution to the European future or to French literature?

[*To European civilization.*]

I'll say it is zero, frankly.

[*Is European diversity a handicap or a hope of salvation?*]

It is a hope of salvation for the excellent reason that, in history, whenever a vast empire has spread beyond certain limits, it has collapsed. If Alexander had remained within the borders of Macedonia, there would probably still be a Greece today descending in a straight line from Alexander. Diversity clearly has disadvantages. These are precisely the disadvantages of freedom. They are also those of loyalty and objectivity. Nevertheless it is by objectivity and freedom that the world has progressed on the plane that concerns us, and we must accept their disadvantages. But frankly I think the disadvantages of Empires and huge continents, so far as their future development is concerned, can be at least as great as the disadvantages of diversity for Europe. It seems to me, for example, if scientific research today is at the basis of material power, that scientific research will be truly convincing, effective and fertile in the long run only in a climate of freedom.

[*Must European civilization not protect itself from attacks coming from both East and West?*]

This is what people call a trick question. All right. I shall first give you an equivocal reply, and then a direct one. The equivocal reply is that for me the main enemy of any civilization is generally itself. If European civilization is in danger, it is doubtless because Empires or civilizations are exerting pressure on it from outside, but it is mainly because it does not in itself have enough health or enough strength to respond to this challenge of history. On reflection, my reply is not all that equivocal.

But I shall answer you even more directly that I am not one of those people who think that the threat from the East and the threat from the West are equally strong. I think that the threat from the East, given that it is a military threat bringing in its wake a danger of totalitarianism, is a more powerful threat than any that may be presented for our civilization by forms of American culture which are hard for us to assimilate. For the time being, what is involved is a peaceful confrontation between the forms of American civilization and our own, while there is instead a warlike or quasi-warlike confrontation between East and West. This is at least what I think. Obviously I am speaking just for myself here. That said, I think you are basically asking me this question not in order to know my point of view, such as I have just given it to you, but in order to ask me what I think of the dangers that American civilization may present for us. So I shall try to tell you what I think about this personally.

I do not know America well. I have spent just three months there.[4] That said, I am quite well acquainted with her literature and her history. America represents for me the realization of the hopes of the French eighteenth century. Let me at once clarify this. I am referring to what in my country we call the *Encyclopédistes*, who were the first in Europe to identify what they called a philosophy of happiness. It was they who dreamed of a rational happiness based on a harmonious organization of the world, and who above all emphasized the happiness that nature and the world could provide for men. They were philosophers of happiness in general. And there is no doubt—and this is what for my own part I found very attractive in America as soon as I landed there—that in America there is a desire for happiness. This desire is shown by purely negative signs and at other times by positive ones. The purely negative signs are the refusal to accept pessimistic philosophies as really serious; the refusal to consider or stress unhappiness. They bury people quickly in America, for example. They bury them quickly, whereas the custom in Mediterranean civilization, as you know, is on the contrary to prolong contact with death, contact with the loved one you have just lost. This little example, which should absolutely not be extrapolated, strikes me as illustrating a certain rejection of unhappiness and, positively, the wish to organize everything so that life is easier and more luminous. In this sense, there is no doubt that the philosophy of the eighteenth century, via paths that it would moreover be easy to discover, found there, it must be said, a pretty sensational embodiment.

That said, I think—for reasons which could likewise be defined, but it would take too long—that the American temperament lacks the thing which in the philosophy of happiness of our *Encyclopédistes* played the role of brake and regulator. This was what, with a word hard to define, we call "taste." I mean a reluctance to push anything too far. (For example, a man like Benjamin Constant, who was an atheist, used to say with a rather disgusted air, "irreligion has something vulgar and hackneyed about it";[5] because militant atheism, according to him, was exaggerated and not sufficiently nuanced.) People say a lot of stupid things about American culture and very many unjust ones, especially in Europe. This culture offers us first-class intellectuals, literature, science. If today there is less and less tuberculosis in Europe, to whom do we owe it? However, let us say no more about that. Yet, in the application of this philosophy of happiness in your [sic] country, there is a kind of excess which is in the American temperament; a kind of desire for total victory, which has ended up taking forms that have, of course, gone beyond limits and smashed nuances. This is what makes it hard to adapt your [sic] everyday life to the European average. And I speak about this objectively, since as a North African rather than a European I found myself at ease in the rhythm of American life. Nevertheless, this rhythm disorients Europeans. In the same way, this general rejection of general ideas—this taste for the concrete, for empiricism, for facts: in other words, for all that can be perceived directly, understood and grasped directly—has driven American thought to turn away from general ideas. In this, it is in fact directly inspired by the French and English empiricists of the eighteenth century. This mistrust of general ideas has condemned it—and I shall here be far more assertive than in everything I have just said—has condemned it almost irremediably to understand nothing of the European drama. A certain number of what can only be called American blunders in relation to European problems come from this refusal to consider certain foundations of the European tragedy: its ideological and metaphysical foundations. But I shall add that the American people is also young, and the leadership it has exercised since roughly 1945 is a wholly fresh one. It still has time to practice at it. But the kind of danger which may affect us from America is precisely this tendency to drive us to the direct level of the facts of life as it comes, and which—directed at people poorly prepared (the influence of the cinema is especially striking)—risks taking a certain number of sensibilities to levels where it is not desirable that sensibilities should be taken. That is precisely what I think.

[*How are we to explain why French philosophy should be so dependent upon German philosophy?*]

Your profession has taught you, Sir, how difficult the question of influences is in the history of thought. So I shall simply tell you this: it is a question I have asked myself too, since I have escaped the contagion and have in a way been surprised to find so many profound reasons for disagreement with the intellectual society in which I live. Here is the answer to which I have come. I simply believe that Germany discovered the unhappiness of existence before France. Not that she had a more painful history, but because she was born late and with difficulty as a nation. And also, perhaps, because of what Stendhal used to say about the German character, when he spoke about how the Germans were condemned always to make things hard for themselves. In any case, from the nineteenth century onward German philosophers reflected on the unhappiness of existence. Our own philosophy of that time, as you know, was a philosophy that was really cut off from the true problems of our civilization. Those problems were posed in Germany, and in another form in Russia, but not in France. Our nineteenth-century philosophy was the ideology of a satisfied class: one consequently anchored in its own satisfaction, detached from history and by no means intent on re-entering it. Thereupon two wars: one of them ill-fated to begin with and later won at the price of dreadful sacrifices; the other in which everything was lost and saved. The French then found themselves confronted by historical misfortune. If they then turned to their philosophers, what did they find? They found nothing which could speak to them about the misfortune in which they were plunged. So they turned toward philosophers who, for their part, spoke about the unhappiness of history; about the unhappy consciousness; about the difficulty of living; about being for death—in short, about everything you know. And it is quite obvious that this movement, in my view, was far too passionate, far too exclusive; but it can nevertheless be explained. That said, a supplementary explanation can be found for the problem which concerns you in the fact that the majority of French thinkers today are thinkers of the left, hence in part Marxisant. But Marx comes directly from the German ideology. In line with their convictions, they went back to the sources. Whence a renewal of Hegelian studies, a renewal of Marxist studies too, and a renewal of German existentialist philosophy in general. But signs of an evolution are seemingly appearing. A resounding conversion is being prepared, people say. Monsieur Merleau-Ponty, who was one of the representatives of the tendency which concerns us,[6] has just published a book called *Adventures of the Dialectic*, which seems to mark a certain rupture with that tendency, and consequently to initiate a turn in the French ideology, if this terrible word can be used.

[*Are the weakness of Europe and its nihilism not due to the fact that she no longer has a faith, whereas the countries of the East do have one?*]

Very well, but you know I am also a writer. I am rather sorry to be continually confronted by questions which are outside my competence. In literature, I have some small competence—at least I might speak; I might express myself, even eloquently—whereas with these I am somewhat constrained. All right, the East has a faith. Does it have one? Do you know it? We have no faith? Who said so? I know lots of men who have one. We have no faith; it is not written in texts, our Constitutions do not prove faith. But in 1945 all the nations of Europe showed that they had a faith when they were under German domination. That is not so long ago. I am forever confronted by these problems which are rather . . . well, to speak sincerely, I do not think they are fundamentally true. Of course, one can and must discuss them, but I do not believe nihilism is on one side alone. This is the position I have always defended. I think there is just one single capitalism in the world, but it can assume different forms: private capitalism or State capitalism. Lack of faith is not on one side alone; faith does not grow of its own accord on the other. After all, there is also a Christian faith, there is a Christian movement in the West. Why should the Christian faith not produce its own works and institutional forms today? It has attempted—and still is attempting—to do so. Perhaps it will succeed. How can we tell?

I think that the real problem does not lie there. The real problem is to know if we wish to survive as a civilization. And that wish is not necessarily rational. If I say that I wish to go on living, it is not because I entirely know what I am, but because I have an extremely lively and extremely acute feeling of what I am as a being and because I want to continue in my being. So it is not reason which takes precedence, it is the instinct to live. Well then, if young people today in the West do not have that instinct to live, they must rediscover it, because that is where the problem lies. And they will rediscover it, I believe, not by relying on people who will tell them, systematically, what they must believe and do. They will rediscover it by relying on themselves. I mean on their experience of life and their own reflection.

[*Are the rationalism of science and Cartesian rationalism not demolished by the development of science itself (in physics and chemistry the most ele-*

mentary functions escape any possibility of being conceived of in a rational way), and does this evolution not threaten European civilization?]

I think that the discovery of irrational numbers by contemporary science is an advance. It is an advance because, if contemporary science managed to demonstrate total determinism, what would correspond to it in civilizational form is totalitarianism, by a direct path, which would be easy to demonstrate if we really did not have so little time. As for Cartesian rationalism, I was speaking with reference to it just now. It is part of our civilization. But because of the interpretation which has been made of it, the notion of the individual which has been based on it, Cartesian rationalism underlies a certain degeneration of Western society. I should stress that it is not a matter of Descartes himself. Philosophers remain great minds and great men. But what is taken from them is not the best, it is always the dregs. One of the weaknesses of Western civilization, in any case, is its creation of the individual separated from his community: the individual seen as a whole. To summarize somewhat all that I put rather badly just now, it seems to me that Western society today is dying of excessive individualism, whereas Eastern society has not even been born because of an excessive collectivism. Insofar as our individualism is brought back toward a surer notion of the duties of the community, and, in parallel, Eastern collectivism sees the first fermentations of individual freedom arise, we shall make progress. It is in this sense that I do not feel at all concerned if the works of a man like Heisenberg end up by endangering a certain notion—static and purely rational—of man, such as has been established in the West.

[*If the artist must demand freedom to speak in the name of those who are unable to do so, does he not limit that freedom insofar as he has to choose those for whom he is going to speak and exclude the rest?*]

Well, it is limited freedom, Mademoiselle. Freedom without limits is the opposite of freedom. Only tyrants can exercise freedom without limits: Hitler, for example, was relatively a free man—

the only one, moreover, in his whole empire. But if one wishes to exercise an authentic freedom, it cannot be exercised solely in the interest of the individual exercising it. Freedom has always had as a limit—this is an old story—the freedom of others. I shall add to this platitude that it exists, and has meaning and content, only insofar as it is limited by the freedom of others. A freedom involving only rights would not be freedom, it would be omnipotence, it would be tyranny. A freedom involving also rights and duties is a freedom which has a content and which can be experienced. The rest, freedom without limits, cannot be experienced, or can be only at the expense ultimately of the death of others. Limited freedom is the only thing which gives life at the same time to the one exercising it and to those on whose behalf it is exercised.

[*Does the conception of the artist as spokesperson of the suffering people not take us back to the age of cathedrals or to myth, and is it the sole remedy for bourgeois and individualist literature?*]

I understand the question and it aims at truth, does it not? We cannot go back to cathedrals, of course, the issue is settled in advance, nor for that matter to Greek temples. When we speak about Hellenism, I do not think any of us wants to re-create an agora where we would stroll about in short tunics. So we shall not return to the cathedral. Returning to myth is a quite different problem, and this already makes far more sense, because in fact some of the great works of our epoch, like for example Melville's *Moby Dick*,[7] are works which have assigned deep and subtle truths to a myth capable of being understood by everyone. That book, *Moby Dick*, is given as a prize volume to children in American schools, and yet it represents one of the deepest and most poignant reflections an artist could develop on the problem of evil. There is consequently no doubt that myth still remains for us one of the possible forms of literary and artistic rebirth. But the path leading to that artistic rebirth, to that art which will be accessible to all, does not go by way of one genre or another. That rebirth will perhaps be a rebirth of tragedy, or some ample flowering of the novel, or again some epic rebirth, I have no idea. But what is far more important for that rebirth is the inner attitude of the artist. This inner attitude can only be sincerity. You will understand better what I mean by sincerity if you consider that, in my view, such sincerity cannot be practiced in solitude. Artists who voluntarily separate themselves from the world are obliged to sacrifice a certain portion of sincerity, for the excellent reason that sincerity is not that state of purity, that iron raised to a white heat; it is a way of presenting oneself to the other—to the reader, as it may be, or to the spectator if a picture or play is involved—presenting oneself to the other in the simplest and truest way. Which seems all very easy, after all, yet clearly it is the peak of art, which none of us attains. At present all of us in Europe are, as artists, so fettered by obstacles, considerations, the weight of history, the acceleration of things, the multiplicity of information— we are so fettered by all this that the simple, natural sincerity of Homer, for example, is something impossible for us. But it is at such sincerity, such simplicity, that we must aim, for the excellent reason that it is the point where artist and public meet. For the rest, I am no prophet and cannot tell what form that rebirth will take.

[*Why accept to speak about the future of European civilization when you say you are mainly concerned with the present?*]

Well, in the first place I have an appropriate answer for you, which is that I accept the subjects proposed to me.

In the second place, this subject interests me. I did indeed say that only the present concerned me, but I understand by present something that goes beyond the coming day or year. The historical present is, roughly speaking, the living generation. Which, in spite of everything, implies the future of Europe. At the moment when my generation quits the stage in order finally to take its leave, it is my own present which in a certain way will end. If I cannot imagine, let us say, the year 2000, I can nevertheless imagine pretty well the coming years. They are years which belong to me. In this sense, they are present to me. Everything that is in front of me in a perceptible way, everything that can make me suffer or give me joy, is my present.

So it is I who am in the wrong. In an abrupt way, I gave a definition of the present that was not correct. Your question is judicious, because my formulation was not.

[*In your lecture on the artist and his time, you criticized art for art's sake and realist art.*[8] *But instead of thinking about the creative process in the context of opposition between subject and object, should we not understand it as the progressive identification of the artist with his object? For a painter such as Braque, for example, there is an entire development through which the painter identifies with the object he is painting. Is this process of identification possible in literature?*]

I think it is possible in poetry, at least I suppose so, not being a poet. I think it is impossible in literature, for the excellent reason that in prose, at any rate, it is impossible wholly to suppress the rational intermediary. Literature passes through language, and language cannot do without the rational intermediary. People have tried it, as you know. The experiments with automatic writing, as it was called, were interesting as experiments. It is even possible, to some extent (we all do it, even the writers seemingly most in control of themselves)—it is possible to indulge in automatic writing. It is not possible to make it into a system of composition, in the way that Braque, in the texts which I know, makes a system of composition out of this almost mystical identification—is that right? What is possible in painting, since the facts are there and Braque has done it, strikes me as impossible in literature. I cannot think of any example.

[*Does the writer not identify with his characters?*]

Yes, to that extent. But it is a partial extent. For the composition of a book, especially of a novel, is a rational composition. It brings in an aesthetic which is itself an exercise of intelligence. This is why I say that one may indulge in a method like this, but one cannot give oneself over to it, if one is a writer.

[*Should we not dissociate European civilization from the geographical area to which people customarily limit it and define culture in the way Isocrates[9] conceived of Hellenic culture: "We consider as Greeks those who participate in our culture"? Does abandoning the universalist character of European civilization, its power to radiate beyond its own geographical area, not amount to hastening its death?*]

My feeling is very favorable to what you say. No spiritual phenomenon can have a properly defined territorial basis. The limits of geography have never been those of the mind. There is no doubt that the influence of European civilization has gone beyond the limits within which it was born. It has gone so far beyond them, moreover, that traces of it can be found in nations or in territories which are not specifically European. Nor is there any doubt that England is only half European, both geographically and culturally.

These diversities, these shadings, these divergences do not prevent us, for ease of discussion, from being able to trace the geographical limits which roughly and conventionally demarcate the area of European civilization.

As for knowing if this civilization must influence other peoples or otherwise perish, well, I rather agree with you, but that is one of the reasons for my hope. For the moment, Europe is threatened primarily by European ideas, and especially by the insurrection of colonies which have learned ideas of freedom in European schools. It strikes me that this represents (at the same time naturally as an anxiety about the future) a degree of optimism.

[*Is the work of Kazantzakis[10] appreciated in France?*]

As I think I have said, it is highly regarded. Two of his novels have been translated. Some collections of poetry, or rather I should say poetic prose, such as *Ascesis: The Saviors of God*, have also been translated. Two of his plays have been translated and published. We do not despair of seeing them staged.

Few foreign writers in our country at present have a similar literary position. There are foreign writers who have a greater literary position, men like Faulkner or Thomas Mann, men who are universally known and far more read, far more translated in France. But among the writers who are beginning to become known in France and who, I hope, will become more and more so, well, Kazantzakis really is one of the greatest. Moreover, your newer literature is also being translated, since Mrs. Liberaki[11] has been translated and two of her novels published by Gallimard.

[*Has the French novel been making progress since Balzac and Stendhal?*]

No living writer would dare to compare themselves today with those great departed souls.

On the Future of Tragedy

1955

On April 29, 1955, a day after participating in the discussion on the future of European civilization at the Graeco-French Cultural Union (see p. 144), Albert Camus gave the following lecture at the French Institute in Athens on the theme of contemporary theater. The text of this lecture remained unpublished until its appearance in 1965 in the volume entitled Essais *in the first version of* Œuvres complètes *by Camus, edited by Roger Quilliot for the Bibliothèque de la Pléiade. The extracts from theatrical works with which Camus peppered his contribution, indicated by "Reading" in square brackets, have not been included.*

An Oriental sage would always ask the deity in his prayers to spare him from living in an interesting age. We have not been spared such a fate. Our age is only too interesting, meaning that it is tragic. To purge us of our misfortunes, do we at least have the theater for our age, or may we hope to have it? In other words, is modern tragedy possible? That is the question I should like to ask myself today. But is this question reasonable? Is it not of the same kind as "Shall we have a good government?," or "Will our writers become modest?," or "Will the rich soon share their wealth out among the poor?"— interesting questions, no doubt, but ones leading to dreams rather than reflection.

I do not think so. I think, on the contrary, and for two reasons, that we may legitimately ask ourselves about modern tragedy. The first reason is that the great periods of tragic art occur in history during centuries of transition, at moments when the life of peoples is heavy with both glory and threat, when the future is uncertain and the present dramatic. After all, Aeschylus fought in two wars and Shakespeare was alive during a quite remarkable succession of horrors. Both stood, moreover, at a kind of dangerous turning point in the history of their civilization.

It is noteworthy, in fact, that in the thirty centuries of Western history, from the Dorians until the atomic bomb, there have existed only two periods of dramatic art, both narrowly compressed in time and space. The first was Greek: it presented an extraordinary unity and lasted a century, from Aeschylus to Euripides. The second lasted barely longer, and for a while flourished—with differing ethics—in countries bordering on the furthest point of Western Europe. It has in fact been too little noticed that the magnificent explosion of Elizabethan theater, the Spanish theater of the Golden Age and French tragedy of the seventeenth century are very close contemporaries. When Shakespeare died, Lope de Vega was fifty-four and had staged most of his plays; Calderón and Corneille were alive. There was indeed no more distance in time between Shakespeare and Racine than between Aeschylus and Euripides. Historically, at least, we may consider that at the time of the Renaissance there was one single magnificent flowering, which was born in the inspired disorder of the Elizabethan stage and reached formal perfection a century later in French tragedy.

Between those two moments of tragedy, almost twenty centuries went by. During those twenty centuries, nothing. Nothing apart from Christian mystery plays, which may be dramatic but are not tragic, as I shall explain later. So we may say that what were involved were two very exceptional periods, which on account of their very singularity should teach us something about the conditions for tragic expression. This is a very exciting subject in my view, which should be pursued with rigor and patience by real historians. But it goes beyond my competence and, regarding it, I should like merely to summon up the reflections of a man of the theater.

When we examine the movement of ideas in those two periods, as well as in the tragic works of the time, we find ourselves confronted by a constant. The two periods in fact mark a transition between forms of cosmic thought, wholly impregnated by the notion of the divine and the sacred, and other forms instead animated by individual and rationalist reflection. The movement from Aeschylus to Euripides is roughly the one from the great pre-Socratic thinkers to Socrates himself (Socrates, who despised tragedy, made an exception for Euripides). Similarly, from Shakespeare to Corneille we are moving from the world of obscure, mysterious forces which is still that of the Middle Ages to the universe of individual values asserted and maintained by human will and reason (almost all Racine's sacrifices are sacrifices of reason). It is the same movement basically as the one from the passionate theologians of the Middle Ages to Descartes. Although in Greece this evolution is clearer, because simpler and more compressed into a single place, it is the same in both cases. Each time, in the history of ideas, the individual gradually breaks free from a sacred body to confront the ancient world of terror and devotion. Each time, in works, we pass from ritual tragedy and quasi-religious celebration to psychological tragedy. And each time the definitive triumph of individual reason, in the fourth century in Greece and in the eighteenth century in Europe, dries up tragic production for long centuries.

So far as we are concerned, what can we draw from these observations? First this very general remark, that the tragic age seems to coincide each time with an evolution where man, consciously or not, breaks free from an ancient form of civilization and finds himself confronting it in a state of turmoil, without, for all that, having found a new form capable of satisfying him. In 1955, it seems to me that this is where we are. And at once the question may be asked of knowing whether this inner laceration will find a tragic expression among us. Plainly the twenty centuries of silence separating Euripides from Shakespeare must invite caution. After all, tragedy is a very rare flower and the chance of seeing it bloom in our age remains slender.

But a second reason still encourages us to wonder about that chance. This time, what is involved is a very special phenomenon which we have been able to observe in France for the past thirty

years, precisely since the reforms of Jacques Copeau.¹ This phenomenon is the arrival of writers in the theater, hitherto colonized
by brokers and businessmen. The intervention of writers is thus
bringing about the resurrection of tragic forms that tend to restore
dramatic art to its true place, at the apex of the literary arts. Before
Copeau (exception made for Claudel, whom nobody staged),² the
favorite place for theatrical sacrifice in our country was the double
bed. When the play was particularly successful, the sacrifices would
multiply and the beds too. In short, a business like so many others, where everything was paid for—dare I say—according to the
animal's weight. Anyway, here is what Copeau had to say about it:

> [. . .] if you wish us to specify more clearly the feeling
> which inspires us—the passion driving us, compelling
> us, obliging us and to which we must basically yield—it
> is *indignation*.
>
> An unbridled industrialization which, more cynically
> every day, degrades our French stage and turns the
> cultivated public away from it; the monopolization of
> most theaters by a handful of entertainers in the pay of
> shameless merchants; everywhere, even where great tra-
> ditions should ensure some decency, the same spirit of
> ham-acting and speculation, the same baseness; every-
> where bluff, exaggeration of every kind and all man-
> ner of exhibitionism sponging off a dying art that is no
> longer involved at all; everywhere cowardice, disorder,
> undiscipline, ignorance and stupidity, scorn for the cre-
> ator, hatred for beauty; ever crazier and more pointless
> production, ever more compliant criticism, ever more
> errant public taste: that is what incenses us and makes
> us revolt.³

Since that noble cry, followed by the creation of the Vieux-
Colombier, the theater in our country—and this is our eternal
debt to Copeau—has gradually recovered its former glory: in other
words, a style. Gide, Martin du Gard,⁴ Giraudoux,⁵ Montherlant,⁶

Claudel and so many others have given it back a splendor and ambition lost for a century. At the same time a movement of ideas and reflection about the theater, whose most significant product is the fine book by Antonin Artaud, *Le Théâtre et son double*,[7] and the influence of foreign theorists such as Gordon Craig and Appia,[8] have reinstalled the tragic dimension at the center of our concerns.

By comparing all these observations, I shall thus be able to set clear limits to the problem I was seeking to evoke for you. Our epoch coincides with a drama of civilization which, today as in past times, might encourage tragic expression. At the same time many writers, in France and elsewhere, are concerned to give the epoch its tragedy. Is that dream sensible, is that project feasible and on what conditions—this is the burning question, in my view, for all in thrall to theater as if to a second life. Of course, nobody today is able to give that question a decisive response of the "conditions favorable—tragedy follows" type. So I shall confine myself to a few suggestions regarding this great hope of Western men of culture.

First, what is a tragedy? How to define the tragic has greatly preoccupied historians of literature and writers themselves, though no formula has won general agreement. Without claiming to settle a problem confronted by which so many intelligent minds hesitate, we may at least proceed by comparison and try to see wherein, for example, tragedy differs from drama or melodrama. Here is what strikes me as being the difference: the forces confronting each other in tragedy are equally legitimate, equally armed with reason. In drama or melodrama, on the other hand, just one is legitimate. In other words, tragedy is ambiguous, drama simplistic. In the former, each force is simultaneously good and bad. In the latter, one of the forces is good, the other evil (which is why in our day propaganda plays are nothing but the resurrection of melodrama). Antigone is right, but Creon is not wrong. Similarly Prometheus is at once just and unjust, and Zeus who oppresses him mercilessly is also within his rights. The formula for melodrama would basically be: "Only one is just and justifiable," while the tragic formula par excellence is: "All are justifiable, nobody is just." This is why the chorus in ancient tragedies mainly advises caution. For it knows that within certain limits everybody is right; and the person who from blindness or passion ignores those limits rushes toward disaster, in order to make a right prevail which he believes he alone possesses.

The constant theme of ancient tragedy is thus the line which must not be crossed. On either side of this line, equally legitimate forces meet in a vibrant and perpetual confrontation. To mistake the line or seek to break the balance is to perish. You will similarly find in *Macbeth* or in *Phèdre* (though in a less pure fashion than in Greek tragedy) this idea of the line that must not be crossed, beyond which lie death or disaster. And you will find the explanation of why the ideal drama, such as the romantic drama, is primarily movement and action, since it presents the struggle of good against evil with all its ups and downs; while the ideal tragedy, especially the Greek, is primarily tension, since it is the conflict in a frenzied immobility between two powers, each covered by the twofold masks of good and evil. It goes without saying, of course, that between these two extreme types of drama and tragedy, dramatic literature provides every kind of intermediary.

But sticking with pure forms, what are the two powers confronting each other in ancient tragedy, for instance? If we take *Prometheus Unbound* as a typical example of that tragedy,[9] it may be said that on the one hand there is man and his wish for power, on the other the divine principle reflected in the world. There is tragedy when man, out of pride (or even out of stupidity, like Ajax), enters into rivalry with the divine order personified by a god or embodied in society. And the tragedy will be all the greater, the more legitimate that revolt is and the more necessary that order.

Consequently, everything within tragedy tending to break this balance destroys tragedy itself. If the divine order implies no rivalry, allowing only for transgression and repentance, there is no tragedy. There can only be mystery or parable, or again what the Spanish used to call "act of faith" or "sacramental act," that is to say a spectacle in which the one truth is solemnly proclaimed. Religious drama is thus possible, but not religious tragedy. This is how the silence of tragedy up to the Renaissance is to be explained. Christianity submerges the whole universe, man and the world, in the divine order. So there is no tension between man and the divine principle, but at most ignorance, and difficulty in stripping man of the flesh, renouncing passions in order to embrace spiritual truth. And perhaps after all there is only one Christian tragedy in history. It was observed on Golgotha, for an imperceptible instant, at the moment of "My God, why hast thou forsaken me?" That fleeting doubt, and that doubt alone, consecrated the ambiguity of a tragic situation. Afterward Christ's divinity was no longer in doubt. The Mass consecrating that divinity daily is the true form of religious theater in the West. But it is not invention or creation, it is repetition.

Conversely, all that frees the individual and subjects the universe to his wholly human law, especially through denial of the mystery of existence, destroys tragedy anew. Atheistic and rationalist tragedy too is thus impossible. If all is mystery, there is no tragedy. Nor if all is reason. Tragedy is born between shadow and light, and through their rivalry. And that is understandable. In religious or atheistic drama, the problem is basically resolved in advance. In the ideal tragedy, by contrast, it is not resolved. The hero rebels and denies the order oppressing him; divine power, through oppression, asserts itself precisely insofar as it is denied. In other words, rebellion alone does not make a tragedy. Nor does affirmation of the divine order. A rebellion and an order are needed, each buttressed by the other and each reinforcing the other through its own strength. No Oedipus without the fate summarized by the oracle. But the fate would not have all its fatality if Oedipus did not reject it.

And if the tragedy ends in death or punishment, it is important to note that what is punished is not the crime itself, but the blindness of the hero who has denied balance and tension. Of course, we are dealing with the ideal tragic situation. Aeschylus, for example, who remained quite close to the religious and Dionysiac origins of tragedy, granted Prometheus a pardon in the final phase of his trilogy: his Eumenides replaced the Erinyes.[10] But in Sophocles, for most of the time, the balance was absolute, which is the reason why he is the greatest tragedian of all time. Euripides, by contrast, was to upset the tragic balance in the direction of the individual and psychology. He thus heralded individualistic drama: in other words, the decline of tragedy. Similarly, the great Shakespearian tragedies were still rooted in a kind of vast cosmic mystery providing an obscure resistance to the ventures of their impassioned individuals, while Corneille promotes individual morality and, by his very perfection, heralds the end of the genre.

So it has been written that tragedy swings between the poles of extreme nihilism and unbounded hope. Nothing is more true, in my view. The hero denies the order which strikes him down and the divine order strikes because it is denied. Both thus assert their reciprocal existence at the very instant when it is challenged. Thus all is justifiable and nothing is. The chorus draws the lesson, namely that there is an order, that this order may be painful, but that worse still is not to acknowledge its existence. The only purification comes down to neither denying nor excluding anything, thus accepting the mystery of existence, man's limitation and, in short, this order where a man knows without knowing. "All's well," Oedipus then declares after his eyes are gouged out. Henceforth he knows though he never sees again, his darkness is light, and from that face with its dead eyes shines forth the supreme lesson of the tragic universe.

What is to be drawn from these observations? A suggestion and a working hypothesis, nothing more. For it seems that tragedy is born in the West whenever the pendulum of civilization finds itself at equal distance from a sacred society and a society built around man. On two occasions, and twenty centuries apart, we find locked in battle a world still interpreted in terms of the sacred and a man already engaged in his singularity, that is to say armed with his ability to challenge. In both cases, the individual later asserted himself more and more, the balance was gradually destroyed and the tragic spirit at last fell silent. When Nietzsche accused Socrates of being the gravedigger of ancient tragedy,[11] to some extent he was right. To precisely the same extent as Descartes marked the end of the tragic movement of the Renaissance. For in the age of the Renaissance it was the traditional Christian universe that was called into question by the Reformation, the discovery of the world and the flowering of the scientific spirit. The individual gradually rose up against the sacred and against fate. Shakespeare then unleashed his impassioned creations against the simultaneously evil and rightful order of the world. Death and pity invaded the stage and, once again, the definitive words of tragedy rang out: "My desolation does begin to make a better life."[12] Then once again the balance tipped more and more in the other direction. Racine and French tragedy completed the tragic movement with the perfection of chamber music. Armed by Descartes and the scientific spirit, triumphant reason then proclaimed the rights of the individual and emptied the stage. Tragedy descended into the street on the bloody trestles of revolution. Romanticism was to write no tragedy, but merely dramas, among which only those of Kleist and Schiller attained real greatness. Man was alone, so was confronted by nothing apart from himself. He was no longer tragic, he was an adventurer; drama and novel would depict him better than any other art. The spirit of tragedy had thus disappeared up until our own days, when the most monstrous wars in history failed to inspire any tragic poet.

So what might give us hope for a rebirth of tragedy among us? If our hypothesis is valid, our only reason for hope is that individualism is visibly being transformed today, and under the pressure of history the individual is gradually recognizing his limits. The world that the eighteenth-century individual believed he could subjugate and model through reason and science has indeed taken shape, but a monstrous shape. At once rational and excessive, it is the world of history. But with such a degree of excess, history has assumed the aspect of fate. Man doubts being able to dominate it, but can only struggle in it. A curious paradox: humanity, with the same weapons with which it had rejected fatality, has refashioned for itself a hostile fate. Having made a god of human rule, man is once again turning against that god. He is in opposition, at once battling and perplexed, torn between absolute hope and definitive doubt. So he is living in a tragic climate. This explains perhaps why tragedy might seek to be reborn. Man today shouting out his revolt, in full knowledge that this revolt has limits, demanding freedom while subject to necessity—this contradictory man, torn and henceforth aware of the ambiguity of man and his history—this man is the tragic man par excellence. He is perhaps advancing toward a formulation of his own tragedy, which will be obtained on the day when *All's Well*.[13]

And precisely, what we can observe in the French dramatic rebirth, for example, are gropings in that direction. Our dramatic authors are in search of a tragic language, because there is no tragedy without language, and because that language is all the harder to create insofar as it must reflect the contradictions of the tragic situation. It must be at once hieratic and familiar, barbaric and learned, mysterious and plain, haughty and pathetic. So our authors, in search of this language, went back instinctively to the sources—in other words, to the tragic periods of which I have spoken. Thus we have seen a rebirth in our country of Greek tragedy, but in the only forms possible for highly individualistic minds. Those forms are derision, or mannered and literary transposition; in other words, basically humor and fantasy, the comic alone belonging to the realm of the individual. Two good examples of this attitude are provided for us by Gide's *Oedipus* and *The Trojan War [Will Not Take Place]* by Giraudoux.[14] [*Reading*]

We have also been able to observe in France an effort to reintroduce the sacred to the stage. Which was logical. For this, however, ancient images of the sacred had to be called upon, whereas the problem of modern tragedy consists in re-creating a new sacred. So we have seen either a kind of pastiche, in style and feeling, as in Montherlant's *Port-Royal*,[15] which is having a success currently in Paris [*Reading*], or the resurrection of an authentic Christian feeling, for example in the admirable *Partage de midi*.[16] [*Reading*] But it can be seen here how religious theater is not tragic: it is a theater not of rivalry between creature and creation but of renunciation of the creature. In one sense, Claudel's works prior to his conversion, such as *Tête d'or* or *La Ville* [The City], were more significant for what concerns us.

In any case, however, religious theater always precedes tragedy. In a certain sense, it heralds it. So it is not surprising that the dramatic work in which the tragic style if not the tragic situation is already perceptible remains the work by Henry de Montherlant, *Le Maître de Santiago*,[17] from which I should like to read you the two principal scenes. [*Reading*]

Conclusion

In such a work, in my view, we find an authentic tension, though somewhat rhetorical and above all highly individualistic. But it seems to me that tragic language is created in it, and then provides us with more material than the drama itself. At all events, the attempts and studies I have sought to acquaint you with through a few magnificent examples, if they do not give us the certainty that a tragic rebirth is possible, at least leave us with that hope. The path remaining ahead of us must first be traced by our society itself, in search of a synthesis of freedom and necessity, and by each one of us who must preserve within ourselves our power of revolt, without yielding to our power of negation. At this price, the tragic sensibility taking shape in our epoch will find its flowering and its expression. Which amounts to saying that the true modern tragedy is that which I shall not read to you, since it does not yet exist. In order to be born, it needs our patience—and a genius.

But I wanted simply to make you feel that there exists today in French dramatic art a kind of tragic nebula within which nodes of coagulation are beginning to form. A cosmic tempest may, of course, sweep the nebula away and with it the future planets. But if this movement continues despite the storms of time, these promises will bear their fruit, and the West will perhaps experience a dramatic rebirth. It is assuredly being prepared in all countries. However, and I say this without nationalism (I love my country too much to be a nationalist), it is in France that the preliminary signs of this rebirth can be perceived.

In France, yes, but I have said enough for you already to be sure like me that the model, and the inexhaustible source, remains for us Greek genius. In order to express to you at once this hope and a twofold gratitude—first that of French writers toward Greece, the common fatherland, then my own toward your welcome—I cannot finish this last lecture better than by reading to you a passage from the superb and learnedly barbaric transposition which Paul Claudel made of Aeschylus's *Eumenides*, in which our two languages are mutually transfigured into a single strange and magnificent Word. [*Reading*]

Spain and Don Quixotism

1955

On October 23, 1955, a ceremony took place in the Sorbonne's Richelieu amphitheater to celebrate the three hundred and fiftieth anniversary of the publication of Don Quixote.[1] *Albert Camus took advantage of the opportunity given him to speak in order to honor not just the classic work by Cervantes, which he rated among "the three or four works [. . .] which crown the vast pile of creations of the spirit" (see p. 189), but also the memory of Miguel de Unamuno. The Spanish intellectual had been seen as an important anti-Francoist figure since his famous speech on October 12, 1936, at the University of Salamanca, of which he had then been rector. On that day, in front of an assemblage of Francoist and Falangist officials, Unamuno had invoked reason and the law in denouncing the brutal force of Franco's troops. Stripped of his post and placed under house arrest, Unamuno died there of grief a few months later. The speech by Camus was published in* Le Monde libertaire *on November 12, 1955.*

In the year 1085, during the years of reconquest, Alfonso VI, an energetic king who had five wives, including three Frenchwomen, took the mosque of Toledo from the Arabs. Informed that this victory had been made possible by a betrayal, he had the mosque handed back to his adversaries, then conquered Toledo and the mosque again by force of arms. Spanish tradition abounds in such features, which are not just indications of honor but, more significantly, of the madness of honor.

At the other extremity of Spanish history, Unamuno, confronting those wont to deplore Spain's feeble contributions to scientific discovery, made the following incredible rejoinder of disdain and humility: "Inventing is their business." "Their" referred to other nations. As for Spain, she had her own discovery which, without betraying Unamuno, we may call the madness of immortality.

In these two examples, as much with the warrior king as with the tragic philosopher, we encounter in its pure state the paradoxical genius of Spain. And it is not surprising that, at the high point of its history, this paradoxical genius should have been embodied in a work itself ironic, ambiguous by definition, destined to become the gospel of Spain and, through an additional paradox, the greatest book of a Europe nevertheless intoxicated by its own rationalism. The haughty, upright renunciation of a stolen victory, the stubborn refusal of the century's truths, non-actuality in effect elevated to a philosophy, found in *Don Quixote* a ridiculous and royal spokesman.

But it is important to note that these refusals are not passive. Don Quixote fights and never gives up. "Ingenious and formidable," according to the title of an old French translation, he is perpetual combat. His non-actuality is thus active, it constantly embraces the century it rejects and leaves its marks upon it. A rejection that is the opposite of a renunciation, an honor that bends the knee to humility, a charity that takes up arms—this is what Cervantes embodied in his character, mocking him with a mockery itself ambiguous, that of Molière for Alceste, which persuades better than any highflown sermon. For it is true that Don Quixote fails in his own century and the lackeys hoax him. But all the same, when Sancho is governing his island with the success we all know, he does so remembering his master's precepts, of which the two greatest concern honor: "Glory in your humble stock, Sancho [. . .] when people see that this does not embarrass you, nobody will try to make you embarrassed about it"; and charity: "[. . .] but when there were any doubts about justice I should go for leniency and mercy."[2]

Nobody will deny that these words of honor and mercy have a sinister air today. They are mistrusted in curio shops; and, as for tomorrow's executioners, from the pen of an official poet we could read a fine case against *Don Quixote*, seen as a manual of reactionary idealism. In truth, that non-actuality has grown continually greater, and we have today reached the summit of the Spanish paradox, the moment when Don Quixote is thrown into prison and his Spain out of Spain.

To be sure, all Spaniards can claim Cervantes. But no tyranny has ever been able to claim genius. Tyranny mutilates and simplifies what genius brings together in complexity. As for paradox, tyranny prefers Bouvard and Pécuchet[3] to Don Quixote, who for three centuries has likewise been a perpetual exile among us. But that man in exile is on his own a fatherland we claim as ours.

So this morning we are celebrating three hundred and fifty years of non-actuality. And we are celebrating it with that part of Spain which, in the eyes of the powerful and the strategists, is non-actual. The irony of life and the loyalty of men have thus resulted in this solemn anniversary taking place among us in the very spirit of Quixotism. In the catacombs of exile, it reunites the true faithful of the religion of Don Quixote. It is an act of faith in the man whom Unamuno already called Our Lord Don Quixote, patron of the persecuted and humiliated, himself persecuted in the kingdom of shopkeepers and police. Those like me who have always shared this faith, and who even have no other religion, know moreover that it is a hope at the same time as a certainty. The certainty that, with a certain degree of determination, defeat culminates in victory; misfortune burns joyfully; and non-actuality itself, maintained and pushed to the end, finishes by becoming actuality.

But for that it is necessary to go all the way; necessary for Don Quixote, as in the Spanish philosopher's dream, to descend into Hell to open the gates for the lowest wretches. Then, on that day when according to Quixote's moving remark "the spade and hoe will go hand in hand with knight-errantry,"[4] perhaps the persecuted and the exiled will finally be reunited, the crazy, fevered dream of life transfigured in that last reality which Cervantes and his people invented and bequeathed to us, for us to defend it tirelessly until history and men decide to recognize and salute it.

Homage to an Exiled Journalist

1955

On December 7, 1955, Albert Camus spoke at a banquet organized in Paris in homage to Eduardo Santos, president of the Republic of Colombia from 1938 to 1942, then editor of the great liberal Bogotá daily newspaper El Tiempo. *During the Colombian civil war between liberals and conservatives after 1948, the daily's premises were the target of numerous attacks, and were even burned down in 1952. After the military coup of General Gustavo Rojas Minilla in 1953,* El Tiempo *was finally banned when Eduardo Santos refused to publish a communiqué imposed by the government. The speech delivered by Camus at the banquet appeared for the first time in the journal* Les Cahiers des droits de l'homme *(January–February 1956), then for a second time, with an additional postscript, in the review* La Révolution prolétarienne *in November 1957. It is the latter version which is reproduced here.*

We are proud to welcome among us this evening an ambassador who is unlike any other. For I have read that the government which had the sorry privilege of suspending the greatest newspaper in South America had previously offered its editor, President Eduardo Santos, an embassy in Paris. You rejected that honor, Mr. President, not out of disdain for Paris, as we know, but out of love for Colombia, and doubtless because you know that governments sometimes consider embassies abroad as places of gilded banishment for troublesome citizens. You remained in Bogotá, so you made trouble in accordance with your vocation, and you were censored, this time without diplomatic niceties and with the utmost cynicism.

But by that very token, you earned the sole qualifications that warrant your being seen by everyone today as the true ambassador of Colombia, not only in Paris, but in all capitals where just the word freedom makes hearts quicken.

It is not as easy as people think to be a free man. The truth is that the only ones declaring it to be easy are those who have decided to repudiate freedom. For it is not because of its privileges that freedom is rejected, as people would like us to believe, but because of its exhausting tasks. As for those, by contrast, whose job and passion it is to endow freedom with its content of rights and duties, they know this is a ceaseless effort, an unfailing vigilance, and a daily testimony in which pride and humility partake in equal measure. If we are tempted today to tell you of our affection, it is because you have delivered that testimony in full, without sparing yourself. By rejecting the dishonor you were being offered, which consisted in agreeing to take responsibility for the disavowal and contrition that a government was daring to dictate to you, and by allowing your fine paper to be destroyed rather than placing it at the service of falsehood and despotism, you have assuredly been one of those unbending witnesses who always deserve respect. But that would not yet suffice to make you into a witness for freedom. Many men have sacrificed everything mistakenly, and I have always thought that heroism and sacrifice were not enough to justify a cause. Stubbornness alone is not a virtue. But what gives your resistance its true significance, what makes you into the exemplary companion whom we wish to salute, is that in the same circumstances, when you were the respected president of Colombia, not only did you not use your power to censor your opponents, but you prevented the paper of your political enemies from being suspended.

That act is enough for you to be saluted as a truly free man. Freedom has children who are not all legitimate and admirable. Those who applaud it only when it covers their privileges, and who have only censorship on their lips when it threatens them, do not belong among us. But those who, in the words of Benjamin Constant, wish neither to endure nor to possess the means of oppression; those who want freedom at once for themselves and for others[1]—in a century doomed to the excesses of oppression, those are the seeds beneath the snow about which one of the greatest of our number spoke.[2] Once the storm is over, the world will be fed by them.

Such men, we know, are rare. Freedom today does not have many allies. I have sometimes said that the true passion of the twentieth century was slavery. That was a bitter comment which did injustice to all those men, of whom you are one, whose sacrifice and whose example help us every day to live. But I was simply seeking to express the anguish I feel every day, confronted by the abasement of liberal energies, the prostitution of words, the slandered victims, the smug justification of oppression, the manic admiration of strength. We see a proliferation of minds that could be described as seeming to make a taste for slavery into a component of virtue. We see intelligence seeking justifications for fear, and finding them with ease, since every baseness has its own philosophy. Indignation is weighed up, silences are concerted, history is merely the garment of Noah spread over the obscenity of the victims. In short, all flee true responsibility, the weariness of being loyal or having an opinion of their own, in order to flock into the parties or phalanxes which will think, grow indignant and basically decide in their stead. Contemporary intelligence seems no longer to measure the truth of doctrines and causes except by the number of armored divisions they can field. From now on everything is good that justifies the assassination of freedom, be it the nation, the people or the size of the State. The people's welfare in particular has always been the alibi of tyrants, and it offers moreover the advantage of giving the lackeys of tyranny a clear conscience. Yet it would be easy to destroy that clear conscience by shouting at them: if you want the people to be happy let them speak, so that they can tell us what kind of happiness they want and what they do not! But the truth is that even those making use of such alibis know they are lies; they leave to their tame intellectuals the chore of believing the lies and showing that religion, patriotism or justice require the sacrifice of freedom in order to survive. As if freedom, when it departs from anywhere, were not the last to disappear, after everything which once constituted our reasons for living. No, freedom does not die alone. Along with it, justice is banished forever, the fatherland lies dying, innocence is crucified daily.

To be sure, freedom is not enough for everything and has boundaries. The freedom of each individual finds its own limits in those of others; no one has a right to absolute freedom. The limit where freedom begins and ends, where its rights and duties are adjusted, is called law, and the State itself must be subjected to law. If it evades this, if it deprives its citizens of the benefits of this law, there is malfeasance. Last August there was malfeasance in Colombia, just as for the past twenty years there has been malfeasance in Spain. And there, as everywhere, your example helps us remember that one cannot compromise with malfeasance. One rejects it and fights it.

Your battlefield was the press. Freedom of the press is perhaps what has suffered most from the slow erosion of the idea of freedom. The press has its pimps just as it has its policemen. The pimp debases it, the policeman subjugates it, each using the other as a pretext to justify his encroachments. These gentlemen vie to protect the orphan and give her refuge, be that refuge a prison or a brothel. The orphan is entirely justified in declining so many solicitous services, and in deciding she must struggle alone and alone determine her fate.

Not that the press is in itself an absolute good. Victor Hugo said in a speech that it was intelligence, progress and so forth.[3] As an old journalist already, I know it is nothing of the kind and the reality is less comforting. But in another sense, the press is better than intelligence or progress; it is the possibility of all this and other things too. The free press can doubtless be good or bad, but without freedom it will assuredly never be anything but bad. When one knows the worst and the best of which man is capable, one knows equally well that it is not the human person in itself that must be protected, but the possibilities it embodies—in short, ultimately its freedom. I confess for my own part that I cannot love the whole of humanity, other than with an immense and somewhat abstract love. But I do love a number of men, living or dead, with so much strength and admiration that I am always anxious to preserve in others what will perhaps one day make them resemble those I love. Freedom is nothing but the chance of being better, while servitude is certainty of the worst.

So if, despite so much compromise and subservience, we must continue to see in journalism, when it is free, one of the greatest professions of this age, it is only insofar as it allows men like you and your colleagues to serve their country and their age at the highest level. With freedom of the press, peoples are not certain to move toward justice and peace. But without it, they are certain not to do so. For justice is done to peoples only when their rights are recognized, and there are no rights without expression of this right. On this point we can believe Rosa Luxemburg, who was already saying: "Without a free and untrammeled press, without the unlimited right of association and assemblage, the rule of the broad masses of the people is entirely unthinkable."[4]

So we must be intransigent on the principle of this freedom. It underpins not merely the privileges of culture, as people hypocritically seek to persuade us. It also underpins the rights of labor. Those who, in order to justify their tyrannies, pit labor and culture against each other will never make us forget that everything which enslaves intelligence puts labor in chains, and vice versa. When intelligence is gagged, the worker is soon enslaved, just as when the proletarian is in chains, the intellectual is soon reduced to holding his peace or lying. In short, the person who violates truth or its expression ultimately mutilates justice, even when he thinks he is serving it. From this point of view, we shall deny to the end that a press is true because it is revolutionary; it will be revolutionary only if it is true, and never otherwise. So long as we keep these obvious facts in mind, your resistance, Mr. President, will keep its true meaning and, far from being isolated, illuminate the long struggle you will thus help us not to abandon.

The Colombian government accused *El Tiempo* of being a super-State within the State and you were right to refute that argument. But your government was right too, although in a sense that it would not accept. For, in saying this, it was paying homage to the power of words. Censorship and oppression merely provide proof that words are enough to make a tyrant tremble, provided only that they are supported by sacrifice. For nourished by heart and blood, words alone can bring men together, whereas the silence of tyrannies separates them. Tyrants soliloquize over millions of solitudes. If we, by contrast, reject oppression and falsehood, it is because we reject solitude. Every resister, when he stands up against oppression, is thereby affirming the solidarity of all men. No, it is not you yourself or a far-off newspaper which you defended by resisting oppression, but the whole community that unites us across frontiers.

Is it not true, moreover, that your name has always been linked throughout the world to the cause of freedoms? And how should we not recall here that you have been and remain one of the most loyal friends of our Spain, Republican Spain, today scattered across the world, betrayed by its allies and its friends, forgotten by all, the humiliated Spain which still stands precisely only by crying out so forcefully. On the day when the other Spain, Christian and penitentiary, along with its jailers and its censorship re-enters the organization of so-called free nations—on that day I know you will stand with us all, in silence but without a backward glance, by the side of free, unhappy Spain.

For this loyalty, allow me to thank you in the name of my second fatherland and in the name of all those who, assembled here, are telling you of their gratitude and their friendship. Take our thanks for being among the few who, in the time of servitude and fear, stand firm on their rights. More or less everywhere people complain about how the sense of duty is disappearing. How would it be otherwise, since people are no longer bothered about their rights? The one who is intransigent about his rights alone retains the power of duty. Great citizens of a country are not those who bend the knee before authority, but those who—against authority, if need be—do not compromise on the country's honor and freedom. And your own country will always salute in you its great citizen, as we do here, for having succeeded, scorning all opportunism, in facing up to the total injustice being inflicted upon you. At the moment when the world is being disfigured by the most meager realism, a debased conception of power, passion for dishonor and the ravages of fear, at the very moment when it might be thought that all is lost, on the contrary something is beginning, since we no longer have anything to lose. What is beginning is the time of the diehards, henceforth condemned to defend freedom unconditionally. This is why your isolation serves as an example and comfort for all those who, like me, are separating today from many of their traditional friends, by rejecting all complicity, even temporary, even and above all tactical, with regimes or parties, be they of right or left, which justify however minimally the suppression of a single one of our freedoms!

To conclude, allow me to tell you that while reading the other day the admirable message you addressed to your people, along with your resolution and loyalty I reflected on the long sorrow that must have been your lot. When oppression triumphs, as we all here know, those who nevertheless believe that their cause is just suffer from a kind of astonished unhappiness at discovering the apparent impotence of justice. Then come the hours of exile and solitude, which we have all experienced. But I should like to tell you that, in my view, the worst that can happen in the world in which we live is for one of those men of freedom and courage about whom I have spoken to stagger beneath the weight of isolation and long adversity, and then doubt himself and what he represents. And it seems to me that, at that moment, those who resemble him must draw close to him, forgetting titles and formalities, with solely the language of the heart, to tell him that he is not alone and his action is not futile; that a day always comes when the palaces of oppression crumble, when exile is over, when freedom blazes forth. This calm hope justifies your action. If men, after all, cannot always ensure that history has a meaning, they can always act so that their own life has one. Believe me if I tell you that across thousands of kilometers, from far-off Colombia, you and your colleagues have shown a little of the hard road we still have to travel together, toward freedom. And in the name of the loyal and grateful friends welcoming you here today, please allow me to salute fraternally in you and your colleagues the great companions of our common liberation.

For Dostoyevsky

1955

In a 1958 interview, Albert Camus described Dostoyevsky as a "true prophet" of the twentieth century. A prophet whose work he discovered at the age of twenty, when he was a student in Algiers. It was there that in 1938, with the company of the Théâtre de l'Équipe which he then led, he staged an adaptation of The Brothers Karamazov *in which he played the part of Ivan. Subsequently the author would develop a whole number of reflections upon Dostoyevsky's work in his essays—*The Myth of Sisyphus, The Rebel—*and his* Notebooks. *In 1959, after "several years of work and persistence," Camus realized one of his oldest and dearest projects: the stage adaptation of the novel* Demons. *A few years earlier, in 1955, he had taken part in a collective homage to Dostoyevsky organized on the initiative of Radio Europe. The text he drafted for the occasion, reproduced below, was published in 1957 in the review* Témoins.*

A few months ago I was welcoming a likable young Soviet man who greatly surprised me by complaining that the great Russian writers were not translated enough into French. I informed him that the great Russian literature of the nineteenth century was, of all the literature of that period, the one which has been translated most and best here. And, in my turn, I capped his surprise by assuring him that without Dostoyevsky twentieth-century French literature would not be what it is. To finish convincing him, I told him: "You're in the study of a French writer very much involved in the movement of ideas of his time. Which are the only two portraits to be found in this study?" Turning in the direction I was pointing, his face lit up to see the portraits of Tolstoy and Dostoyevsky.

The light which I saw in my young friend's face, and which alone would erase the memory of all the stupidities and cruelties being amassed today to divide men, I did not ascribe to Russia or to France, but to the genius of creation shining out across frontiers, which you sense at work almost unceasingly in all Dostoyevsky's writings.

I encountered those writings at the age of twenty, and the shock they gave me still persists twenty years later. I place *Demons* alongside three or four other great works, such as the *Odyssey*, *War and Peace*, *Don Quixote* and the plays of Shakespeare, which crown the vast pile of creations of the spirit. At first I admired Dostoyevsky because of what he revealed to me about human nature. "Reveal" is the word. For he teaches us only what we know but refuse to recognize. Moreover, he satisfies in me a rather indulgent taste for lucidity for its own sake. But very quickly, as I experienced more cruelly the drama of my epoch, I came to love in Dostoyevsky the man who has lived and expressed our historical destiny most profoundly. For me, Dostoyevsky is above all the writer who, well before Nietzsche, managed to discern contemporary nihilism, define it, predict its monstrous consequences, and seek to indicate the paths of salvation. His main subject is what he himself calls "the deep spirit, the spirit of negation and death";[1] the spirit which, invoking the limitless freedom of "everything is allowed," ends up in the destruction of everything or the servitude of everyone. His personal suffering is at once to take part in it and to reject it. His tragic hope is to cure humiliation by humility and nihilism by renunciation.

The man who wrote, "The questions of God and immortality are the same as the questions of socialism, but from a different angle,"[2] knew that henceforth our civilization would demand salvation for all or for no one. But he knew that salvation could not be extended to all if you forgot about the suffering of one individual. In other words, he wanted no religion that was not socialist, in the broadest sense of the word; but he rejected a socialism that was not religious, in the broadest sense of the term. In this way he saved the future of true religion and of true socialism, although the world of today seems to prove him wrong on both counts. Dostoyevsky's greatness, however (like that of Tolstoy, who said nothing else, albeit in a different way), will not cease to grow; for our world will die or admit that he was right. Whether this world dies or is reborn, Dostoyevsky in either case will be justified. This is why, despite and because of his infirmities, he towers over our literature and our history. He still helps us today to live and hope.

Appeal for a Civilian Truce
in Algeria

1956

In articles published in L'Express *in autumn 1955, Albert Camus invited the various forces involved in the Algerian conflict to a dialogue, request-ing them to give priority to sparing the civilian populations. He moved from writing to action by launching on January 22, 1956, at the Cercle du Progrès in Algiers,[1] his "Appeal for a Civilian Truce." Although the atmosphere inside was relatively fraternal between Arabs and French, violent demonstrations took place at the same time outside, where Algérie Française extremists shouted "Death to Camus!" The meeting came to a tense end and clashes were only just avoided. Conscious of the project's failure, Camus left* L'Express *and decided no longer to express himself publicly on the subject of Algeria. However, he continued to act behind the scenes by asking for numerous individuals under sentence of death to be pardoned. The appeal by Camus was published in the weekly* Demain *on January 26, 1956, before being included by the author in his* Actuelles III—Chroniques algériennes *(1939–1958).*

Ladies and gentlemen,

Despite the precautionary measures needed for this meeting to take place, despite all the difficulties we encountered, I shall speak this evening in order not to divide but to unite. For this is my most ardent wish. Not the least of my disappointments—and the word is inadequate—is having to acknowledge that everything is conspir-ing against such a wish; and, for example, that a man and writer

who has devoted part of his life to serving Algeria should find himself, before it is even known what he wants to say, denied the right
to speak. But at the same time this confirms the urgency of the
calming endeavor we need to undertake. So this meeting had to
take place, in order to show at least that all chance of dialogue is
not lost, and so that general discouragement does not lead to acceptance of the worst.

I have indeed spoken about "dialogue," so have not come to
deliver any formal lecture. To be honest, in the current circumstances I would not have the heart to do so. But it struck me as
possible—and I even considered it my duty—to come and transmit
to you a purely human appeal, capable on one point at least of quell-
ing passions and bringing together most Algerians, French or Arab,
without obliging them to abandon any of their convictions. This
appeal, sponsored by the committee which organized this meeting,
addresses both camps and asks them to accept a truce that would
affect innocent civilians alone.

So all I need to do today is justify this initiative to you. I shall
attempt to do so briefly.

Let us first say, and insist upon this point, that by force of circumstance our appeal is situated outside all politics. If it were otherwise,
I should not be competent to speak about it. I am not a politician,
my passions and tastes lead me elsewhere than to public platforms. I
step on to them only when obliged by the pressure of circumstance,
and by the idea I sometimes have of my job as a writer. With regard
to the core of the Algerian problem, moreover, as events accelerate
and the mistrust on both sides grows, I would perhaps have more
doubt than certainty to express. My sole qualification for intervening on this issue is to have experienced the Algerian misfortune as
a personal tragedy, and especially to have been unable to feel joy
over any death whatsoever. For twenty years, with slender means,
I have done what I could to contribute to the harmony of our two
peoples. You may doubtless laugh at the sight of the preacher of
reconciliation confronted by the reply that history is offering him,
when it shows him the two peoples he loved locked together only in
an identical mortal rage. But he himself, at any rate, is not moved to

laugh about it. Before such a failure, his one concern can no longer be anything other than to spare his country excessive suffering.

It must also be added that neither are the men who have taken the initiative to support this appeal acting in a political capacity. Among them are members of great religious families, who have been willing, in accordance with their highest vocation, to support a duty of humanity. Or again, men who were not obliged by profession or temperament to become involved in public affairs. For the most part, indeed, their profession, useful in itself to the community, sufficed to fill their lives. They could have remained on one side, like so many others, counting the blows, at most from time to time uttering a few fine, melancholic strains. But they thought that building, teaching or creating were works of life and generosity which could not be continued in the realm of hatred and blood. Such a decision, so heavy with consequences and commitments, gives them no right except just one: the right to ask people to reflect on what they are proposing.

Lastly it must be said that we do not wish to obtain from you any political support. If we sought to raise the core issue, we would risk not receiving the backing we need. We may differ on the necessary solutions, and even on the means of achieving these. Confronting anew positions defined—and distorted—a hundred times would for the moment mean only adding to the burden of insult and loathing beneath which our country is struggling and suffocating.

But one thing at least does unite all of us, which is love of our common land—and anguish. Anguish before a future that closes in a little more every day; before the threat of a deteriorating conflict, and an already serious economic imbalance aggravated daily, which risks becoming such that before long no force will any longer be able to revive Algeria again.

It is this anguish which we all wish to address, even and especially among those who have already chosen their camp. For even among the most determined of them, even at the very heart of the fray, I know there are some who are not resigned to murder and hatred, and who dream of a happy Algeria.

It is to this element in each one of you, French or Arab, that we are appealing. It is to those who are not resigned to seeing this great country break in two and drift apart that—without recalling yet again the mistakes of the past and concerned only about the future—we would like to say that it is possible today, on one particular issue, first to unite, then to save human lives, and thus to prepare a more favorable climate for a reasonable discussion at last. The deliberate modesty of this aim, and yet its importance, should in my view earn it your broad assent.

What is involved? Persuading the Arab movement and the French authorities, without having to enter into contact or commit to anything else, to declare simultaneously that for the duration of the troubles the civilian population will always be respected and protected. Why this measure? The first reason, upon which I shall not insist unduly, is, as I have said, purely humanitarian. Whatever the long-standing, deep-seated origins of the Algerian tragedy, one fact remains: no cause justifies the death of innocents. Throughout history men, unable to suppress war itself, have concentrated on limiting its effects; and however dreadful and abhorrent the recent world wars may have been, aid and solidarity organizations did nevertheless manage to pierce their darkness with that feeble ray of pity which prevents us from despairing of man entirely. This need appears all the more urgent when what is involved is a struggle that, in so many respects, takes on the semblance of a fratricidal fight; and where in the murky fray weapons no longer distinguish between men and women, or between soldiers and workers. From this point of view, even were our initiative to save just one innocent life it would be justified.

But it is justified by other reasons too. However gloomy it may be, the Algerian future is not yet wholly compromised. If each individual, Arab or French, made the effort to reflect on their opponent's arguments, the elements at least of a fertile discussion might emerge. But if the two Algerian populations, each accusing the other of having started the conflict, were to hurl themselves against one another in a kind of xenophobic frenzy, then all chance of understanding would be drowned definitively in blood. It is possible, and this is our greatest anguish, that we are advancing toward these horrors. But that must not and cannot happen without those among us, Arab and French, who reject the madness and destruction of nihilism, issuing one last appeal to reason.

Reason, here, proves clearly that on this point at least French and Arab solidarity is inevitable, in death as in life, in destruction as in hope. The terrible visage of this solidarity appears in the infernal dialectic ensuring that what kills one party kills the other too, each casting the blame on the other and justifying its own violence by its opponent's. The eternal dispute over who was originally responsible then loses its meaning. And for having been unable to live together, two populations—at once similar and different, but equally deserving of respect—condemn themselves to die together, with anger in their hearts.

But there is also a community of hope justifying our appeal. This community is based on realities against which we can do nothing. This country has been home for a century to a million Frenchmen and for centuries to millions of Muslims, both Arab and Berber, and several religious communities, vigorous and thriving. These men must live together, at this crossroads of routes and races where history has placed them. They can do so, on the sole condition of taking a few steps toward each other in a free encounter. Our differences should then help us instead of pitting us against one another. For my own part, here as everywhere, I believe only in differences, not in uniformity. And first of all, because the former are the roots without which the tree of freedom withers and the sap of creation and civilization dries up. Yet we remain rooted to the spot, facing one another, as if struck by a form of paralysis relieved only by short, brutal bouts of violence. For the struggle has taken on a merciless character, arousing irrepressible indignation on both sides, and passions that leave room only for escalation.

"No further discussion is possible": this is the cry stifling every future, and every chance of life. Thereafter it is a blind conflict in which the Frenchman decides to take no heed of the Arab, even if he knows somewhere within himself that the latter's demand for dignity is justified, and the Arab decides to take no heed of the Frenchman, even if he knows somewhere within himself that the

French of Algeria too have a right to security and dignity in our common territory. Trapped in their resentment and hatred, all are then deaf to each other. Every proposal, with whatever intention it is advanced, is met with mistrust, at once distorted and made unusable. We gradually become entangled in an inextricable knot of old and new accusations, hardened vengefulness, unflagging grudges succeeding one another as in old family trials where complaints and arguments accumulate over generations, to the point where the fairest and most humane of judges can no longer sort things out. It is hard then to envisage an end to such a situation, and the hope for any French and Arab partnership, leading to a peaceful and creative Algeria, fades away a little bit more every day.

So if we wish to preserve something of this hope, at least until the day when discussion gets going on the core issue; if we wish to ensure that this discussion has a chance of succeeding, thanks to a mutual endeavor to understand—we must act upon the very nature of the struggle. We are too tightly fettered by the scale of the drama and the complexity of the passions unleashed by it to hope to secure a cessation of hostilities straight away. For such an act would imply the adoption of purely political positions, which for the time being would perhaps divide us even more.

But we can act at least upon what is hateful about the struggle and propose, without changing anything in the current situation, to renounce only what makes it unpardonable: that is to say, the murder of innocents. The fact that such a meeting would bring together French and Arabs, equally concerned not to proceed to irreparable harm and irreversible disaster, would give it a serious chance of intervening vis-à-vis both camps.

If our proposal were to have a chance of being accepted, and it does have one, we would not merely save precious lives, we would restore a climate favoring a healthy discussion not spoiled by absurd intransigence; we would prepare the ground for a better and more nuanced understanding of the Algerian problem. By bringing about this slight thaw on a specific issue, we could hope one day to dismantle the whole hardened mass of hatreds and crazy demands in which we are all immobilized. The word would then belong to the politicians, and everyone would have the right to defend anew his own convictions and explain his dissent.

This at any rate is the narrow position on which we can, to begin with, hope to unite. Any broader platform would for the moment offer us only an additional area of disagreement. We must restrain ourselves.

But I do not believe, after mature reflection, that any Frenchman or any Arab could refuse his assent to this action, at once limited and vital. In order to convince ourselves wholly of this, we need only to imagine what will happen if this initiative should fail, despite the precautions and the narrow limits we are setting for it. What will happen is final divorce, destruction of all hope and a disaster of which we have as yet only the faintest idea. Those of our Arab friends who stand courageously beside us today in this no-man's-land where we are threatened from both sides—and who, themselves torn, already have such difficulties in resisting escalation—will be forced to yield to it and abandon themselves to a fatality which will crush any possibility of dialogue. Directly or indirectly, they will be drawn into the struggle, whereas they might have been the peacemakers. So it is in the interests of all Frenchmen to help them escape this outcome.

But, similarly, the direct interest of Arab moderates is to help us escape a different type of fatality. For if we fail in our initiative and thus prove impotent, those liberal Frenchmen who think we can make the French presence and the Arab presence coexist, who believe that such coexistence will do justice to the rights of both, who are sure at any rate that it alone can save the people of this country from misfortune—those Frenchmen will find their lips sealed.

Instead of the broad community of which they dream, they will then be sent back to the only living community which gives them legitimacy—that is, to France. Which means that, through our silence or with deliberate intent, we shall in turn be drawn into the struggle. To illustrate this twofold outcome, which is to be feared and which dictates the urgency of our appeal, I cannot speak in the name of our Arab friends. But I can testify that it is possible in France. Just as I have sensed here the Arab mistrust toward everything proposed to them, we can sense in France, as you must know, the rise of doubt and a parallel mistrust which risk becoming established if the French—already upset by the continuation of war in the Rif after the sultan's return,[2] and by the resurgence of Fellaghism in Tunisia[3]—see themselves obliged by the spread of a merciless conflict to think that the aims of this struggle are not merely justice for a people, but the realization of foreign ambitions at France's expense and for its definitive ruin. The reasoning that many Frenchmen will then adopt, should they lose all hope and come to accept the inevitable, is diametrically opposed to that of the majority of Arabs. This reasoning will consist in saying: "We are French. Consideration for what is just in our opponents' cause will not lead us to disregard what, in France and her people, deserves to survive and grow. We cannot be asked to applaud all nationalism apart from French nationalism, to absolve all sins apart from those of France. In our present plight and since we must choose, we cannot choose anything but our own country."

So, through the same reasoning but argued in reverse, our two peoples will separate definitively and for a long while Algeria will become a heap of ruins, whereas a simple pause for reflection now could still change the face of things and avoid the worst.

This is the twofold danger threatening us, the deadly stakes before us. Either, in one respect at least, we shall succeed in coming together to limit the damage, thus encouraging a satisfactory development; or we shall fail to unite and to convince, and this failure will have repercussions on the whole future of Algeria. This is what justifies our initiative and determines its urgency. It is why my appeal will be more than imperative. If I had the power to give voice to the solitude and anguish of each one of us, it is with that voice that I would address you. So far as I am concerned, I have loved with passion this land in which I was born; I have drawn from her everything that I am; and within my friendship I have never separated any of the men who live there, whatever their race. Although I have known and shared the miseries of which she has no lack, she has remained for me the land of happiness, energy and creation. And I cannot resign myself to seeing her become for a long while the land of misfortune and hatred.

I know that the great tragedies of history often fascinate men by their dreadful aspect. So they stand motionless facing these tragedies without managing to decide on anything apart from waiting. They wait, and one day the Gorgon devours them. I would like instead to make you share my conviction that this spell can be broken, that this impotence is an illusion, that sheer strength of heart, intelligence and courage are enough to check fate and sometimes reverse it. One must simply want that, not blindly, but with a resolute and meditated will.

People resign themselves too easily to fatality. They accept too easily the idea that blood alone moves history forward, and the stronger then progresses due to the other's weakness. This fatality does perhaps exist. But the task of men is not to accept it, nor to submit to its laws. If they had accepted it in the earliest times, we would still be in prehistory. The task of men of culture and faith is, in any case, neither to desert historic struggles nor to serve what is cruel and inhumane in them. It is to survive in them, to help man in them against what oppresses him, to encourage his freedom against the fatalities that surround him.

It is on this condition that history really advances, innovates and, in a word, creates. For all the rest, it repeats itself, like a bloody mouth spewing forth only a furious stammer. We have only reached the stammer today, and yet the broadest perspectives open up in our century. We are at the level of knife fights, or almost so, and yet the world is advancing at the speed of supersonic aircraft. On the same day when our newspapers are publishing the appalling account of our provincial disputes, they announce the formation of the European Atomic Energy Community. Tomorrow, if only Europe reaches a common agreement, floods of wealth will sweep the continent and, overflowing as far as here, will make our problems seem outdated and our enmity obsolete.

It is for this still unimaginable but imminent future that we must prepare ourselves and stick together. What is absurd and distressing in the tragedy through which we are living may be seen in the fact that, in order one day to embrace perspectives that are on a world scale, we must today assemble miserably and in small numbers to ask merely, without as yet aspiring to anything more, for a handful of innocent victims to be spared in one small isolated spot on the globe. But since that is our task, however humble and ungrateful it may be, we must tackle it with determination, in order to deserve one day to live as free men: in short, as men who refuse to either practice or be subjected to terror.

Poznań

1956

In early 1956 Poland's political and social climate was unstable. At Poznań the living conditions of the metalworkers were deteriorating, while their working standards were frequently being raised. After a vain attempt at negotiation, a strike broke out on June 28. More than a hundred thousand people took to the streets, and official buildings were attacked. Very quickly the minister of defense, Konstantin Rokossovsky, brought in the army, which bloodily repressed the uprising: fifty-odd demonstrators were killed, hundreds wounded. Nothing indicates that Camus delivered this speech in public, but as the text did not appear in any publication put out during the author's lifetime, the decision was taken to include it in the present volume.

An international communist leader, who sometimes calls himself a trade unionist, has declared that the Poznań uprising was caused by agitators inspired from abroad. Until then, this political genius was basically saying nothing more than any bourgeois journalist confronted by working-class or colonial uprisings which come to disturb his notion of happiness. Nevertheless, the argument he then invoked deserves our full support. In a normal country, he said, you do not attack police stations in order to satisfy working-class demands. For in a normal country, it is true, trade-union freedoms authorize peaceful struggle for working-class demands. But where the right to strike no longer exists, where labor laws with a stroke of the pen annul a century of trade-union achievements, when workers who receive just the bare minimum see government decisions eroding wages that are no longer enough even for survival, what is left for them but shouting and anger?

No, the regime under which the worker finds himself forced to choose between destitution and death is not a normal one. And those who, from nearby or from afar, with qualifications or without, slander or criticize the martyrs of Poznań, those people wall themselves off definitively from the community of free men and dishonor the revolution that they claim to defend. Mr. Cyrankiewicz,[1] whom a certain press presents to us as a mild liberal, and who does indeed dispense fine words while his security services are executing workers, likewise made an unfortunate statement in announcing the repression. Anybody, he said, raising a hand against the people can rest assured that it will be cut off. If that punishment is as certain as the Polish head of government says, then we may be sure that his country and several others will soon be ruled by a bevy of one-armed generals. For those rulers and bureaucrats have done better than raise their hand against the people: they have struck the people and laid it low in blood. But working-class blood does not bring happiness! Those frightened tyrants who shoot and talk nonsense are united today in the same conscious complicity. They know—never doubt it—they know they are guilty!

This is why we cannot fail to greet with indignation the attitude in this matter of the Yugoslav government and its official press. By insulting and slandering the Poznań victims, the Yugoslav government has just offered Stalin a quite splendid tribute. It has dashed the expectations of all those who actually trusted it, and has condemned itself in the eyes of the free left for a long time to come. But these slanders, after all, like the qualifications we see our own progressive individuals adopting even here, teach us only what we already knew. They teach us that reaction today is also on the left. Or would be, at least, if the sacrifices of the Polish workers, and the solidarity they have awoken in the world among so many people like those present in this hall, did not still testify to the honor and indefatigable courage of the working-class movement. But those people who, at the sight of workers advancing shoulder to shoulder against tanks to demand bread and freedom, have no other reaction than to treat these martyrs as fascists and virtuously to regret that they do not have the patience to die silently of hunger, while waiting for the regime to be so good as to do what is called liberalize— those people have excluded themselves from the working-class movement and its honor.

For my own part, I shall certainly refrain from giving even the slightest encouragement to the rebellion and struggle of men whose battle I cannot share. But now that these men, sick to death of humiliation, have risen and been murdered, I should despise myself for displaying the slightest hesitation and, faced with their sacrifice, expressing anything but my respect and my absolute solidarity. They assuredly have no need for us to congratulate them. They need only for their cry to be echoed by a thousand voices wherever freedom reigns; for their distress to be relayed and exposed to the eyes of the world; for people to know and respect their will to have done with that mystification which claimed they had freely consented to the sacrifice of their freedoms, in order to obtain bread for all. The truth, they have shouted out to us, is that they had neither bread nor freedom; that they neither wish nor are able to do without either; that they know, as we all do, that the two are inseparable, and that, deprived of freedom, the slave still receives his bread only at his master's pleasure.

For a few months now, a myth has been crumbling irresistibly before our eyes. Today we know the sadness of having been right to refuse to see the regimes in the East as revolutionary and proletarian. Sadness indeed: who would rejoice at having been right to declare that millions of men really were suffering misery and oppression? Today the truth, the terrible truth explodes, the myth splinters. But we know that this myth has for years perverted the conscience and the intelligence of Europe. Even faced with the break of dawn, these blind men will still say it is night. But they will say so with more difficulty today. The workers of Poznań have just delivered the final blow to a cynical myth that held sway. Before the eyes of all, the fires of the Polish insurrection illuminate the degradation and tragedy of a revolution perverted. No longer can anyone be blind or naive about this degradation today. There can only be accomplices.

We shall not be, we shall never be such accomplices! Nor shall we be triumphant Pharisees. This victory of truth has been paid for by too many deaths and too much blood for us to be able to greet it other than with a grim determination. Still today, those unarmed workers being shot in the shadows to save what is left of dying regimes make us feel only the horror and grief which have accompanied that prolonged lie. But those desperate deaths impose on us a loyalty that must be pledged once again. Loyalty to the word they shouted out in the face of repression; the word which converted soldiers even in the ranks of the army; the word that has survived all the oppression with which it was crushed and all the mystification in which it was cloaked: loyalty to indefatigable freedom, to invincible and sacred freedom. Yes, we can only respond from afar to that harrowing cry of the workers of Poznań and echo it throughout the world. But we must do so unceasingly, so that the cry will never again be silenced. Freedom or barbarism, this is what we have learned in the long years of history that have just gone by; this is what we are learning in this new tragedy. So the choice will not be hard. We shall choose freedom against the old and new barbarisms, and we shall choose it once and for all, until the end, so that we do not prove unworthy of a single day in the sacrifice of the still oppressed working-class militants of Poland.

The Option of Freedom

Tribute to Salvador de Madariaga
1956

On October 30, 1956, an event was organized in Paris to honor the seventi-
eth birthday of the Spanish intellectual Salvador de Madariaga (1886–1978).
It was sponsored by a committee including numerous French and foreign
personalities, such as Édouard Herriot, Eduardo Santos (see p. 181), Robert
Schuman, Paul-Henri Spaak, Victoria Ocampo, Pablo Casals, Karl Jaspers
and André Malraux. Briefly minister of public education and then of jus-
tice during the Second Republic in Spain (1931–1939), Salvador de Madar-
iaga also represented Spain at the League of Nations at the beginning of the
civil war, before being forced into exile (in England, Mexico and then the
United States) after the victory of Franco. The speech delivered by Camus
during this evening of homage was published in April 1957 in the review
Monde nouveau, *with the title "The Option of Freedom."*

As we pay tribute today to a man whom all of us here admire and
love, I should like to inscribe words at the entrance which I know
will strike a chord in many of those assembled here, and which
in any case summarize with some pride the destiny and the vocation of our friend Salvador de Madariaga. Already eighty years ago
those words were proposed to the free spirit by Nietzsche: "Thou
shalt prefer exile in order to be able to say the truth."[1] It is doubtless not certain that people always choose to go into exile. But they
certainly do choose to stay there and live there. And to accept such
a hard option does indeed require nothing less than love of truth
and freedom.

At any rate, nothing could better define Salvador de Madariaga than this twofold passion, provided we also acknowledge that he has known how to live and exemplify it without spectacular contortions, with the refinement and humor which we love in him, and which in certain individuals of quality are expressions of decency. But however decent it may be, his passion for truth is no less indomitable; that courteous wrestler is also, as we know, a proud fighter. This does not mean—and Salvador de Madariaga would never allow me to say—that a ready-made, carefully wrapped truth greets us in his work. But we do find in it the tireless striving for truth, the cautious yet bold action of a mind that refuses to be satisfied with fine words: a mind that scorns all intellectual comforts and is ready to yield only to hard evidence. As the author of so many powerful, sagacious books, when he offers us some idea or solution, we can be sure he has not gone off beforehand to request the recipe from any political party or church.

Like so many great Spanish minds—and contrary to the widespread opinion (when some idiot one day declared that there was no Spanish philosophy, he at once found a hundred intelligent men to repeat it)—he is one of our rare contemporaries who can legitimately sport the title of philosopher. Despite his encyclopedic knowledge, he does not—like our official thinkers—believe that philosophy consists in teaching the history of philosophy. But he appears to know that it consists, at the same time as uncovering the secrets of the world, in exercising one's powers of reason to set out the rules of behavior; and, in short, to try to live according to how one thinks, at the same time as striving to reflect in depth upon one's life and one's era. Which means that this seeker of truth is also one of our rare upholders of truth. What he believes, he is ready to defend. And if he spends half his life in studious retreat reflecting upon man today, he devotes the other half to serving him. So I might have summed up my thoughts by saying it is no man of letters we are honoring today, but a gentleman of letters.

But I should like to reassure our friend and tell him my intention is not to overwhelm him with academic encomia. Be assured that my aim is both less formal and perhaps more serious. We have already celebrated, even with music, your seventieth birthday, and paid your work the homage it deserves. You will simply allow a forty-year-old to say why, with all the respect and deference he feels for you, he sees you as his comrade in arms.

I am sure that this assertion will not surprise you. If it were to surprise you, however, I would beg you to consider the state of our intellectual society, the gurus strutting about everywhere, the rotten scraps they offer essentially to our appetite for truth and dignity. You will then appreciate better the kind of solitude in which some of us were living in search of great lessons, if a handful of men—of whom you are one—were not stubbornly upholding across frontiers the rights, the duties and the honor of the mind.

For it must be said we have not been spoiled for great examples. I am not speaking even of the general enfeeblement of character and intelligence among those whose function was to govern or represent us. But remaining in the realm of thought alone, men of my generation, born to historical life with Hitler's seizure of power and the Moscow Trials, first saw philosophers of the right, through hatred for one part of the nation, justify enslavement of the whole nation beneath a foreign army and police force. It then became necessary for intelligence too to take up arms, in order to rectify that deplorable line of argument.

Scarcely had we recovered peace and honor than a fresh conspiracy against intelligence and its freedoms, even more painful for us, developed. We saw—and still see—thinkers of the left, through hatred for another part of the nation, justify with fine arguments: suppression of the right to strike and other working-class achievements; the concentration-camp system; the abolition of all freedom of thought and expression; and even anti-Semitism, provided only that it be professed and practiced in the guise of humanism. A cold frenzy of self-punishment thus—with a ten-year gap—made our theorists of the nation or of freedom fervent supporters of the worst tyrannies to have spread across the world and, in a word, worshippers of the accomplished fact. Too many of our intellectuals and artists, caught up in this frenzy, ended by resembling those daughters who sang their hearts out in front of the Peirebeilhe inn,[2] to cover the screams of travelers having their throats slit by their virtuous parents. In the name of history and its realism, at all events, a vast conspiracy against the mind and freedom has developed over years when it was still necessary to fight for every inch.

In this interminable struggle which is still continuing, on whom might we rely in thought and in action except on men like you? You have helped us understand through your example, as through your writings, why cynical and realist positions have compelling prestige. They permit judgment and contempt, whereas those who hold other attitudes such as your own are obliged to try to understand, implying constant effort on their part. Whence the prestige of the former among certain intellectuals, prone to the least effort. Intelligence without character is ultimately far worse than blissful idiocy. Lacking any firm will, it readily yields to some implacable doctrine, which is why we have seen the birth of this type so specific to our era: the tough intellectual, ready to justify all manner of terrors in the name of realism alone.

Faced with this attitude and these fine speeches, we have been able to learn from your patience and firmness. Glass too is hard, diamond alone scratches it, yet at the first blow it shatters. One must simply wait and hold fast, with a smile if possible, to remain faithful to your teaching. In short, you have prevented us from despairing of our era's intelligence, showing us by the power of example that the tough intellectual can be countered by the firm intellectual.

When in our specialist journals we read fine apologies for hatred, relying on denunciation of its opposite which is supposed to be bleating softness, thanks to you we do not regard ourselves as either soft or bleating, and can answer that the opposite of hatred is not timid idealism, but generous justice. We then have only to wait, leaving our enemies to shout that there is no effective justice without a little hatred. History, their notorious history, is there to teach them sooner or later that justice vanishes in hatred like a stream in the ocean. For the flies swarming today around the historical coach do not alter the speed of history.[3] They buzz, they lie, they shout that the people are happy to be enslaved. But one day, a truly his-

toric day this time, a capital city instead swarms with rebels dying
and conquering under the sole banner of freedom.

Yes, dear Don Salvador, it is men like you who have prevented
us from despairing. And when I was asked to address you today, I
thought this was the first thing I would say. Those who feel they
were made primarily to admire and to love, and who in the desert
of the contemporary world were in danger of perishing of hunger
and thirst, have an infinite debt of gratitude toward all those who,
in these dishonored times, have offered them a worthy and proud
image of men and intellectuals. It is this gratitude which I wish to
express to you, with all my affection. Thanks to you and very few
others, the perpetual mavericks like us have a party. What party?
Well, the party of men whom the hard-line and totalitarian insult,
while at the same time coming to ask them for a signature to save
the lives of their militants! From this definition you will recognize
that I am talking about liberals!

But you have given—and here lies your originality—a content
to that notion of liberalism which was in its death throes, expiring
at once under the slanders of its enemies and from the cowardice of
its advocates. You were able to say that freedom was not the freedom to prosper or starve, but to take responsibility for one's civic
duty. You refused to choose any of the orthodoxies of our age, and
managed to set the boundaries beyond which the ideas by which
we live lose their meaning. You have been heard tirelessly repeating
that freedom was nothing without authority, but authority without
freedom was merely a tyrant's dream; that the privileges of money
were unacceptable, but there was no society without hierarchy, and
leveling was the opposite of true justice; that power was legitimate
only through popular consent, but direct popular suffrage gave
rise to anarchy or tyranny; that nationalism was the plague of our
era, but international society could not do without nations, since in
order to be surpassed these first needed to exist.

A philosophy so attentive, so vigilant, so concerned with verac-
ity, and the way you have illustrated it through your own life,
make you the worthy heir to that great Spanish tradition which
still remains the only living one beyond the Pyrenees. You too have

concerned yourself with history, but you have seen in it "an illustrious war against death," in Ortega's superb formulation,[4] consequently the privileged site where man tirelessly wages war against the forces of darkness, for life and freedom.

This is the secret of your youth and your strength, you who have never fallen asleep in any prejudice. To take just one example, I know without having talked to you about it what your emotion is, faced with the heroic and deeply moving revolt by workers and students in Hungary. But I know too that you must have laughed to learn that General Franco was protesting, doubtless in memory of Guernica, against the appeal to a foreign army to crush a people in arms. You laughed, as I did, with the appropriate contempt. For we are in fact entirely in solidarity with the Hungarian people arisen against its foreign masters. But this is because we are entirely in solidarity with the Spanish people, likewise oppressed, and awaiting a liberation that the disunited nations have stolen from it.

You were writing recently with some bitterness about the decline of indignation. It is true that indignation is declining. What is worse, it is becoming organized; it is practiced at fixed times and in one direction. Our protesters have become hemiplegic. They choose among victims and decree that some are touching while others are loathsome. So you were denouncing, with your customary clear-sightedness, one of the ills from which we are suffering. And you were then able to add: "We have been reduced to seeking our hope in our very despair. Humanity has fallen so low that it can only rise up again." But in doing so you forgot, in one of those moments of discouragement which we all know, your own teaching. You forgot that the long struggle which you and your fellows have waged is beginning to bear fruit. So, in conclusion, allow one of your readers to remind you: according to you, there is no truce in man's battle for light and freedom. History is never stabilized, in either the prosperity of peoples or their distress. Today, just when we were thinking we had reached the point of utmost distress, hope is reawakening, humanity is indeed arising, freedom is once again lighting up with its flames cities hitherto imprisoned!

The Europe being created today in innocent blood will be paid for at dreadful cost; and we, for whom each human life is irreplaceable, will be unable to greet its rebirth with shouts of joy. But it will be reborn, and we shall greet it solemnly; it will be reborn in the West as in the East, in Madrid as in Budapest, and it will have your countenance and recognize its true masters, since it is already rejecting its false prophets. It will be that great schoolmistress of freedom and order about which you have dreamed.

"The earth always turns," said Foreign Minister Shepilov,[5] after giving a report on the savage intervention of Russian troops. It does indeed turn, and along with it the long-triumphant lie fades, the long-obscured truth begins to enlighten us. Artificial worlds, cemented only by blood and terror, crumble amid the disarray and silence of those who used to hymn their virtues. Freedom—whose futility and necessary disappearance had been proclaimed and proved to us—in a day disperses the thousands of learned volumes and the armies beneath which it was kept buried. It is on the march again, and millions of men again know that it is the only leaven of history, the only reason for them to live, and the only bread of which they can never get their fill.

If this hope is being reborn today, if the honor of living is finally returning to us, know that we owe it to men like you, to men like many of those who, without fear and without hatred, have simply held fast. Which is why, in winding up, I shall not wish for you the repose which others might consider well merited. For we still have need of you. We have need of you to continue what we have begun. And in the knowledge that I shall thus be responding to the desire of your young heart, I wish you the everlasting, proud struggle for truth and freedom that you and we place above all else.

To this uncomfortable wish, I shall add only the personal expression of a gratitude and friendship which you know will not be feigned. How could I ever forget that, amid so many betrayals, you have remained faithful to our shared reasons for living? So how should we not be tempted to tell you in unison this evening what the dying Turgenev wrote to Tolstoy: "I have been fortunate to be your contemporary."[6] But we have, after all, been more than your contemporaries (there are some contemporaries of whom we are not proud): we have shared your anguish and your hope, our defeats have been yours, just as the liberation we all await we shall owe to your example and your action—which continues—for our common honor.

Message to Young French Supporters of Hungary

1956

In October 1956, Hungary gave birth to a significant dissident movement involving intellectuals, students and workers, which on October 23 developed into a popular insurrection. On October 28 the reformer Imre Nagy became prime minister for the second time and launched the country upon a path toward democracy and emancipation from Moscow. Whereas at first he had supported Nagy's policy, the general secretary of the Hungarian communist party, János Kádár, secretly formed a shadow government, in the name of which he negotiated intervention by the Red Army. On November 4, Russian tanks entered Budapest. The repression cost more than two and a half thousand deaths and drove two hundred thousand Hungarians into exile. Imre Nagy was executed on June 16, 1958. In Paris on November 23, 1956, the Free French Association organized a meeting of support for the Hungarians. Although invited, Camus was unable to attend; but he asked one of the members of the association, Michelle Dalbret, to read out the message reproduced below.

Mademoiselle,

I was truly sorry not to have been able to respond to your invitation as you wished. I was touched, however, by your arguments and by the kindness you were good enough to show me. But quite apart from my personal dislike of public speaking, I cannot respond to every demand made on an independent writer, simultaneously and from all sides. Furthermore, having turned down other requests, it was hard for me to accept yours. Lastly, I should like to devote myself as far as possible to securing the success of the appeal I have initiated by European writers to the UN.[1]

Still, I should like not to be entirely absent from your company on Tuesday evening. Since you are addressing young listeners, perhaps you might tell them what, if present, I would have told them, which I shall now attempt to summarize.

The one thing I can state publicly today, having taken part directly or indirectly in twenty years of our bloody history, is that the supreme value, the last possession for which it is worth living and fighting, still remains freedom.

Men of my generation were twenty years old at the time when Hitler was taking power and when the first Moscow Trials were being organized. For ten years we had to struggle first and foremost against the Hitlerian tyranny and the men of the right who supported it. And for ten more years we had to fight the Stalinist tyranny and the sophistries of its defenders on the left. Today, despite the successive betrayals and the slanders which all manner of intellectuals have heaped upon it, freedom remains our primary reason for living. I confess that I have been tempted over these past years to despair of freedom's destiny. Betrayed by those whose vocation was to defend it, trampled by our clerisy before peoples who remained silent, I feared it was dead and gone, which is why it sometimes seemed to me that the dishonor of our age was all-embracing. But the young people of Hungary, of Spain and France and of all countries are proving to us today that this is far from being the case; and that nothing lays low, or will ever lay low, that pure and violent force driving men and peoples to claim the honor of living upright. All of you who are now entering our history, do not forget that. Do not forget it anywhere or at any time! And if you can agree honorably to discuss everything, never entertain the idea that freedom of thought, or individual and national freedom, can ever be called into question, even provisionally, for a single second.

You must now know that when thought is in chains, labor is enslaved; that the writer is muzzled when the worker is oppressed;

and that when the nation is not free, socialism liberates nobody but enslaves everyone.

Let the Hungarian sacrifice, in the face of which we have been brooding over our own shame and impotence, serve at least to remind us of this. We shall be less tempted to condemn our own nation, and it alone, for its historical sins. Without ceasing to demand from it all the justice of which it is capable, we shall be more concerned about its survival and its freedom. You will then not need to imitate us, we who in that long struggle have worn ourselves out fighting to correct watchwords and denounce mystifications, in unending fruitless civil struggles. You will look for what unites you rather than what separates you. You will thus have some chance of being spared a sense of solitude, hard to endure. Then, all together, you will perhaps remake this country which I love today like freedom itself, and which despite its misfortunes, its weaknesses and its faults, continues to deserve our loyalty in this world. But in any case, everywhere and always, retain the memory of what we have just lived through, in order to remain loyal to freedom, with its rights and its duties, and in order never to accept—never— any man, however great, or any party, however strong, thinking for you and dictating your behavior. Forget your masters, those who have lied so much to you, as you now know; and all the rest too, since they were unable to convince you. Forget all masters, forget the outworn ideologies, the moribund concepts, the decrepit slogans which people still try to go on feeding to you. Do not let yourselves be intimidated by any of these forms of blackmail, from the right or the left. And in conclusion, do not accept any more lessons, other than from the young fighters of Budapest dying for freedom. They have not lied to you, in proclaiming that free thought and free work, in a free nation, in the bosom of a free Europe, are the only things in this land and in our history worth fighting and dying for.

This is what, Mademoiselle, I should have wished to say to your audience on Tuesday. And which you will perhaps say on my behalf. Please accept my best regards.

Albert Camus

Kádár Has Had His Day of Fear

1957

Having supported the crushing of the Hungarian insurrection in Buda-
pest by Russian troops on November 4, 1956, János Kádár became head
of the Hungarian government and installed a proletarian communism
approved by the Kremlin. On March 15, 1957, a day commemorating the
1848–1849 Hungarian Revolution against the Austrian Empire, at the
Salle Wagram in Paris, the libertarian association Solidarité Interna-
tionale Antifasciste organized a big meeting of support for the Hungarian
insurrection and its tens of thousands of exiles. Invited to speak alongside
the insurgents György Szabó and Balazs Nagy, Albert Camus delivered
the speech reproduced below, which was published on March 18, 1957, in
Le Franc-Tireur, *before being reprinted as a preface to* That Day in
Budapest: October 23, 1956, *a work by the Hungarian intellectual Tibor*
Méray, who had fled to Paris.[1]

The Hungarian minister Marosán,[2] whose name rings out like a
program, declared a few days ago that there would be no further
counterrevolution in Hungary. For once, one of Kádár's ministers
was telling the truth. How could there be a counterrevolution,
since one had already seized power? There can no longer be anything but a revolution in Hungary.

I am not one of those who want the Hungarian people to take up
arms again, in an insurrection doomed to be crushed, beneath the
gaze of an international community which will lavish on it applause
and virtuous tears, but then return to its slippers like fans from the
terraces on a Sunday evening after a cup match. There are already

too many dead in the stadium, and we can be generous only with our own blood. Hungarian blood has shown itself to be too precious to Europe and to freedom for us not to hoard its every last drop.

But I am not one of those who think there can be some compromise, even resigned, even provisional, with a regime of terror which has as much right to call itself socialist as the executioners of the Inquisition had to call themselves Christians. And on this anniversary of freedom I wish with all my strength for the mute resistance of the Hungarian people to hold out, to swell and—echoed by all the voices we can give it—to obtain from a unanimous international opinion the boycott of its oppressors. And if that opinion is too spineless or selfish to bring justice to a martyred people, if our voices also are too weak, I hope that the Hungarian resistance may still hold out until the counterrevolutionary State collapses everywhere in the East under the weight of its lies and contradictions.

Bloody, Leaden Rituals

For we are indeed dealing with a counterrevolutionary State. How to call otherwise this regime which obliges the father to denounce his son, the son to demand the ultimate punishment for his father, the wife to testify against her husband, and which has raised informing to the level of a virtue? The foreign tanks, the police, the girls of twenty hanged, the workers' councils decapitated and gagged, again the gallows, the writers deported and imprisoned, the lying press, the camps, the censorship, the judges arrested, the criminal making laws, and the gallows again and always—is this socialism? The grand celebration of freedom and justice?

No, we have known and we do know all this: the bloody, leaden rituals of totalitarian religion. Hungarian socialism today is in prison or exile. In the palaces of the State, armed to the teeth, the second-rate tyrants of absolutism lurk, panic-stricken by the very word freedom, outraged by the word truth! The proof is that today, March 15, the day of truth and unconquerable freedom for all Hungarians, has for Kádár been merely one long day of fear.

But for long years these tyrants, helped in the West by accomplices whom nothing and nobody compelled to such zeal, spread dense smokescreens over their real actions. When something did filter through, they or their Western interpreters would explain to us that all would be settled in ten generations or so. And that meanwhile everyone was joyfully advancing toward the future; that the deported peoples had made the mistake of blocking the traffic a little on the splendid path of progress; that those executed were wholly in agreement with their own suppression; that the intellectuals were proclaiming themselves delighted with their pretty gags, because they were dialectical; and that the people were basically filled with joy by their own work, since even if they were working overtime for wretched wages things were all proceeding in the right historical direction.

Alas! the people themselves spoke up. They began to speak in Berlin, in Czechoslovakia,[3] at Poznań,[4] and finally in Budapest. There, along with them, the intellectuals tore off their gags. And both together, with a single voice, declared that they were not moving forward but going backward; that people had been killed for nothing, deported for nothing, enslaved for nothing; and that from now on, in order to be certain of advancing along the right path, everyone must be given truth and freedom.

Thus, at the first shout of insurrection in free Budapest, learned but threadbare philosophies, miles of false arguments and fine deceptive doctrines, were scattered to the four winds. And truth, naked truth, so long abused, burst forth into the world's gaze.

Scornful masters, not even aware they were insulting the working class, had assured us that the people could easily do without freedom, if only they were given bread. And the people themselves were all at once replying that they did not even have bread, but assuming that they did they would still want something else. For it is not a learned professor but a Budapest blacksmith who wrote the following: "I want to be seen as an adult who wants—and knows how—to think. I want to be able to say what I think, without having anything to fear; and I also want to be listened to."

As for the intellectuals to whom people had preached and

shouted that there was no other truth than what served the aims of the cause, here is the oath they swore on the tomb of their comrades murdered by the aforesaid cause: "Never again, even under threats and torture or through a misguided love for the cause, will anything other than truth issue from our lips." (Tibor Méray on the tomb of Rajk.)[5]

The Scaffold Cannot Be Liberalized

After that, the cause is clear. This murdered people is our own. What Spain was for us twenty years ago, Hungary will be today. The subtle nuances, the linguistic tricks and the learned considerations with which people still try to falsify the truth do not concern us. The rivalry we are being told about between Rákosi and Kádár is unimportant. The two are of the same breed. They differ only in the size of their hunting bags, and if Rákosi's is the bloodier, it will not be for long.

At any rate, whether it is the bald killer or the persecuted persecutor[6] who rules Hungary makes no difference in terms of the country's freedom. I am sorry in this respect still to have to play the part of Cassandra and disappoint the fresh hopes of certain indefatigable colleagues; but there is no evolution possible in a totalitarian society. Terror cannot evolve except for the worse, the scaffold cannot be liberalized, the gallows is not tolerant. Nowhere in the world have we seen a party or man wielding absolute power not use it absolutely.

What defines the totalitarian society—of right or left—is first and foremost the single party; and the single party has no reason to destroy itself. Which is why the only society capable of evolution and liberalization, the only one that should retain our sympathy at once critical and active, is the one where plurality of parties is institutionalized. It alone enables us to denounce injustice and crime, hence to correct them. It alone enables us today to denounce torture, ignoble torture, as despicable in Algiers as in Budapest.

What Budapest Was Defending

The idea, which still has support in our country, that a party because it calls itself proletarian can enjoy special privileges with respect to history is an idea of intellectuals weary of their advantages and their freedom. History confers no privileges—it allows them to be won from her.

And it is not the job of intellectuals, or of workers, to bestow any praise at all on the right of the strongest or on the done deed. The truth is that nobody, no man or party, has any right to absolute power or to permanent privileges in a history itself changing. And no privilege or higher reason can justify torture or terror.

On this point, Budapest is still showing us the way. This defeated, enslaved Hungary which our fake realists compare pityingly to Poland, still at the tipping point, has done more for freedom and justice than any other people for the past twenty years. But for the lesson to reach and convince those in the West who were refusing to hear or see, the Hungarian people were obliged—and we shall never be able to console ourselves for this—to shed torrents of blood, already congealing in memory.

At least let us endeavor to be faithful to Hungary, as we have been to Spain. In the solitude in which Europe finds herself today, we have but one means of doing so, which is never to betray, in our own countries or elsewhere, what the Hungarian combatants died for; never to justify, in our own countries or elsewhere, even indirectly, what killed them.

The tireless demand for freedom and truth; the community of the worker and the intellectual (which people still go on stupidly opposing among us, to the great advantage of tyranny); and lastly political democracy as a condition—assuredly not sufficient, but necessary, indeed indispensable—for economic democracy: this is what Budapest was defending. And by doing so the great insurgent city was reminding Western Europe of its forgotten truth and greatness. It was putting paid to that strange sense of inferiority which weakens most of our intellectuals, and which for my own part I refuse to feel.

Reply to Shepilov[7]

The flaws of the West are innumerable, its crimes and errors real. But ultimately let us not forget that we are the only ones to possess this power of improvement and emancipation residing in the free spirit. Let us not forget that when totalitarian society, by its very principles, obliges friend to betray friend, Western society, despite all its errors, always produces that breed of men who maintain the honor of living; I mean the breed of those who stretch out a hand to the enemy himself, in order to save him from misery or death.

When Minister Shepilov, returning from Paris, dares to write that "Western art is fated to tear the human soul apart and create butchers of every kind," it is time to answer him that our writers and artists, they at least, have never butchered anybody; and they nevertheless have enough generosity not to accuse the theory of socialist realism for the massacres covered up or ordered by Shepilov and his ilk.

The truth is that there is room for everything among us, even for evil, and even for Shepilov's own writers; but also for honor, for the free life of desire, for the adventure of intelligence. While there is no room for anything in Stalinist culture, apart from moralistic sermons, a gray life and the catechism of propaganda. To those who were still able to doubt this, Hungarian writers just shouted it out, before demonstrating their definitive choice, since today they prefer to remain silent rather than lie to order.

We shall find it very hard to be worthy of so many sacrifices. But we must try, in a Europe finally united, by forgetting our quarrels, punishing our own mistakes, multiplying our creations and our solidarity. To those finally who have sought to abase us and make us believe that history could justify terror, we shall reply with our own true faith, that which we share as we now know with Hungarian, Polish and even, yes, Russian writers, likewise gagged.

Our faith is that, parallel to the power of constraint and death which darkens history, there is on the march in the world a power of conviction and life, a vast movement of emancipation which is called culture and which is formed at once by free creation and free work.

Our daily task, our long vocation, is to add to this culture by our works, and not to subtract from it anything at all, even temporarily. But our proudest duty is to defend personally, and to the end, against the power of constraint and death from wherever it may come, the freedom of this culture: in other words, the freedom of work and creation.

Those Hungarian workers and intellectuals alongside whom we stand today with such impotent grief understood this and made us understand it better. This is why, if their distress is ours, their hope belongs to us too. Despite their wretchedness, their exile, their chains, they have left us a magnificent heritage that we have to deserve: freedom, which they did not choose but took only a day to restore to us!

A Message to Hungarian Writers in Exile

1957

Following the bloody repression of the Hungarian insurrection by Russian troops in early November 1956, many intellectuals were imprisoned and more than two hundred thousand Hungarians were forced to leave their country. Albert Camus supported them by his public statements, at the same time as making approaches to the Hungarian government in favor of intellectuals imprisoned in Hungary. On November 4, 1957, or a year after the violent events in Budapest, the Association of Hungarian Writers in Exile organized a meeting in London. Invited to take part, Camus was unable to attend, but charged the Hungarian-born French historian Ferenc Fejtő—with whom in 1958 he was to collaborate in the collective work The Truth About the Nagy Affair—*to read out in his name the message reproduced below. The text was published in* Le Monde *on November 6, 1957.*

I wish only to express the solidarity which, for a year now, has bound all free intellectuals in the West to the fate of Hungary.

However hard it is to think of the solitude in which we have allowed the Hungarian combatants to die, and in which we are allowing the survivors to live, the regrouping which has taken place across Europe in this regard does nevertheless give a kind of meaning to that desperate combat.

Totalitarian regimes have no better allies than weariness and neglect. Our watchwords are therefore obvious: they are memory and determination. Only such determination can bring on the day of reparation for Hungary.

The Hungarians have no need for us to weep or lament. They need only for their cries to be echoed, and for their will to destroy the lie oppressing them to be known and respected.

We shall never have paid our debt to the insurgents of October until freedom has been restored to the Hungarian nation and people.

That is the pledge of loyalty which must unite us this evening.

Nobel Prize Acceptance Speech [Stockholm]

1957

On October 16, 1957, the Swedish Academy announced that Albert Camus had been awarded the Nobel Prize in Literature. Despite the panic and distress this news provoked in him, the writer accepted the honor. He thereby submitted to the rule decreeing that the laureate should go to receive the prize in Stockholm and deliver a speech on the occasion. So it was that on December 10, 1957, Camus took the floor, following the grand award ceremony for the Nobel Prizes at the Stockholm Town Hall. In the edition of his speech published by Éditions Gallimard in January 1958, Camus dedicated his prize to Louis Germain, his teacher at the Belcourt primary school in Algiers, to whom he had written on November 19, 1957: "Without you, without that kindly hand which you extended to the impoverished little child that I was, without your example, nothing of all this would have happened."

In receiving the distinction with which your free Academy has been so good as to honor me, my gratitude was all the deeper in that I was aware how much this award exceeded my personal merits. Every man, and especially every artist, wants to be recognized. I want it too. But I could not learn of your decision without comparing its resonance to what I really am. How should a youngish man, possessing only his doubts and a body of work still under construction, accustomed to living in the solitude of labor or the refuges of friendship, not have learned with a kind of panic of a decree which abruptly bore him, alone and reduced to himself, to the center of a blinding light? What could have been the mood in which he received this honor, at a time when in Europe other writers, among her greatest, are reduced to silence, and when the land of his birth is experiencing ceaseless misery?

I did experience that dismay and inner turmoil. In order to rediscover peace, I essentially had to comply with an overgenerous fate. And since I was unable to match it by relying simply on my own merits, I found nothing to help me except what has sustained me in the most unfavorable circumstances throughout my life: the idea I entertain of my art and the writer's role. Please just allow me, in a spirit of gratitude and friendship, to tell you as simply as I can what that idea is.

I personally cannot live without my art. But I have never put that art above everything. If it is necessary to me, however, this is because it does not separate itself off from anyone, but allows me to live, such as I am, at the level of all. Art to my mind is not a solitary enjoyment. It is a means of touching the greatest number of men by offering them a privileged image of common sufferings and joys. So it obliges the artist not to isolate himself, instead subjecting him to the humblest and most universal truth. And the man who has often chosen his destiny as an artist because he felt different very quickly learns that he will sustain his art, and his difference, only by acknowledging what he has in common with others. The artist is molded in this perpetual to-and-fro between himself and others, halfway between the beauty he cannot do without and the community from which he cannot tear himself away. This is why true artists do not despise anything. They compel themselves to understand instead of judging. And if they have a side to take in this world, it can be only that of a society where, in Nietzsche's great words, not the judge but the creator rules, be he worker or intellectual.

The role of the writer is consequently not separated from difficult duties. By definition, he cannot today place himself at the service of those who make history. He is at the service of those who endure it. Or otherwise he is alone and stripped of his art. All the armies of tyranny with their millions of men will not lift him out of solitude, even and above all if he agrees to march with them. But the silence of an unknown prisoner, abandoned to humiliation at the other end of the world, is enough to bring the writer back from exile, each time at least that he manages amid the privileges of freedom not to forget that silence, and to make it resonate by means of art.

None of us is great enough for such a vocation. But in all the circumstances of his life—obscure or temporarily famous, thrown into the irons of tyranny or free for a while to express himself—the writer can rediscover the feeling of a living community which will justify him, provided only that, so far as he can, he accepts the two responsibilities inherent in the greatness of his craft: the service of truth and that of freedom. Since his vocation is to bring together the largest number of men possible, it cannot compromise with the lies and slavery which, wherever they hold sway, engender solitude. Whatever our personal infirmities, the nobility of our craft will always be rooted in two commitments that are difficult to maintain: refusal to lie about what we know, and resistance to oppression.

For more than twenty years of an insane history, hopelessly lost like all men of my age in the convulsions of the era, I was thus sustained by the obscure feeling that writing today was an honor, because this act involved an obligation, and an obligation not just to write. It obliged me in particular, such as I was and depending on my powers, along with all those living the same history, to bear the misery and hope we all shared. Those men—born at the outset of the First World War and twenty years old when Hitler's power and the first revolutionary trials were established; who then to complete their education were confronted by the war in Spain, the Second World War, the concentration camps, the Europe of torture and prisons—today have to raise their children and their works in a world threatened by nuclear destruction. Nobody, I imagine, can ask of them to be optimistic. And I even believe that we must understand, without ceasing to struggle against them, the mistakes of those who, through an exaggeration of despair, claimed the right to dishonor and flocked into the nihilisms of the epoch. But it remains true that most of us, in my own country and throughout Europe, rejected such nihilism and set out in search of some legitimacy. They had to create an art of living at a time of catastrophe, in order to be born anew and then struggle openly against the death instinct at work in our history.

Every generation doubtless believes itself destined to remake the world. Mine, however, knows it will not do so. But its task is perhaps greater. It consists in preventing the world from unraveling. Heir to a corrupt history in which there mingle fallen revolutions, technologies gone mad, dead gods and outworn ideologies; where second-rate powers can today destroy everything, but no longer know how to convince; where intelligence has abased itself to the point of making itself the servant of hatred and oppression—this generation, within and around itself, on the basis of its negations alone, has had to restore a little of what makes the dignity of living and dying. Before a world threatened with disintegration, where our grand inquisitors risk establishing forever the kingdoms of death, it knows it ought, in a kind of mad race against the clock, to restore among nations a peace that would not be that of servitude; to reconcile once more labor and culture, and remake an ark of the covenant with all men. There is no certainty my generation could ever accomplish this huge task. But everywhere in the world it is certainly already making its twofold wager on truth and freedom, and when necessary can die for this without hatred. It is this generation which deserves to be saluted and encouraged wherever it is to be found, and especially wherever it sacrifices itself. In any case, it is to this generation that, confident of your profound agreement, I should like to transfer the honor you have just done me.

In this way, having spoken about the nobility of the craft of writing, I would have restored the writer to his true place, having no other titles than those he shares with his comrades in struggle, vulnerable but obstinate, unjust and with a passion for justice, building his work without shame or pride in view of all, always torn between pain and beauty, and destined in short to draw from his twofold being the creations that he stubbornly strives to erect in the destructive movement of history. After that, who could expect of him ready-made solutions or fine morals? Truth is mysterious, fleeting, always to be won. Freedom is dangerous, as hard to live as it is exalting. We must march toward these two goals, painfully but determinedly, sure in advance of our own lapses on so long a road. What writer would then dare, in all good conscience, to make himself a preacher of virtue? As for me, I have to say once again that I am nothing of all that. I have never been able to renounce the light, the happiness of existence, the free life in which I grew up. But although this nostalgia explains many of my mistakes and failings, it has doubtless helped me understand my craft better, and still helps me blindly to remain close to all those silent men who can endure in this world the life which is made for them only through the memory or return of brief, free joys.

Brought back in this way to what I really am, to my limits, to my debts and to my difficult faith, I feel myself freer to show you, in conclusion, the extent and generosity of the honor you have just granted me, freer to tell you also that I should like to receive it as a homage made to all those who, sharing the same fight, have received no privilege from it, but instead experienced misery and persecution. It will then remain only for me to thank you, from the bottom of my heart; and, as a personal testimony of gratitude, to make you publicly the same age-old promise of loyalty which every true artist, every day, makes to himself in silence.

[The Artist and His Age]

Lecture at Uppsala University
1957

Four days after the official award ceremony for the Nobel Prizes in Stockholm, Albert Camus gave a lecture on December 14, 1957, in the great amphitheater of the oldest Swedish university, at Uppsala. In the edition of Swedish Speeches *published in January 1958 by Éditions Gallimard, the text of this address accompanied the Nobel Prize acceptance speech delivered by Camus on December 10, 1957, at the Stockholm Town Hall.*

An Oriental sage would always ask in his prayers for the deity to spare him from living in interesting times. As we are not sages, the deity has not spared us and we do live in interesting times. At any rate, ones that do not allow us to be uninterested in them. Today's writers know this. If they speak, they are criticized and attacked. If they have grown modest and stay silent, people will speak to them only about their silence and reproach them vociferously for it.

Amid all this racket, the writer can no longer hope to stand aside and pursue reflections or images dear to him. Until now, for better or worse, abstention was always possible in history. The person who did not approve could often remain silent, or speak of something else. Today everything has changed, and even silence takes on a daunting significance. From the moment when abstention itself is considered as a choice, punished or praised as such, the artist is conscripted whether he wants it or not. "Conscripted" strikes me as more accurate here than "committed." What is really involved for the artist is not a voluntary commitment, but rather a compulsory military service. Every artist today is a conscript on the galley of his period. He must resign himself to it, even if he thinks that this galley stinks of herring, there are far too many slave-drivers aboard and, what is more, the course is awry. We are on the open sea. The artist must take his turn at the oars like the rest, without dying if possible: that is to say, while continuing to live and create.

To tell the truth, this is not easy, and I understand that artists may regret their former comfort. The change is rather brutal. To be sure, in the amphitheater of history the martyr and the lion have always existed. The former would sustain himself with eternal consolation, the latter with raw historical scraps. But until now the artist was on the terraces. He would sing for nothing, for himself, or in the best case to encourage the martyr and distract the lion a bit from his meal. Now, however, the artist finds himself in the amphitheater. His voice is necessarily no longer the same, and far less confident.

You can see clearly all that art can lose from this constant obligation. Ease, in the first place, and that divine freedom which breathes in Mozart's work. You understand better the distraught and obstinate look of our works of art, their worried brow and sudden collapses. You can explain that we thus have more journalists than writers, more boy scouts of painting than Cézannes, and finally that tales for girls and thrillers have taken the place of *War and Peace* or *The Charterhouse of Parma*. Of course, you can always counter this state of affairs with the humanist lament, become what Stepan Trofimovich in *Demons* wants to be with all his heart: reproach incarnate.[1] You can also, like him, have bouts of civic sadness. But this sadness changes nothing in reality. It is better, in my view, to give the period its due, since it demands it so vigorously, and acknowledge calmly that the age of dear sirs, artists with camellias and geniuses posing in armchairs is over. To create today is to create dangerously. Every publication is an act, and this act exposes you to the passions of a century which forgives nothing. So the question is not to know if this is, or is not, detrimental to art. For all those who cannot live without art and what it means, the question is merely to know how, among the police forces of so many ideologies (what a host of churches! what solitude!), the strange freedom of creation remains possible.

It is not enough to say in this respect that art is threatened by State powers. For in that case the problem would be simple: the artist fights or surrenders. The problem is more complex, more deadly too, as soon as you realize that the fight is being waged within the artist himself. Hatred of art, of which our society provides such fine examples, is so effective today only because it is fostered by artists themselves. For the artists who went before us, doubt concerned their own talent. For artists today, it concerns the necessity of their art, hence their very existence. In 1957, Racine would apologize for having written *Bérénice* instead of fighting to defend the Edict of Nantes.[2]

This questioning of art by the artist has many reasons, of which only the chief ones need detain us. In the best of cases it can be explained by the impression the contemporary artist may have of lying, or wasting his breath, if he does not take account of history's woes. For what characterizes our age is the way in which the masses and their wretched condition burst into the sight of contemporary sensibility. We now know they exist, whereas we once tended to forget it. And if we know it, this is not because the elites, artistic or other, have become better. No, never fear; it is because the masses have grown stronger and prevent us from forgetting them.

There are other reasons too, and some less noble, for this abdication by the artist. But whatever these reasons may be, they lead to the same end: discouraging free creation by attacking its essential principle, which is the creator's faith in himself. "A man's obedience to his own genius," Emerson said magnificently, "is faith in its purest form."[3] And another nineteenth-century American writer added: "So long as a man is faithful to himself, everything is in his favor, government, society, the very sun, moon, and stars."[4] This astonishing optimism seems dead today. The artist in most cases is ashamed of himself and his privileges, if he has any. Before all else, he must answer the question he puts to himself: is art a deceptive luxury?

I

The first honest answer you can give is the following: art may indeed sometimes be a deceptive luxury. On the poop of galleys, as we know, you can always and everywhere sing about constellations while the slaves are rowing away, exhausting themselves in the hold; in the amphitheater you can always record the polite conversation abuzz on the terraces as the victim is ripped apart in the lion's jaws. It is very hard to reproach such art for anything, when it has scored great successes in the past. Except for this, that things have changed a bit, and in particular the number of galley slaves has increased immensely across the globe. Before so much misery, if it wishes to go on being a luxury, art today has to accept that it must also be a lie.

What indeed should it speak about? If it adapts itself to what our society mostly asks for, it will be trivial amusement. If it blindly rejects that, if the artist decides to isolate himself in his dream, it will express nothing but a negation. We shall thus have a production of either entertainers or formal grammarians, which in both cases culminates in an art cut off from living reality. For the past century or more, we have been living in a society which is not even the society of money (money or gold can arouse carnal passions), but that of abstract symbols of money. The society of merchants can be defined as a society in which things disappear in favor of signs. When a ruling class calculates its wealth no longer by the acre of land or the ingot of gold, but by the number of figures ideally corresponding to a certain number of exchange operations, it at once condemns itself to placing a certain kind of mystification at the center of its experience and its universe. A society based on signs is, in its essence, an artificial society where man's carnal truth finds itself mystified. So it will come as no surprise that this society should have chosen—in order to make of it its religion—an ethics of formal principles; and that it should inscribe the words freedom and equality on its prisons and its financial temples alike. However, words are not prostituted with impunity. The most slandered value today is certainly the value of freedom. Fine minds (I have always thought there were two kinds of intelligence: intelligent intelligence and stupid intelligence) proclaim as a doctrine that freedom is nothing but an obstacle in the path of true progress. But it has been possible to put forward such solemn idiocies because, for a hundred years now, mercantile society has made exclusive and unilateral use of freedom; considered it a right, rather than a duty; and not been afraid, whenever it could, to make freedom in principle serve oppression in practice. So is it any surprise if this society has asked art to be not an instrument of liberation, but an exercise of minor importance—mere entertainment? A whole society of high fashion, where people mainly had money troubles and only romantic problems, thus contented itself for decades with its society novelists and the most futile kind of art: the kind about which Oscar Wilde said—thinking of himself before he knew prison—that the greatest of all vices was to be superficial.[5]

So the manufacturers of art (I have not yet said artists) of bourgeois Europe before and after 1900 accepted irresponsibility, because responsibility implied an exhausting rupture with their society (those who really did make a break were called Rimbaud, Nietzsche or Strindberg, and we know the price they paid). It is from this time that the theory of "art for art's sake" dates, which is simply a demand for such irresponsibility. Art for art's sake, the recreation of a solitary artist, is very precisely the artificial art of a false, abstract society. Its logical culmination is salon art, or the purely formal art sustained by affectation and abstraction, which ends in the destruction of all reality. A few works thus charm a few men, while many crude fabrications corrupt many others. Art is finally constituted outside society, and cuts itself off from its living roots. Little by little the artist, however much fêted, is alone; or at least he is no longer known by his nation, except through the intermediary of the major press or the radio, which will give a convenient, simplified idea of him. The more art is specialized, in fact, the more necessary vulgarization becomes. So millions of men will have the feeling that they know such and such a great artist of our day, because they have learned from the papers that he breeds canaries, or that he only ever marries for six months. The height of renown today consists in being admired or hated without having been read. Every artist who gets caught up in wanting to be famous in our society should know that it is not he who will be famous, but someone else under his name, who will end up escaping him and perhaps, one day, killing the true artist in him.

So how is it surprising that almost all that has been created of value in the mercantile Europe of the nineteenth and twentieth centuries, in literature for example, should have been built against the society of its day? It may be said that until the eve of the French Revolution, the prevailing literature was roughly speaking a literature of consent. From the moment when bourgeois society emerged from the revolution and was stabilized, a literature of revolt developed instead. Official values were then negated, for example in our country, either by the bearers of revolutionary values, from the romantics to Rimbaud, or by the guardians of aristocratic values, of whom Vigny and Balzac are good examples. In both cases, people and aristocracy, which are the two sources of all civilization, enroll against the false society of their day.

But this rejection, too long maintained and grown rigid, became false likewise and led to another kind of sterility. The theme of the accursed poet born in a mercantile society (Chatterton is the finest example)[6] hardened into a prejudice which eventually suggested you could not be a great artist except against the society of your day, whatever its nature. Legitimate initially, when it asserted that an authentic artist could not compromise with the world of money, the principle became false when people interpreted it to mean that an artist could express himself only by being against everything in general. This is why many of our artists aspire to being accursed, have a bad conscience about not being accursed, and want simultaneously to be applauded and booed. Society, of course, being tired or indifferent today, applauds and boos only at random. The intellectual of our day then never stops bracing himself to appear taller. But by dint of rejecting everything, and even the tradition of his art, the contemporary artist gives himself the illusion of creating his own rule book and ends up by believing that he is God. He thus thinks he can create his own reality. Far away from his society, however, he will create only formal or abstract works, moving as experiences, but devoid of the fecundity proper to authentic art, whose vocation is to unite. Eventually there will be as great a difference between contemporary subtleties or abstractions and the work of a Tolstoy or Molière as there is between a draft discounted against invisible wheat and the thick soil of the furrow itself.

II

Art may thus be a deceptive luxury. So we shall not be surprised if men or artists wished to backtrack and return to truth. They at once denied that the artist had any right to solitude, offering him for a subject not his own dreams but the reality lived and suffered by all. Certain that art for art's sake—through its subjects as through its style—eludes the understanding of the masses, or else expresses nothing of their truth, these men wished the artist to set out instead to speak about—and for—the majority. If he translates the sufferings and joy of all into the language of all, he will be universally understood. In return for being absolutely faithful to reality, he will obtain total communication between men.

This ideal of universal communication is indeed that of every great artist. Contrary to the common prejudice, if anyone does not have a right to solitude it is precisely the artist. Art cannot be a monologue. The solitary and unknown artist himself, when he invokes posterity, does nothing but reassert his deep vocation. Judging dialogue impossible with deaf or inattentive contemporaries, he invokes a broader dialogue with generations to come.

But in order to speak about and for all, it is necessary to speak about what we all know and about the reality we share. The sea, the rain, need, desire, the struggle against death—this is what unites us all. We resemble each other in what we see together, in what we suffer together. Dreams change with men, but the reality of the world is our common country. So the ambition of realism is legitimate, for it is deeply bound up with the artistic adventure.

So let us be realists. Or rather let us try to be, if only it is possible.

For it is not certain that the word has any meaning; not certain that realism, even if desirable, is possible. Let us first ask ourselves if pure realism is possible in art. If we are to believe the declarations of the last-century naturalists, it is the exact reproduction of reality. So it would be to art what photography is to painting: the former reproduces while the latter selects. But what does it reproduce and what is reality? Even the best photograph, after all, is not a sufficiently faithful reproduction, not yet sufficiently realistic. What is more real in our universe, for example, than a man's life? And how could we hope to bring him to life better than in a realistic film? But under what conditions will such a film be possible? Under purely imaginary conditions. It would in fact imply an ideal camera fixed day and night on that man, and constantly recording his slightest movements. The result would be a film whose projection would itself last a man's lifetime, and which could be seen only by spectators resigned to wasting their lives being concerned exclusively with the details of another man's existence. Even under those conditions, this unimaginable film would not be realistic. For the simple reason that the reality of a man's life is not to be found only where he stands. It is to be found in other lives which give shape to his: lives of loved ones, in the first place, who would have to be filmed in their turn; but also lives of unknown men, powerful and wretched, fellow-citizens, policemen, teachers, invisible comrades from mines and building sites, diplomats and dictators, religious reformers, artists who create myths determining our behavior—humble representatives, finally, of the sovereign chance ruling the most ordered existence. So there is only one possible realistic film, the very one that is forever projected before us by an invisible camera onto the screen of the world. The only realistic artist would be God, if he exists. Other artists are necessarily unfaithful to the real.

Artists who reject bourgeois society and its formal art, who wish to speak about reality and that alone, at once find themselves in a painful impasse. They must be realistic, but cannot be. They want to subject their art to reality, but reality cannot be described without making a choice from it which subjects it to the originality of an art. The fine and tragic production of the early years of the Russian Revolution shows us this torment clearly. What Russia gave us at that time with Blok[7] and the great Pasternak,[8] Mayakovsky[9] and Yesenin,[10] Eisenstein[11] and the first novelists of concrete and steel, was a magnificent laboratory of forms and themes, a fertile turmoil, a frenzy of research. It was necessary to draw conclusions, however, and say how one could be realistic when realism was impossible. Dictatorship, here as elsewhere, cut to the chase: in its view, realism was first of all necessary, and then it was possible, provided that it aspired to be socialist. What does that decree mean?

In essence, it recognizes frankly that you cannot reproduce reality without making a choice from it, and rejects the theory of realism as formulated in the nineteenth century. All that remains for it is to find a principle of selection around which the world will be organized. And it finds this not in the reality we know, but in the reality to come: that is to say, the future. In order to reproduce properly what is, you must also depict what will be. In other words, the true object of socialist realism is precisely what does not yet have any reality.

The contradiction is indeed superb. But, after all, the very expression "socialist realism" was contradictory. For how is any socialist realism possible when reality is not wholly socialist? It is not socialist, for example, either in the past or entirely in the present. The answer is simple: you will select from the reality of today or yesterday that which prepares and serves the perfect city of the future. So you will devote yourself, on the one hand, to denying and condemning what is not socialist in reality, on the other to extolling what is or will become socialist. We inevitably get propaganda art, with its heroes and villains: in short, a collection of stories for young girls, as much cut off from complex, living reality as formal art. Ultimately, this art will be socialist precisely insofar as it will not be realistic.

This aesthetic which aspired to be realistic then becomes a new idealism, as sterile for any authentic artist as bourgeois idealism. Reality is ostensibly allotted a sovereign rank, only the better to be liquidated. Art finds itself reduced to nothing. It serves, and by serving is enslaved. Only those who precisely take care not to describe reality will be called realistic and praised. The rest will be censured, with applause from the former. The renown that in bourgeois society used to consist in not being read, or being misunderstood, in totalitarian society will consist in preventing others from being read. Here again true art will be disfigured, or gagged, and universal communication rendered impossible by the very people who used to desire it most intensely.

The easiest thing, in the face of such a failure, would be to acknowledge that so-called socialist realism has little to do with great art; and that, in the very interest of revolution, revolutionaries should seek another aesthetic. Instead, we know how its defenders loudly proclaim that no art is possible outside of it. They do indeed proclaim this. But my deep conviction is that they do not believe it, but have come to an inner decision that artistic values had to be subordinated to the values of revolutionary action. If this were stated clearly, discussion would be easier. You can respect this great renunciation on the part of men who suffer too much from the contrast between the misery of all and the privileges sometimes attached to an artist's destiny; who reject the intolerable distance separating those gagged by destitution and those whose vocation is instead always to express themselves. You might then understand these men, try to have a dialogue with them, attempt for example to tell them that suppression of creative freedom is perhaps not the best way to triumph over servitude, and that while waiting to speak for all people, it is stupid to strip yourself of the power of speaking at least for some people. Yes, socialist realism should admit its kinship, and that it is the twin brother of political realism. It sacrifices art for an aim foreign to art, but which on the scale of values may strike it as being superior. In short, it temporarily suppresses art in order first to build justice. When in some still vague future justice exists, art will come back to life. In matters of art, you thus apply the golden rule of contemporary intelligence, which argues that you cannot make an omelette without breaking eggs. But this ponderous good sense ought not to mislead us. It is not enough to break thousands of eggs to make a good omelette, and it does not seem to me that we should judge the quality of the cook by the amount of broken eggshells. The artistic cooks of our day should instead fear overturning more baskets of eggs than they intended, and that as a result the omelette of civilization may never set and, in short, art may never return to life. Barbarism is never temporary. People do not allow for it, and it is normal that from art it should spread to social behavior. Then you see emerge, from the misery and blood of men, trivial literature, a compliant press, photographic portraits, and parish-hall plays with hatred taking the place of religion. Art here culminates in a forced optimism, precisely the worst of luxuries and most pathetic of lies.

Why should this be any surprise? Men's anguish is so large a subject that apparently no one could touch it, unless they were like Keats, said to be so sensitive that he could touch pain itself with his hands. This becomes clear when a controlled literature involves itself in bringing official consolation to such anguish. The lie of art for art's sake pretended to be unaware of evil and so took responsibility for it. But the realist lie, even if it does bravely face up to acknowledging men's present woe, also seriously betrays it, by using it to extol a happiness to come, about which nobody knows anything and which thus authorizes every kind of mystification.

The two aesthetics which long clashed—the one recommending total rejection of actuality and the one claiming to reject all that is not part of actuality—nevertheless end up converging far away from reality, in a single lie and in the suppression of art. Academicism of the right ignores a distress that academicism of the left exploits. But in both cases, the distress is reinforced at the same time as art is negated.

III

Must we conclude that this lie is the very essence of art? On the contrary, I shall say that the attitudes about which I have so far spoken are lies only insofar as they do not have much to do with art. So what is art? Nothing simple, to be sure. And it is even harder to discover amid the shouts of so many people intent on simplifying everything. On the one hand, people want the genius to be splendid and solitary; on the other, they urge him to be like everyone else. Alas! reality is more complex. And Balzac conveyed it in a sentence: "A man of genius has this beauty, that he looks like everyone and that no one looks like him."[12] The same with art, which is nothing without reality, and without which reality is not worth much. For how could art do without the real? But how could it subject itself to the real? The artist chooses his object as much as he is chosen by it. Art, in a certain sense, is a revolt against the world in its fleeting, unfinished aspect: so it sets out merely to give another form to a reality it is nevertheless obliged to preserve, because that reality is the source of its emotion. In this respect, we are all realists and no one is. Art is neither total rejection, nor total consent to what exists. It is simultaneously rejection and consent, which is why it can only be a perpetually renewed rift. The artist always finds himself in this ambiguity, unable to deny the real and yet forever fated to contest it, inasmuch as it is forever unfinished. In order to make a still life, a painter and an apple must confront one another and reciprocally correct one another. And if forms are nothing without the light of the world, they add to this light in their turn. The real universe which, through its splendor, creates bodies and statues, at the same time receives from them a second light that reflects that of heaven. Great style is thus to be found halfway between the artist and his object.

So it is not a question of knowing if art should flee the real or submit to it, but simply of what precise dose of reality the work should cram into itself, in order not to disappear into the clouds or, on the contrary, drag itself along with leaden soles. Every artist resolves this problem as he feels it and as he can. The stronger an artist's revolt against the world's reality is, the greater may be the weight of the real which will balance it. But this weight can never stifle the artist's solitary imperative. The loftiest work will always, as with the Greek tragedians, with Melville, Tolstoy or Molière, be the one which balances the real with the rejection man opposes to this real, each giving the other new impetus in a ceaseless outpouring which is that of joyous, tormented life itself. Now and again a new world emerges, different from the everyday one and yet the same, particular but universal, full of innocent insecurity, aroused for a few hours by the power and dissatisfaction of genius. This is it and yet is not it; the world is nothing and the world is everything. There you have the twofold, tireless cry of every true artist; the cry that holds him upright, his eyes always open, and which now and again wakens for everyone within the sleeping world the fleeting, insistent image of a reality which we recognize without ever having encountered it.

Similarly, confronted by his century, the artist can never turn away from it or lose himself in it. If he turns away from it, he talks to empty space. But conversely, insofar as he takes it as his object, he affirms his own existence as a subject and cannot submit to it entirely. In other words, it is at the very moment when the artist chooses to share the common lot that he affirms the individual who he is. And he will not be able to escape this ambiguity. The artist takes from history what he can see of it in himself, or can suffer there himself, directly or indirectly: that is to say, actuality in the strict sense of the word and the men who are alive today, not the relationship between this actuality and a future which the living artist cannot foretell. To judge contemporary man in the name of a man who does not yet exist is the role of prophecy. The artist, for his part, can only appreciate the myths proposed to him in terms of how they affect the living man. The religious or political prophet can judge absolutely and, as we know, does not hesitate to do so. But the artist cannot. If he were to judge absolutely, he would apportion reality between good and evil without nuance and create melodrama. The aim of art, however, is not to legislate or rule, but first of all to understand. It sometimes does rule by understanding. But no work of genius has ever been based on hatred and contempt. This is why the artist, once his long journey is over, absolves instead of condemning. He is not a judge but a justifier. He is the everlasting advocate of the living creature, just because it is alive. He truly does argue for love of his fellows, not for that love of the stranger which debases contemporary humanism into a courtroom doctrine. Instead the great work ends up confounding all judges.

Through it, the artist at once pays homage to the loftiest figure of mankind and bows down before the lowest of criminals. As Wilde wrote: "There is not a single wretched man in this wretched place along with me who does not stand in symbolic relation to the very secret of life."[13] Yes, and this secret of life coincides with that of art.

For a hundred and fifty years the writers of mercantile society, with a few rare exceptions, thought they could live in happy irresponsibility. They did indeed live, then died alone as they had lived. As for us writers of the twentieth century, we shall no longer ever be alone. Instead we have to know that we cannot escape the common woe. And our only justification—if we have one—is to speak, so far as we are able, for those who cannot do so. But in fact we must do it for all those who are suffering at this time, whatever the past or future greatness of the States and parties oppressing them: for the artist, there are no privileged executioners. This is why beauty, even today, above all today, can serve no party; in the long term or the short, it serves only men's pain or men's freedom. The only committed artist is the one who, while in no way refusing to fight, at least refuses to join the regular forces. I mean the maverick. The lesson he then finds in beauty, if this is honestly depicted, is not a selfish lesson but one of hard brotherhood. Conceived in this way, beauty has never enslaved anyone. And for millennia, every day and at every instant, it has instead relieved the servitude of thousands of men, sometimes freeing a few of them forever. In conclusion, perhaps we here touch the greatness of art, in this perpetual tension between beauty and pain, love of mankind and the frenzy of creation, intolerable solitude and the besetting crowd, rejection and consent. It advances between two chasms, which are frivolity and propaganda. On this ridge upon which the great artist progresses, each step is an adventure, an extreme risk. Yet in this risk, and in it alone, the freedom of art is to be found. A difficult freedom, more akin to an ascetic discipline? Which artist would deny that? Which artist would dare to say he is up to this unending task? Such freedom presupposes a sound heart and body, a style resembling a spiritual power, and patient application. Like every freedom, it is a perpetual risk, an exhausting adventure; which is why people today flee this risk as they flee the demands of freedom, only to flock into every kind of servitude and obtain at least peace of mind. But if art is not an adventure, what then is it and where is its justification? No, the free artist is not—any more than the free man—a man of comfort. The free artist is the one who with great difficulty creates his own order. The more uncontrollable what he must set in order, the stricter his rule will be—and the more he will have asserted his freedom. There is a saying of Gide's that I have always agreed with, though it can easily be misunderstood: "Art lives from constraint and dies from freedom."[14] This is true. But it should not be taken to mean that art can be directed. Art lives only from the constraints it imposes upon itself. It dies from the rest. On the other hand, if it does not constrain itself, it goes crazy and enslaves itself to shadows. The freest art, and the most rebellious, will thus be the most classic, which will crown the greatest effort. So long as a society and its artists do not agree to this prolonged, free effort; so long as they succumb to the comfort of entertainment or conformism, to the games of art for art's sake or the homilies of realist art—artists are left in nihilism and sterility. Saying this means saying that rebirth today depends upon our daring and clear-sighted determination.

Yes, this rebirth is in the hands of us all. It depends on us whether the West will produce those anti-Alexanders who had to retie the Gordian knot of civilization, severed by the power of the sword. For this, we must take all the risks and travails of freedom. It is not a matter of knowing if, by pursuing justice, we shall succeed in preserving freedom. It is a matter of knowing that without freedom we shall not accomplish anything, but lose both future justice and former beauty. Freedom alone removes men from isolation; as for servitude, it hovers over only a host of solitudes. And art, because of that free essence I have tried to define, unites where tyranny divides. Why, then, is it any surprise that it should be the enemy singled out by all oppressions? Why is it any surprise that artists and intellectuals should have been the first victims of modern tyrannies, whether of the right or the left? Tyrants know there is an emancipatory power in the work of art, which is mysterious only for those who do not revere it. Every great work makes the human face more admirable and richer; this is the whole secret of it. And all the thousands of camps and prison bars will not suffice to obscure this deeply moving testimony to dignity. Which is why it is not true that culture can be suspended, even temporarily, in order to prepare a new one. One cannot suspend man's unceasing testimony to his destitution and his greatness; one cannot suspend the act of breathing. There is no culture without heritage, and we neither can nor should reject anything of our own heritage: that of the West. Whatever the works of the future may be, they will all be entrusted with the same secret, made from courage and freedom, sustained by the bravery of thousands of artists from every century and every nation. Yes, when modern tyranny shows us that, even confined to his craft, the artist is a public enemy, it is quite right. But in this way it pays homage through him to a human figure which nothing has so far managed to crush.

My conclusion will be simple. It will consist in saying, even amid all the sound and fury of our history: "Let us rejoice." Let us indeed rejoice at having seen the death of a lying Europe used to comfort, and at finding ourselves confronted by cruel truths. Let us rejoice as men, since a long mystification has collapsed and we can see clearly into what threatens us. And let us rejoice as artists, torn from slumber and deafness, forcibly held in front of wretchedness, prisons and blood. If before this spectacle we manage to keep the memory of days and faces, if conversely before the beauty of the world we manage not to forget the humiliated, then Western art will gradually regain its power and royalty. There are certainly few examples in history of artists confronted by such hard problems. But precisely, when even the simplest words and sentences are paid for in weight of freedom and blood, the artist learns to handle them carefully. Danger renders men classic, and all greatness ultimately has its roots in risk.

The age of irresponsible artists is over. We shall regret it for its small joys. But we shall be able to recognize that this test at the same time serves our chances of authenticity, and we shall accept the challenge. The freedom of art is not worth much when its only meaning is to ensure the artist's comfort. For a value or virtue to take root in a society, it is best not to lie about it: in other words, to pay for it whenever you can. If freedom has become dangerous, then it is on the way to no longer being prostituted. And I cannot agree with those who complain today about the decline of wisdom. They may appear to be right. But actually wisdom has never declined so much as at the time when it was the riskless pleasure of a few humanists in libraries. Today, when it is confronted at last by real dangers, there is instead some chance that it might once again stand upright and be respected.

It is said that Nietzsche, after his break with Lou Salomé[15]—submerged in total solitude, at once crushed and exalted by the perspective of the vast work he would have to carry out without any help—used to walk by night on the mountains overlooking the Gulf of Genoa, and light great bonfires of leaves and branches which he would watch being consumed. I have often dreamed about those fires, and sometimes I have placed certain men and certain works before them in my mind's eye, to put them to the test. Well, our age is one of those fires, whose unbearable burning will doubtless reduce many works to ashes! But for those which remain, their metal will be intact; in their regard, we shall be able to yield unhesitatingly to that supreme joy of intelligence we call "admiration."

One may doubtless wish, as I also do, for a gentler flame, a respite, a pause conducive to dreaming. But perhaps there is no peace for artists, other than that to be found in the heat of battle. "Every wall is a gate," Emerson rightly said.[16] Let us not look for the gate, and the way out, anywhere except in the wall against which we live. Instead let us look for respite where it is to be found: I mean in the very thick of the battle. For in my view—and I shall end here—it is to be found there. Great ideas, it has been said, come into the world on doves' feet.[17] So perhaps if we listened hard we would hear, amid the din of empires and nations, something like a faint sound of wings, the gentle commotion of life and hope. Some will say that this hope resides in a people, others in a man. I believe instead that it is aroused, rekindled and maintained by millions of isolated individuals, whose actions and works every day negate the frontiers and the crudest features of history to make shine forth fleetingly the ever-threatened truth which each person erects for all upon his sufferings and his joys.

What I Owe to Spain

1958

On January 22, 1958, the Cercle des Amitiés Méditerranéennes organized an evening in honor of Albert Camus and the Nobel Prize in Literature that had been awarded to him a month earlier in Stockholm. Among the speakers preceding Camus on the platform were notably the Israeli minister for trade and industry Peretz Bernstein, the former president of Colombia and former editor of the Colombian daily El Tiempo *Eduardo Santos (see p. 181), and the vice president of the Conseil d'État, René Cassin. Last to speak, Camus delivered the address reproduced below, which was published the following March in No. 85 of the review* Preuves.*

On the last occasions when I found myself among you, at the invitation of Amitiés Méditerranéennes and some Spanish organizations, I felt myself altogether more at ease. It was a matter of paying homage to men whom we all loved and respected, and my role was to tell them something of what we all felt. I spoke then with warmth, from my heart, and without the awkwardness I feel this evening.

To tell the truth, I have been feeling more or less the same awkwardness since the month of October.[1] For in fact I have never sought honors. Not for any virtuous reason, by the way, but because of my failings. On this point, my indifference borders on conviction. So it has often happened that I refused, and sometimes perhaps refused too much, judging by the reactions that my refusals provoked. However, certain honors did seek me out, which decency obliged me to receive in silence and as simply as I could. But I never felt easy about them. I know why, to tell the truth, but my reasons will be of no interest to you this evening. I have merely wished to begin by expressing and conveying to you this awkwardness, first in order to be forgiven for my occasional reticence, and also to excuse in advance the clumsiness I shall certainly display this evening in thanking you.

Although I have now decided to take a retreat, I was nevertheless eager to accept your invitation. You know why. In the first place, because among you there are men of my blood to whom I have never been able to refuse anything; then because I knew how warmly these men would welcome me; and lastly because these men—and this is what I wanted to say this evening—are the ones who sustained me at moments of discouragement in an often difficult vocation.

Yes, this vocation is difficult. I should like to speak freely to you about it, and this will be easy for me. At the stage of experience where I am, I need spare nothing: neither party, nor church, nor any of the orthodoxies from which our society is dying—nothing apart from the truth, insofar as I know it. I have read recently that I was a solitary man. Perhaps, but along with millions of men who are my brothers and whom I have outstripped. At all events, I try to follow my vocation, and if I sometimes find it hard, that is because it is mainly practiced in the dreadful intellectual society in which we live, where disloyalty is made a point of honor, where reflexes have replaced reflection, where people think at the sound of a slogan, just as Pavlov's dog salivated at the sound of a bell, and where spite too often tries to pass itself off as intelligence.

If the writer is eager to read and listen to what people say, he no longer knows to which saint he should devote himself. A certain Right will reproach him for signing too many manifestos, the Left (the new one at least, though I belong to the old) for not signing enough. The Right reproaches him for being a woolly-minded humanitarian, whereas the Left reproaches him for being an aristocrat. The Right accuses him of writing too badly, while the Left reproaches him for writing too well. Remain an artist or feel ashamed to be one, speak or keep silent, you will be condemned in any case. What else then can you do, except trust your star and stubbornly pursue the blind, hesitant advance which is that of every artist, and which nevertheless justifies him provided only that he properly grasps both the greatness of his vocation and his personal weakness.

This often comes down to displeasing everybody. However, although I feel most cruelly the degradation of this society, I do not separate myself from it, but include myself too in the accusation. But at least I refuse to add to its weaknesses. I am not one of those Christians who rush to set fire to the church for the sole satisfaction of having carried out this fine deed before the materialists do. I am not one of those lovers of freedom who wish to adorn it with extra chains, nor one of those servants of justice who think it is served well only by condemning several generations to injustice. I live as I can, in an unhappy country rich in its people and its youth but temporarily poor in its elites, engaged in searching for an order and a rebirth in which I believe. But if I live in this country and in this society, if I believe it is both inevitable and right to suffer from the common ill, it is not because I cannot imagine another life; it is not because I am satisfied by that phantom of freedom which survives among us, hemmed in by masters of servitude. Without true freedom and without a certain honor, I cannot live. And having once recognized this, having judged that these benefits are supreme, it has seemed to me that they should be guaranteed to everybody. And that while waiting for their kingdom to arrive, we should strive unceasingly, so far as we are able, to testify on their behalf.

This is how I conceive of my vocation. I do not know if I have given too many or not enough signatures, if I am a prince or a road-sweeper. But I do know that, since I was unable naively to esteem myself, I have tried to respect my vocation. I know too that I have tried especially to respect the words I was writing, since through them I wished to respect those who might read them and whom I did not want to deceive. I had to do this in occasionally exhausting struggles, the traces of which—to speak frankly—I still carry within me. Such struggles are inevitable. I have accepted them and shall accept them. But I know that they are also in danger of hardening me, causing me to feel kinds of bitterness for which I am not made. In a word, they are in danger of making me miserly, and stripping me of that great power of joy and life without which an artist is nothing.

If I have finally escaped that danger—and this is what I was trying to get at—it is to some of you that I owe it, even if they are unaware of it. Consequently I owe them almost everything. These men are from all parties and all countries. They are my friends from France, who know I cannot speak about them publicly. They are my friends from Israel, from the exemplary Israel that people want to destroy on the convenient pretext of anti-colonialism, but whose right to live we shall defend, we who have witnessed the massacre of all those millions of Jews and who find it right and proper that their sons should create the country that we were unable to give them. They are also my friends from South America, particularly those from free Colombia, finally free thanks to men whose tireless activity has borne fruit.[2]

But you will allow me to symbolize all these friends, this evening, in exiled Spain. Spanish friends, we are in fact of the same blood, and toward your country, its literature and people, its tradition, I have an undying debt. But I have another debt toward you that you do not and cannot know. In the life of a battling writer, warm springs are needed to help fight the darkening and desiccation one encounters in the struggle. You have been, and still are, one of these springs. On my path I have always found your active and generous friendship. Spain in exile has often shown me gratitude, but this gratitude is disproportionate. The Spanish exiles have fought for years, then accepted with pride the endless pain of exile. As for me, I have merely written that they were right. And merely for this I have received for years, and again this evening in the looks I encounter, the faithful, loyal Spanish friendship which has helped me live. This friendship, though it may be partly undeserved, is the pride of my life. To tell the truth, it is the only reward for which I could wish. And I should like to thank you, you and many others at the same time, for having so long fed in me a hunger to which men do not easily admit, and which I have no need to name this evening.

I want only to tell you all that I shall try not to be unworthy of that friendship. I am not leaving you, I remain faithful to you. The additional influence which has just been attached to my name by the free academy of a free country—it will be easier for me to accept it in the knowledge that I can place it at your service. It is not my custom, as you know, to announce imminent victories and feast days. As you and I know, our struggles are unending. But they are the framework of our life, they are our life itself, and the essential thing is for us to live them together, loyally, warmly, with the same courage I feel in me today, in thanking you for one last time and telling you of your faithful friend's gratitude.

My Debt to Algeria

Lecture at the Algerian Club
1958

Created in 1951 by Colonel Pierre Furnari, the association L'Algérienne fostered the ambition to bring Algerians living in Paris together regularly, without distinction of origin or confession, usually around debates or dinners in the presence of some political or literary celebrity. Although he had not spoken about Algeria in public since the failure of his "Appeal for a Civilian Truce" (see p. 191), Albert Camus accepted Colonel Furnari's invitation and on November 13, 1958, delivered the address reproduced below at a dinner organized in his honor. Since no handwritten trace of this contribution has been found in the author's archives, it is likely that Camus improvised his speech. The first paragraph and the informal style of the text would seem to support this hypothesis.

Ladies and gentlemen,

I'm sorry not to have anything prepared, but to be essaying an improvisation for which I'm not sure I'm cut out. I'd been invited to drink a glass in the company of a few Algerians, and naturally I'm a bit surprised to find so many of them, though I'm glad all the same to see that the Algerians have colonized Paris in their turn.

I'm also a bit hampered in replying by the excessive praise that Colonel Furnari has been so good as to heap upon me, and I'd simply like to say that, since we're all Algerians together, the fact of being Algerian is the reason for my presence here. And that personally, throughout a life in which good fortune has basically outweighed misfortune—I mean my own life—the main example of good fortune, as I see it, is the fact that I was born in Algeria. An opportunity was given to me recently to say that I've written nothing that was not, whether closely or distantly, connected with that land.[1] As it happens, I expressed only something which I feel deeply and have long done so.

I owe to Algeria not just my lessons of happiness, but also—which are not least in a man's life—my lessons of suffering and hardship. These lessons have for some time become rather painful; but they are still there. It was necessary to accept them. Amid the terrible tragedy in which our shared land is submerged, I think there may be not just a reason to hope, but perhaps also for all of us, Arab and French alike, a reason to advance in a common initiative toward what can be called truth. I'm not proud of many things, and in particular I'm not proud of all that Colonel Furnari, for example, is good enough to ascribe to me. But one of the things of which I am proud as a writer, and as an Algerian writer—and my friend Audisio[2] will not contradict me here, since he was the inspirer of this movement—is that we Algerian writers have done our duty and done it for a long while.

What I mean, more precisely, is that there are many of us hoping for what is now called the Algeria of tomorrow. I don't know if that Algeria will be created. Nor do I know in what conditions it will be created. Nor do I know what it will still cost us in blood and misfortune. But what I can say is that this Algeria of tomorrow is something that we Algerian writers made yesterday. I mean that we have been a school of Algerian writers; and when I say school, I don't mean a group of men obeying doctrines or rules, I simply mean a group of men expressing a certain strength of life, a certain land, a certain way of approaching people.

So we've been a school in which, in my opinion, in terms of talent, there were as many Arab names as French ones. Audisio has already said it better than I, but I'll repeat it after him with all the strength I can muster. Essentially, a land which has produced men calling themselves Roy,[3] Roblès,[4] Audisio on the one hand, and on the other Mammeri,[5] Feraoun[6] and a number of others; which has allowed these writers to express themselves at the same time, in the same language, and in freedom—this land . . . for finally, let's be clear, it's not institutions which have allowed us this, it's simply the work we've done, all together, and especially the way in which we've approached each other. Well, this school has in my view given a good example, a fine model, of what might be the Algeria of tomorrow. That's what I'm personally most proud of.

The honors that sometimes rain down on our heads are rather like storms, insofar as they happen to you and you try to endure them modestly, which is a way of avoiding them. Such honors don't have much importance in my view. And speaking to Algerians, I won't surprise them by saying this. We place much higher value on virtues that are much simpler: those of courage, loyalty, tenacity and determination. Those virtues we have practiced within this group of North African writers; and when it befalls me, as late as possible, to make a balance sheet of my endeavors and my life, I'll think how this collaboration, this creation of a North African literature that several of us have carried out jointly and with the utmost fraternity, will count among the positive sides of my life and my endeavors.

That's more or less what I'm aware that I represent among you— far more, I must say, than international literature. And I ask you simply . . . though sometimes Algeria hasn't always agreed with my propositions, and I think I recall that some of the statements which Colonel Furnari read out just now, and to which I'd still subscribe today, were not welcomed with as much favor as they deserved, given what they were saying . . . But be that as it may, whatever the welcome or whatever may be thought of my stance and my mistakes—for I've made mistakes and shall go on making them—I'd simply like you to receive me at *L'Algérienne*, directly and sincerely, as a representative of this Algeria which we've tried to prefigure in our literature.

Notes

The notes below are primarily those of the original French edition, with additions by the translator. Titles of speeches and lectures given in brackets have been chosen for this English-language edition.

Foreword

1 *man a wolf to himself*: *"Homo homini lupus est"* is a Latin proverb meaning "Man is a wolf to man," with variants appearing over the centuries, reaching a peak in 1941, in Plautus, Erasmus, Hobbes (in the dedication to his *De Cive*), Freud, etc.

2 *"I prefer committed men . . . not too bad"*: Camus, *Notebooks 1942–1951*, from mid-1946.

Indigenous Culture

1 *Maurras*: Charles Maurras (1868–1952), a dominant leader of the French intellectual Right from the Dreyfus Affair to the end of the Second World War, and in particular of Action Française; he was authoritarian, royalist, anti-Semitic, xenophobic and an agnostic supporter of Catholicism as a force for order.

2 *not the lie . . . but the truth being murdered in Spain*: Independent Ethiopia was invaded by Fascist Italy in October 1935, subdued and occupied by a murderous campaign that lasted until 1941, after which the country's independence was reestablished by the Allies in the Second World War. The Spanish Republic was plunged into civil war by a military insurrec-

tion led by General Francisco Franco (El Caudillo) in July 1936, which was eventually to triumph with German and Italian help in April 1939.

3 *Audisio*: Gabriel Audisio (1900–1978), French writer and poet, promoter of the wealth and diversity of the Mediterranean identity. He had recently published an essay, *Jeunesse de la Méditerranée* (1935), many of whose themes coincided with those of Camus.

Defense of Intelligence

1 *"When people . . . my revolver"*: The quotation usually goes: "When I hear the word culture, I reach for my Browning." It was in fact misattributed to Göring, actually coming from the 1933 play *Schlageter* by Hanns Johst, about the Nazi hero Albert Leo Schlageter.

2 Paris-Soir: When he arrived in Paris in early 1940, Camus worked briefly as an editorial assistant at *Paris-Soir*. He left the paper after the exodus of June 1940, without having published a single article in it. *Combat*, a newspaper of which Camus became chief editor in 1944, was to present itself as a counter-model to the pre-war press, seen by Camus as sensationalist and compromised, and of which he considered *Paris-Soir* the embodiment.

3 *Fernandel*: Fernand Contandin (1903–1971), better known as Fernandel, was the most successful French comic actor from 1930 until his death. Although called up at the start of the Second World War, following the defeat of France in 1940 he returned to his career and accommodated himself to Vichy and the Occupation.

Informal Talk by Monsieur Albert Camus [to the Romanians]

1 Combat *of which Camus was then chief editor*: See "Defense of Intelligence," note 2.

The Crisis of Man

1 *II*: No "I" occurs in the French original.

2 *"Man is . . . History for Man"*: References to Hegel by Camus are for the most part probably not actual quotations, but paraphrases. Camus did not know German, and will have based himself on French translations, them-

selves not necessarily accurate; perhaps university textbooks rather than scholarly works.

3 *the United Nations . . . in this very city*: From March 25 to August 18, 1946, the UN Security Council met in New York. Twenty sessions took place at Hunter College (now Lehman College) in the Bronx.

Are We Pessimists?

1 *"So I think . . . sense nor wisdom"*: Louis Antoine de Saint-Just, *Fragments sur les institutions républicaines*, part III ("Institutions"), section 4 ("République et gouvernement"), collected and published after his execution in 1793 (9 Thermidor).

2 *Folly of the Cross*: Debate in Christian theology inspired by Saint Paul's words in 1 Corinthians 1:18: "For the preaching of the cross is to them that perish foolishness; but unto us which are saved it is the power of God."

[The Individual and Freedom]

1 *Maurice Merleau-Ponty*: The French philosopher Maurice Merleau-Ponty (1908–1961) and Camus quarrelled following the publication in *Les Temps modernes* in October 1946 of the first of three parts of the former's "Le Yogi et le prolétaire" (reprinted in 1947 in *Humanisme et terreur*). Camus thought that this ironical response made by Merleau-Ponty to Arthur Koestler's book *The Yogi and the Commissar* (1946) came close to justifying the Moscow Trials. Koestler and Camus retained a mutual respect reinforced by shared convictions, testified to by the work *Réflexions sur la peine capitale* (Reflections on the Death Penalty), which they co-signed in 1957.

2 *mystified consciousness in Marx*: For Marxists, this is a form of consciousness whereby social and especially capitalist forms are viewed as natural.

3 *the Barbu community*: During the Occupation, Marcel Barbu (1907–1984), owner of a watch-case factory, founded a labor community at Valence by surrendering the property rights in his firm to his workers. Beyond sharing the means and returns of production, the Barbu community proposed an ideal of communitarian existence incorporating family, material, moral, cultural and spiritual life. After the war, Barbu was elected as a deputy in the Drôme, and proposed bills on labor communities that did not prove successful. Often mocked by his peers in the National Assembly, he resigned his mandate in June 1946.

[Knowledge Is Universal]

1 *Éditions Charlot*: Les Éditions Charlot, called after their founder Edmond Charlot, published the first works by Camus in Algiers, including *L'Envers et l'endroit* (Betwixt and Between) in 1937 and *Noces* (Nuptials) in 1938. Camus was editor, moreover, of their "Poetry and Theater" collection.

2 *L'Arche*: Jean Amrouche founded the review *L'Arche* in Algiers in February 1944, under the patronage of André Gide. The review published Camus's *Le Minotaure ou La Halte d'Oran* (The Minotaur or The Halt at Oran) in its thirteenth issue.

3 *"For years we lived . . . indifferent heaven"*: Quotation from *The Seven Pillars of Wisdom* by T. E. Lawrence ("Lawrence of Arabia"), first published in 1926.

The Unbeliever and Christians

1 *Three years ago . . . not one of the least*: In 1944–1945, a lively polemic pitted the novelist François Mauriac (1885–1970) against Albert Camus on the subject of purges aimed at collaborators. When the former worried in *Le Figaro* about the excesses of popular justice, the latter defended in *Combat* a remedial justice "without hatred but without pity" for compromised elites.

2 *Monsieur Marcel . . . Sartre's play to be banned*: The philosopher, playwright and theater critic Gabriel Marcel (1889–1973) considered shameful the scenes of torture in Jean-Paul Sartre's play *Morts sans sépulture* (Men Without Shadows), regretting that the play had not been banned in France after having provoked violent incidents in Copenhagen (*Les Nouvelles littéraires*, November 10, 1946).

3 Nemo bonus: "None good"; see Mark 10:18: "And Jesus said unto him, Why callest thou me good? There is none good but one, that is, God."

4 *"I was looking . . . never see the way"*: Perhaps a reference to *Confessions of Saint Augustine* (AD 397–400), book VII.

5 *as I have said elsewhere . . . victims or executioners*: Camus is referring here to his article *Sauvez les corps* (Save the Bodies), which appeared in the series "Neither Victims Nor Executioners," *Combat*, November 19–30, 1946.

6 *"Man is . . . History for man"*: See "The Crisis of Man," note 2.

7 *MRP*: Mouvement Révolutionnaire Populaire, the main Christian Democratic political party in France under the Fourth Republic, founded

in 1944 by Georges Bidault and a component of most governing coalitions until 1954 (it was dissolved in 1967). It played an especially important role in foreign policy, including in forming the Iron and Steel Community that was the forerunner of the European Common Market.

8 *Saint-Sulpice*: The church of Saint-Sulpice in the Latin Quarter is the second-largest Paris church after Notre-Dame and a fashionable place to take Mass.

9 *Monsieur Duhamel . . . similar level*: Georges Duhamel (1884–1966) was a distinguished writer, Academician, pacifist and internationalist, opponent of the Occupation and the Vichy regime, editor of the literary review *Mercure de France*. After the Second World War, he was named president of the Alliance Française.

"Spain? I don't think I can speak about it anymore . . ."

1 *Machado*: Antonio Machado (1875–1939), Spanish poet, initially modernist (symbolist) but in his later years increasingly social realist. A strong supporter of the republic in the civil war, he died shortly after arriving as an exile in France.

2 *land of mercury*: Mercury was mined in Spain (Almadén) from Roman times, and eventually came to represent about one-third of the world's production, often by using slave or convict labor, reaching a peak in 1941.

I Reply . . .

1 Combat: See "Defense of Intelligence," note 2.

2 Le Rassemblement: The weekly publication of General de Gaulle's Rassemblement du Peuple de France, *Le Rassemblement* was edited by Albert Ollivier, with whom Camus had rubbed shoulders at *Combat*.

3 *the Ruhr*: After the Second World War, German sovereignty over the Ruhr was restricted by the victorious Allies, both directly by occupation and indirectly through incorporation of its industry into the European Iron and Steel Community. German sovereignty was restored as part of the process leading to the establishment of the German Federal Republic.

Witness for Freedom

1 Empédocle: Founded by Camus, Albert Béguin, René Char, Guido Meister and Jean Vagne, the monthly review *Empédocle* appeared from April 1949 to July/August 1950.

2 *two initials*: "DP" or "Displaced Person."

3 *the philosopher . . . Such indeed is the stance of Hegel*: See "The Crisis of Man," note 2. The reference to the "city" (*ville, Stadt*) may plausibly, in fact, originate as a mistranslation of "state" (*Staat*).

4 *they kill Péguy and thousands of young poets*: Charles Péguy (1873–1914), independent socialist, prominent Dreyfusard, poet and prose writer, founder and editor of *Cahiers de la quinzaine* (Fortnightly Notebooks), returned to his childhood Catholicism in 1912 and was killed at the front at the start of the First World War.

5 *Girondins . . . Montagnards*: In the French Revolution at the end of the eighteenth century, its Jacobin protagonists were divided between the more conservative Girondins, defeated in 1793, and the more radical Montagnards, who thereafter introduced the Reign of Terror.

Time of the Murderers

1 *Train anecdote*: Note by Camus to himself, referring to "The Crisis of Man," p. 18: "The Frenchmen of the Resistance whom I knew, and who used to read Montaigne on the train while carrying leaflets, proved that in our country, at least, it was possible to understand skeptics at the same time as having an idea of honor."

2 *"A pair of boots . . . Shakespeare"*: Dmitry Pisarev (1840–1868) was a leading radical Russian writer in the 1860s, associated with the movement that became known as "nihilism." The remark here, often mistakenly attributed to Pisarev (even by Gorky), appears to have its true origins in a satirical "extract" from a "novel" (entitled *Shchedrodarov*), which Dostoyevsky contributed to the May 1864 issue (No. 5) of his journal *Epokha* (Epoch).

3 *"Official history . . . their word"*: In 1949 Albert Camus published posthumously Simone Weil's work *L'Enracinement* (The Need for Roots) in the "Espoir" imprint that he edited for Éditions Gallimard. He is here rephrasing a passage from it: "It is moreover only because the historical spirit consists in taking murderers at their word that this dogma [of progress] seems to correspond so well to the facts."

4 *"Man is . . . History for Man"*: See "The Crisis of Man," note 2.

5 *two initials*: See "Witness for Freedom," note 2.

6 *the philosopher . . . Such indeed is the stance of Hegel*: See "Witness for Freedom," note 3.

7 *German anecdote*: Note by Camus to himself, referring to the following anecdote, recounted by Herbert Lottman in his biography *Albert Camus* (1978): "German officers had heard some young Frenchmen discussing philosophy in a restaurant. One of these lads had declared that no idea was worth dying for. The Germans called him over to their table and one of them, putting a revolver to his temple, asked him to repeat what he had just said. He repeated the sentence, and the officer congratulated him: 'I think you have just proved your mistake. You have just shown that certain ideas are indeed worth dying for.'"

8 *"Courage . . . merely a subaltern's virtue"*: Arthur Schopenhauer, "The Wisdom of Life," chapter 4 ("Position"), section 4 ("Honor"): "personal courage is really a very subordinate virtue—merely the distinguishing mark of a subaltern."

9 *"It is putting . . . on their account"*: Michel de Montaigne, *Essays* (1580), III, 11: "On the Lame."

10 *"Poets . . . of the world"*: Percy Bysshe Shelley, "The Defense of Poetry" (1821).

The Europe of Loyalty

1 La Révolution prolétarienne: As soon as it began to be published again in 1947, Camus took a close interest in this journal, for which he wrote a dozen texts.

2 *Serrano Suñer*: Ramón Serrano Suñer (1901–2003) was a government minister under Franco from 1938 to 1940, then minister of foreign affairs from 1940 to 1942. A high Francoist dignitary, he notably organized the meeting between Hitler and Franco at Hendaye on October 23, 1940.

3 *the Glières*: The Glières plateau, in the Bornes range, was a Resistance hot spot. More than one hundred maquisards were killed by the Wehrmacht after the plateau was stormed in late March 1944.

4 *Leclerc Division . . . deserts of Libya*: The Leclerc Division was a Free French component of the Allied forces that landed in Normandy in 1944 and subsequently participated in the liberation of France from Nazi occupation. It was commanded by General (later Marshal) Philippe Leclerc, who had previously as a colonel led Free French forces from Chad in

French Equatorial Africa into Libya, where they notably captured the town of Kufra after a long and bloody siege.

5 *students and workers of Barcelona . . . once again claiming its place*: In March 1951, a call to boycott Barcelona trams following an increase in the ticket price was transformed into a general strike movement that paralyzed the city for two weeks.

6 *Anouilh*: Jean Anouilh (1910–1987) was a French playwright, author notably of *Antigone* (1944), widely taken to be an attack on the Vichy government.

7 *Marcel Aymé*: Marcel Aymé (1902–1967) was a popular French novelist, playwright and children's author.

8 *Benavente*: Jacinto Benavente y Martínez (1866–1954) was a Spanish writer and playwright, author of more than one hundred and fifty plays, and winner of the Nobel Prize in Literature in 1922.

9 *Joseph Prudhomme*: The caricature of a stereotypical French bourgeois philistine, plump, pompous and foolish, "Joseph Prudhomme" was created by the playwright Henry Monnier in 1830. He is invoked here in a sarcastic comment on Franco's sententious platitude.

10 *CNT*: Founded in 1911 and espousing libertarian or anarcho-syndicalist ideas, the Confederación Nacional del Trabajo (National Confederation of Labor) was in the early twentieth century the largest workers' union in Spain.

11 *Unamuno . . . Monsieur Rocamora*: On Miguel de Unamuno, see introduction to "Spain and Don Quixotism," p. 178. Pedro Rocamora (1912–1993) was at the time the director-general of propaganda within the undersecretariat for people's education, attached to the national education ministry of the Franco government.

12 *"Error on this side . . . truth on the other"*: "The truth on this side of the Pyrenees, error on the other." Blaise Pascal, *Pensées* (1670), V, 294.

13 *irreproachable militants of the CNT like José Peirats*: José Peirats Valls (1908–1989), worker and journalist, was secretary of the CNT and an editor on the anarcho-syndicalist paper *Solidaridad obrera* (Workers' Solidarity). Forced into exile following Franco's victory, he published in the early 1950s a reference work on Spanish anarcho-syndicalism: *La CNT en la revolución española*.

[Spain and War]

1 Solidaridad obrera, *weekly of the Spanish CNT*: See "The Europe of Loyalty," notes 10 and 13.

2 *I have read . . . believe any longer in the Republic*: In July 1951, *Le Monde* published a series of articles by Jean Créach under the title "Elements of the Spanish Problem."

3 *Franco's Moors*: General Franco built his military career mainly as a successful commander in Spain's North African colonies, especially Morocco, and at the outset of the civil war he led the Army of Africa, made up of Moroccan troops with Spanish officers, with which he invaded the mainland.

4 *as it has just proved*: See "The Europe of Loyalty," p. 102.

Albert Camus Talks About the General Election in Britain

1 *there are good marriages, but no delightful ones*: The reference is to François de La Rochefoucauld, *Maxims* (1678), no. 113.

Appeal for Those Under Sentence of Death

1 *CNT*: See "The Europe of Loyalty," note 10.

Spain and Culture

1 Solidaridad obrera: See "The Europe of Loyalty," note 13.

2 *Unamuno*: On Miguel de Unamuno, see introduction to "Spain and Don Quixotism," p. 178.

3 *Calderón or Lope de Vega*: For the Angers Festival, Albert Camus adapted Pedro Calderón de la Barca's *La devoción de la Cruz* (Devotion to the Cross) in 1953 and Lope de Vega's *El caballero de Olmedo* (The Knight from Olmedo) in 1957.

4 *the government of Monsieur Pinay*: In the course of various ministries in the 1950s, the moderate conservative Antoine Pinay (1891–1994) played an important role in Franco-Spanish reconciliation by encouraging cooperation between the two countries.

5 *a poet they have previously shot*: Camus is referring to the poet and playwright Federico García Lorca (1898–1936), shot at the outset of the Spanish Civil War.

6 *Mussolini himself . . . not so long ago*: Mussolini's Italy invaded Ethiopia in October 1935 and occupied the country until 1941.

7 *"Grande hazaña! Con muertos!"*: "A heroic feat! With dead men!" Title of one of the eighty-two prints in the "Disasters of War" series (1810–1820) by Francisco de Goya (1746–1828).

Bread and Freedom

1 *Africa battalions . . . vice squad*: The Battalions of Light Infantry of Africa (colloquially the Bat' d'Af') were French infantry and construction units serving in North Africa made up of men with prison records or soldiers with serious disciplinary problems. The Brigade de Répression du Proxénétisme, later Brigade Mondaine (1930), was a specialized unit of the French police service dealing with prostitution which had its roots in the eighteenth century.

2 *murder in Prague . . . Kalandra*: The Czech historian, journalist and essayist Záviš Kalandra joined the Communist Party in the 1920s, before being expelled in 1936 for Trotskyism. For the same reason, he was arrested in 1949 and sentenced to death in 1950 after a mock trial. Despite appeals for clemency from across the world, he was hanged in Prague on June 27, 1953.

3 *Kravchenko, from being a profiteer . . . bourgeois regime*: Viktor Kravchenko (1905–1966), a captain in the Red Army, was sent during the Second World War to the Soviet purchasing mission in Washington, D.C. In 1944 he asked for political asylum in the United States and denounced the Stalinist regime in his book *I Chose Freedom*, published in 1946.

[The Berlin Events and Us]

1 *the Rosenbergs were led off to their death*: Sentenced to death in 1951 for spying on behalf of the Soviet Union, American citizens Julius and Ethel Rosenberg were executed in the United States on June 19, 1953. Their trial, seen as unjust and biased, provoked widespread protests throughout the world.

2 *uprising of workers . . . free elections*: On June 1, 1953, a strike at the Škoda factory in Plzeň (Pilsen) sparked off a vast protest movement in several Czechoslovak cities. Repression of the demonstrations by the police and

army did not result in deaths, but more than two thousand individuals were arrested.

3 *Goettling*: Accused of being one of the ringleaders of the insurrection, Willi Goettling, a West Berlin worker born in 1918, was sentenced to death by a court-martial and executed on June 18, 1953.

4 *our progressive organs . . . inspired by the Russian government*: It was a strike movement on the part of Stalin Allee construction workers in Berlin which sparked the uprising.

The Future of European Civilization

1 *watchword of Voltaire . . . watchword of European thought*: This quotation, often misattributed to Voltaire, was in fact coined by the English historian and biographer Evelyn Beatrice Hall (1868–1956) under the pseudonym S. G. Tallentyre, as a summary of Voltaire's view on free speech, in her work *The Friends of Voltaire* (1906).

2 *Ortega y Gasset . . . The Revolt of the Masses*: José Ortega y Gasset (1883–1955), Spanish philosopher, sociologist and essayist. His book *La rebelión de las masas* was published in 1930.

3 *The Mandarins . . . The Story of O*: Published in 1954, Simone de Beauvoir's novel *Les Mandarins* won that year's Prix Goncourt. *Histoire d'O*, a novel by Dominique Aury published in 1954 under the pseudonym Pauline Réage, is a classic of twentieth-century erotic literature.

4 *I do not know . . . three months there*: See introduction to "The Crisis of Man," p. 18, and to "Are We Pessimists?," p. 35.

5 *"irreligion has something vulgar and hackneyed about it"*: Benjamin Constant, *Journaux intimes* ("Intimate Diaries"; first published in full in 1952), in an entry from 1804.

6 *Monsieur Merleau-Ponty . . . the tendency which concerns us*: On the relationship between Camus and Merleau-Ponty, see "[The Individual and Freedom]," note 1.

7 *great works . . . Melville's* Moby Dick: Camus greatly admired the American author, whom he placed among "the greatest geniuses of the West" ("Herman Melville," text published in *Les Écrivains célèbres*, 1952).

8 *In your lecture . . . realist art*: The reference is to a 1951 radio broadcast in which Camus adumbrated some of the themes later expanded in his 1957 Uppsala lecture (see "[The Artist and His Age]," p. 230). Transcript included in *Actuelles II 1945–1953*.

9 *Isocrates*: The ancient Greek philosopher (436–338 BC) is frequently invoked in discussions about Greek nationalism, and ambiguous paraphrases of his views frequently offered—as here—to support one position or another.

10 *Kazantzakis*: Nikos Kazantzakis (1883–1957), a Greek writer, philosopher, playwright and poet, known in particular for his novels *Zorba the Greek* (1946) and *The Last Temptation of Christ* (1954).

11 *Mrs. Liberaki*: Margarita Liberaki (1919–2001), Greek writer and poet; her novels *The Other Alexander* and *Three Summers* were published by Gallimard in 1950 and 1953, respectively.

On the Future of Tragedy

1 *Jacques Copeau*: Camus saw Jacques Copeau (1879–1949), founder of the Vieux-Colombier theater and stage company, as one of his theatrical masters. Back in 1937 he staged *The Brothers Karamazov* at Algiers in Copeau's adaptation. In 1959, on the tenth anniversary of Copeau's death, Camus was to compile a homage entitled *Copeau, seul maître* (Copeau, Only Master), published in a booklet with the title *Cahier Jacques Copeau* (October–November 1959).

2 *Claudel, whom nobody staged*: Paul Claudel (1868–1955), French poet, dramatist and diplomat, converted from unbelief to Catholicism at the age of eighteen. He joined the diplomatic corps in 1893, serving in the USA, China, Europe, Brazil and Japan until 1936, obliging him at first to publish either anonymously or under a pseudonym. His talent was recognized early on, but the fact that his plays were written in verse and often very long—combined with his controversial old-style conservative views and devout Catholicism—meant that they were staged only infrequently.

3 *if you wish . . . makes us revolt*: Jacques Copeau, "Un essai de rénovation dramatique" (An Attempt at Dramatic Renewal), *La Nouvelle Revue française*, September 1, 1913.

4 *Martin du Gard*: Roger Martin du Gard (1881–1958), French novelist, author notably of a multivolume *roman-fleuve* about the Thibault family, winner of the Nobel Prize in Literature in 1937.

5 *Giraudoux*: Jean Giraudoux (1882–1944), French novelist, essayist, playwright and diplomat, influential throughout the interwar period, mainly for his plays, which were widely translated and staged.

6 *Montherlant*: Henry de Montherlant (1895–1972), French novelist, dramatist and essayist, author notably of the tetralogy *Les Jeunes Filles*, but remembered mainly for his plays. He extolled male heroism and especially bullfighting, was a collaborationist in the Second World War, and committed suicide not long after being attacked and wounded by a street gang angered by his having groped a young member.

7 *Antonin Artaud*, Le Théâtre et son double: Antonin Artaud (1896–1948), French poet, dramatist, essayist, actor and theater director, an outstanding figure of twentieth-century theater and the European avant-garde. He conceptualized the Theater of Cruelty movement and was known for his surreal and transgressive themes, influencing such diverse individuals as Salvador Dalí, Luis Buñuel, Jean Genet, Samuel Beckett and the stage director Peter Brooks. His seminal collection of texts *Le Théâtre et son double* (The Theater and Its Double) was first published in 1938.

8 *foreign theorists such as Gordon Craig and Appia*: Gordon Craig (1872–1966), the British actor, director and set designer, ranks among the greatest theorists of dramatic art. The Swiss set designer and director Adolphe Appia (1862–1928) is considered one of the pioneers of modern theater.

9 Prometheus Unbound *as a typical example of that tragedy*: In March 1937, Camus had adapted and directed Aeschylus's *Prometheus Unbound* for the Théâtre du Travail in Algiers.

10 *Aeschylus . . . his* Eumenides *replaced the* Erinyes: The Erinyes or Furies, who appear as the chorus in the first two plays of Aeschylus's *Oresteia* trilogy, are euphemistically termed "the Kindly Ones" in the third.

11 *When Nietzsche accused Socrates of being the gravedigger of ancient tragedy*: Thesis developed by Nietzsche in *The Birth of Tragedy* (1872).

12 *"My desolation does begin to make a better life"*: Antony and Cleopatra, Act V, Scene 2.

13 All's Well: Probably echoing Oedipus's cry quoted on p. 173. But the italics in Camus's original text might possibly indicate an allusion to Voltaire's "Poème sur le désastre de Lisbonne," composed after the great 1755 earthquake, especially the famous couplet: "Un jour tout sera bien, voilà notre espérance; / Tout est bien aujourd'hui, voilà l'illusion" (One day all will be well, that's our hope; / All's well today, that's the illusion).

14 The Trojan War [Will Not Take Place] *by Giraudoux*: Jean Giraudoux's play was put on for the first time in Paris on November 21, 1935.

15 *Montherlant's* Port-Royal: The first staging of *Port-Royal* took place in Paris on December 8, 1954.

16 Partage de midi: Paul Claudel's *Partage de midi* (Break of Noon) had its first staging, by Jean-Louis Barrault, at the Marigny theater in Paris on December 16, 1948.

17 *Henry de Montherlant,* Le Maître de Santiago: The first night of *Le Maître de Santiago* (The Grand Master of Santiago) took place at the Théâtre Hébertot in Paris on January 26, 1948, with Paul Œttly directing.

Spain and Don Quixotism

1 *the publication of* Don Quixote: The first part of Cervantes's novel was published in Madrid in 1605, the second part in 1615.

2 *"Glory . . . leniency and mercy"*: *Don Quixote*, part II, chapters 42 and 51.

3 Bouvard and Pécuchet: An unfinished satirical novel by Gustave Flaubert, published in 1881 after his death the previous year, *Bouvard et Pécuchet* tells the story of two copy clerks who, with the aid of an inheritance, retire to the country and set about compiling a kind of encyclopedia of contemporary knowledge, moving from topic to topic without successfully mastering any, and with often disastrous results, while increasingly alienating their neighbors. For many later writers, seen as a modernist masterpiece.

4 *"the spade and hoe . . . knight-errantry"*: A reference to lines from a burlesque sonnet at the beginning of *Don Quixote*.

Homage to an Exiled Journalist

1 *in the words . . . for others*: Benjamin Constant developed this idea in the second part of his essay *De l'esprit de conquête et de l'usurpation, dans leurs rapports avec la civilisation européenne* (On the Spirit of Conquest and Usurpation, in Their Relations with European Civilization; 1814).

2 *the seeds beneath the snow . . . our number spoke*: Camus is alluding here to the novel *Il seme sotto la neve* (The Seed Beneath the Snow; 1940), by the Italian writer Ignazio Silone (1900–1978).

3 *Victor Hugo said . . . and so forth*: Probably a reference to the speech Victor Hugo gave to the Constituent Assembly on October 11, 1848.

4 *"Without a free . . . entirely unthinkable"*: This quotation taken from Rosa Luxemburg's *The Russian Revolution*, published posthumously in 1918, appears in Albert Camus's *Carnets II* (Notebooks II; 1965).

For Dostoyevsky

1 *"the deep spirit, the spirit of negation and death"*: Perhaps a reference to Fyodor Dostoyevsky, *The Brothers Karamazov* (1879–1880), part II, book V, chapter 5.
2 *"The questions of God . . . from a different angle"*: Ibid., part II, book V, chapter 3.

Appeal for a Civilian Truce in Algeria

1 *Cercle du Progrès in Algiers*: Le Nadi el Taraqqi or Cercle du Progrès was established in 1927 (under a law passed in 1901) by Algerian Muslim families from the Casbah in Algiers as their main meeting place, to help "the intellectual, economic and social education of the Muslims of Algeria." It therefore represented a symbolic choice for launching the "Appeal for a Civilian Truce" in 1956.
2 *continuation of war in the Rif after the sultan's return*: In Morocco, despite the return from exile of Mohammed V and the signature in November 1955 of the La Celle-Saint-Cloud accords heralding the end of the French protectorate, insurrection continued in the Rif in the north.
3 *resurgence of Fellaghism in Tunisia*: After winning autonomy by signing the June 3, 1955, accords, Tunisia demanded independence. This period was marked by a resurgence of armed militancy. Anti-colonial fighters in French-ruled North Africa were regularly known by the Arabic term *Fellagha*, meaning "bandits."

Poznań

1 *Mr. Cyrankiewicz*: Józef Cyrankiewicz (1911–1989) headed the Polish government from 1947 until 1952, then from 1954 until 1970.

The Option of Freedom

1 *"Thou shalt prefer exile . . . say the truth"*: "Ten Commandments of the Free Spirit," written probably in 1876, but published only posthumously.
2 *Peirebeilhe inn*: Inn located at Peyrebeille or Peirebeilhe in the Ardèche,

commonly known as the "red" or "bloody inn," with reference to as many as fifty murders supposedly committed there by its owners between 1805 and 1830.

3 *For the flies . . . speed of history*: A reference to the fable "Le Coche et la Mouche" (The Coach and the Fly) by Jean de La Fontaine (1621–1695), which recounts how a fly, buzzing around the head of one of a team of six horses pulling a heavy coach up a slope, boasts of himself accomplishing the arduous task.

4 *Ortega's superb formulation*: For José Ortega y Gasset, see "The Future of European Civilization," note 2.

5 *foreign minister Shepilov*: Dmitri Shepilov (1905–1995), foreign minister of the USSR from June 1956 to February 1957.

6 *"I have been fortunate to be your contemporary"*: Letter from Ivan Turgenev to Leo Tolstoy, July 11, 1883.

Message to Young French Supporters of Hungary

1 *the appeal I have initiated by European writers to the UN*: In early November 1956, the Hungarian Writers' Union launched a radio appeal for help to intellectuals throughout the world. Called upon in person, Albert Camus on November 10, 1956, signed a text in *Le Franc-Tireur* entitled "For a Common Approach to the UN by French Intellectuals."

Kádár Has Had His Day of Fear

1 *Tibor Méray who had fled to Paris*: Tibor Méray (1924–2020), Hungarian-French journalist and strong supporter of Imre Nagy (see p. 213), fled to Paris in 1956 after the suppression of the Hungarian revolt.

2 *The Hungarian minister Marosán*: György Marosán (1908–1992), deputy premier in 1956, was a key figure in the Hungarian Politburo until 1962.

3 *They began to speak in Berlin, in Czechoslovakia*: See "[The Berlin Events and Us]," p. 139.

4 *Poznań*: See "Poznań," p. 201.

5 *Rajk*: László Rajk (1909–1949), Hungarian communist leader during the Second World War. Accused of being a Titoist spy, he was sentenced to death in purge trials organized on the initiative of Mátyás Rákosi (see next note) and hanged on October 15, 1949. His name was rehabilitated in 1956.

6 *bald killer or the persecuted persecutor*: Mátyás Rákosi (1892–1971), member of the Communist International, spent the Second World War in Russia. Returning to Hungary in 1945, he became general secretary of the Hungarian Communist Party, a post that he was to occupy until 1956. He is here described as "the bald killer," while his replacement, János Kádár, who had been disgraced in 1951 and rehabilitated in 1954, is called "the persecuted persecutor."

7 *Shepilov*: See "The Option of Freedom," note 5.

[The Artist and His Age]

1 *what Stepan Trofimovich in* Demons . . . *reproach incarnate*: Fyodor Dostoyevsky, *Demons* (1871–1872), part I, chapter 1. See also "For Dostoyevsky," p. 188.

2 *Racine would apologize . . . the Edict of Nantes*: Jean Racine (1639–1699) received a mainly Jansenist education at Port-Royal. His tragedy *Bérénice* appeared in 1670. The Edict of Nantes (1598) had given French Huguenots (Calvinist Protestants) the right to practice their religion without persecution from the State, but it was revoked in 1685 by the Edict of Fontainebleau, leading to a large-scale Huguenot exodus from France. The Jansenists, although subjected to periodic repression for their beliefs, made the concessions necessary to avoid similar State condemnation.

3 *"A man's obedience . . . faith in its purest form"*: Ralph Waldo Emerson, *Self-Reliance* (1841).

4 *"So long as a man is faithful . . . the very sun, moon, and stars"*: Henry David Thoreau, *Walden, or Life in the Woods* (1854), and *On the Duty of Civil Disobedience* (1851).

5 *the greatest of all vices was to be superficial*: Oscar Wilde, *De Profundis* (1905). In 1952, Camus wrote a preface for the French edition of Wilde's *The Ballad of Reading Gaol* (1898) published by Éditions Falaize.

6 *Chatterton is the finest example*: Thomas Chatterton (1752–1770), an English poet who, unable to earn enough to live from his art, committed suicide at the age of seventeen, after several days of battling against hunger. His life inspired Alfred de Vigny to compose his eponymous drama, *Chatterton* (1835).

7 *Blok*: Aleksandr Blok (1880–1921), Russian revolutionary poet, playwright, critic and translator.

8 *the great Pasternak*: Boris Pasternak (1890–1960), Russian poet and novelist. After the publication of his novel *Doctor Zhivago* in Italy (1957) and the

award to him of the Nobel Prize in 1958, the Russian regime unleashed a violent campaign against him. Camus supported him publicly in an article on November 1, 1958, published in *Le Figaro littéraire* with the title: "Pasternak sera-t-il un paria?" (Will Pasternak Become a Pariah?).

9 *Mayakovsky*: Vladimir Mayakovsky (1893–1930), Russian poet and playwright, was one of the pioneers of the futurist movement.

10 *Yesenin*: Sergei Yesenin (1895–1925), Russian poet close to peasant milieux and a supporter of the Left Social-Revolutionaries. He was the husband of the American dancer Isadora Duncan from 1922 to 1924.

11 *Eisenstein*: Sergei Eisenstein (1898–1948), Russian filmmaker, notably director of *The Battleship Potemkin* (1925).

12 *"A man of genius . . . looks like him"*: Honoré de Balzac, *Le Curé de village* (The Country Parson; 1839), chapter 4.

13 *"There is not a single . . . very secret of life"*: Oscar Wilde, *De Profundis* (1905).

14 *"Art lives from constraint and dies from freedom"*: André Gide, "L'évolution du théâtre," in *Nouveaux Prétextes* (1918).

15 *Nietzsche, after his break with Lou Salomé*: Lou Andreas-Salomé (1861–1937), Russian-born psychoanalyst and author, had a relationship with Nietzsche in 1883, but rejected his repeated proposals of marriage, before the relationship was broken off under pressure from Nietzsche's sister.

16 *"Every wall is a gate," Emerson rightly said*: Ralph Waldo Emerson, *Natural History of the Intellect* (1871).

17 *Great ideas . . . come into the world on doves' feet*: Friedrich Nietzsche, *Thus Spoke Zarathustra* (1883–1885): "Thoughts that come on doves' feet guide the world."

What I Owe to Spain

1 *I have been feeling . . . since the month of October*: Camus is referring to the Nobel Prize in Literature, which was awarded him on October 16, 1957. See "Nobel Prize Acceptance Speech [Stockholm]," p. 225.

2 *those from free Colombia . . . whose tireless activity has borne fruit*: On May 10, 1957, the Colombian dictator Gustavo Rojas Pinilla left power in favor of a transitional military government. In 1958, the country restored democracy following an agreement on the system of governance reached between the conservative party and the liberal party. See "Homage to an Exiled Journalist," p. 181.

My Debt to Algeria

1 *An opportunity was given to me . . . connected with that land*: Interview with *Le Franc-Tireur*, October 18, 1957.

2 *my friend Audisio*: For Audisio, see "Indigenous Culture," note 3.

3 *Roy*: Born in Algeria, Jules Roy (1907–2000) met Camus in Paris in 1945. In 1947 Camus devoted a laudatory review to Roy's novel *La Vallée heureuse* (The Happy Valley; 1946) in the review *L'Arche*.

4 *Roblès*: Originally from Oran, Emmanuel Roblès (1914–1995) met Camus in Algiers in 1937. A member of the Théâtre de l'Équipe, he founded with Camus the review *Rivages* (1938) and signed several articles in *Alger républicain*. A novelist and playwright, editor of the Méditerranée collection at Éditions du Seuil, he was to be at Camus's side in 1956 when the latter launched his "Appeal for a Civilian Truce in Algeria" (see p. 191).

5 *Mammeri*: Mouloud Mammeri (1917–1989), a Kabyle writer, poet, linguist and anthropologist, was a pioneer of Algerian francophone literature. He was notably the author of *La Colline oubliée* (The Forgotten Hill; 1952).

6 *Feraoun*: Mouloud Feraoun (1913–1962), a Kabyle francophone writer, author of *Le Fils du pauvre* (The Poor Man's Son; 1950) and *La Terre et le sang* (Earth and Blood; 1953). He met Camus through Emmanuel Roblès (see note 4 above). The two men formed a firm friendship unmarred by their differences on the Algerian conflict. A teacher then an inspector of social centers, he was assassinated by the OAS (the Organisation Armée Secrète, a French paramilitary organization) on March 15, 1962, at El Biar near Algiers.

From

ALBERT CAMUS

The classic novel in a new translation by Laura Marris

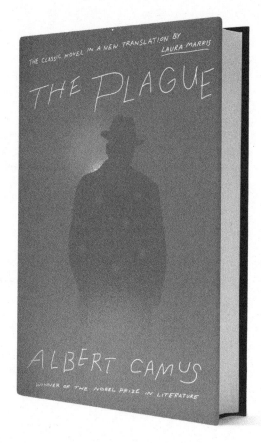

The first American translation in more than seventy years, bringing the
Nobel Prize winner's iconic novel to a new generation of readers

Available now from Alfred A. Knopf
For more information: aaknopf.com